Your Child Can Win

JOAN NOYES
AND NORMA MACNEILL

Your Child Can Win

Strategies, Activities, and Games for Parents of Children with Learning Disabilities

WILLIAM MORROW AND COMPANY, INC.
New York   1983

Library of Congress Cataloging in Publication Data

Noyes, Joan, 1935-
   Your child can win.

   Bibliography: p.
   1. Learning disabilities. 2. Child development.
3. Creative activities and seat work. 4. Games.
I. Macneill, Norma, 1922-   II. Title.
HQ773.N69 1983   649'.15   82-23934
ISBN 0-688-01942-0

Printed in the United States of America

First Edition

1 2 3 4 5 6 7 8 9 10
BOOK DESIGN BY ROBERT BURGESS GARBUTT

Contents

Preface

There are few emotions more overwhelming than the feeling of helplessness parents experience upon learning that a child has a learning disability. Most have heard about learning disabilities but know nothing about them. They are filled with questions. Is my child mentally retarded? What kind of a future is ahead for him? How will it affect my life and the lives of other family members? How do I handle a child who is different? Can I help at home? Will the school be able to cope with his special needs, or will he need a special school or outside tutoring? The list is endless.

We have attempted in this book to give parents suggestions about how they can help their child at home. This is not intended to supersede what the school is doing but is intended, rather, to supplement it. For those of you who live in smaller centers of the country where specialized assistance is difficult or impossible to find, we have tried to provide a temporary solution until you can find some place or person who can give your child the help he needs.

It is hard for us as parents and teachers to understand what this learning-disabled child is going through. Before he gets help, his whole life is a constant series of failures. He suffers despair, discouragement, and frustration. He cannot understand why others succeed when he always seems to fail and his outlook becomes one of hopelessness. He experiences rejection from peers, brothers and sisters, teachers, and even from his parents, who often suspect that he just isn't trying hard enough. His schoolwork is below standard. Often he cannot fit into the regular classroom because of behavioral difficulties. He may not be able to succeed comfortably in such organizations as Scouts, Guides, and the YM/YWCA. His ego becomes badly bruised at an early age when he sees his friends succeed where he cannot. If they are badly coordinated, boys, especially, suffer the torture of constant teasing and often ostracism from their peer group. If failure is not to become a permanent way of life for the learning-disabled child, at some early point in his life he must learn what it feels like to succeed.

We have been working with children with learning disabilities for many years. Joan was a substitute teacher in Danvers, Mass., when the Board of Education asked her if she would like to become part of an innovative program designed to help learning-disabled children. This was more than fifteen years ago when there were few places providing any kind of help for these unfortunate children. Joan, who has always been good with children, jumped at the chance. There were special lecturers from various universities in the area, but everyone was really learning by experience and by actually working with the children. This was when Joan first noted that improving motor control and development helped academic learning as well.

When Joan moved back to Canada, she attended her first meeting of the Association for Children with Learning Disabilities. Twelve years ago there were only a few pilot projects under way to help these children. The ACLD asked Joan to set up an evening program in Mississauga, just to the west of Metropolitan Toronto. Thus the Gym Clubs were born. The object was to improve body-image, coordination, and self-esteem. An additional result was a great improvement in the children's social interaction. They learned to play with other children, some of whom had even worse disabilities than they had. They worked on a one-to-one basis with a teenaged volunteer who often became the family baby-sitter, giving parents the opportunity for some social life of their own. The

Gym Clubs took root and many are still operating throughout Southern Ontario.

Because Joan is constantly being asked for help to set up more clubs, she decided to write this book. Many of the games and strategies devised for the Gym Clubs, and much of what we learned through these clubs, can be used by parents at home. We have also included a chapter on how to set up a Gym Club in your area.

Joan is currently working with children with learning disabilities for the Peel County Board of Education, one of the most forward-looking boards in the country. She has helped with an Early Identification Program, planned curriculum for children with learning problems, worked with parents, conducted seminars, and spoken to many groups, and she is currently working at the secondary-school level with teenagers who are still experiencing difficulties, or whose learning disabilities have never been properly assessed.

Norma knew nothing at all about learning disabilities until the problem was thrust upon her. About fifteen years ago the school informed her that her older daughter, obviously bright and eager, was not able to learn to read. It was a puzzle to teachers and to her parents, because there seemed to be no reason for the problem. Norma happened to read an article about assessments for learning disabilities in a Toronto paper when her daughter was in Grade 3, and this started a chain of events that led to a deep involvement with learning disabilities. Although the school felt that an assessment was not needed and that this bright child was just lazy, spoiled, and probably emotionally disturbed, Norma arranged to have her assessed at one of Toronto's few educational clinics. The results surprised the school and opened a door for Mary Lou. She had secretly assumed that she was "dumb," or "stupid," so that when her assessment arrived in the mail and Norma read the first paragraph to her, her relief was beautiful to see. The paragraph read: "Mary Lou is a delightful child with good average to bright average intelligence. She is very anxious and apprehensive because of trying to please adults and tends to try too hard." So much for the teachers who said she was lazy. Because of the results of the many tests, Mary Lou was given remedial reading to help improve her visual memory and to teach her phonics. When Norma's second daughter showed signs of the same problems, through a test administered on her first day in Grade 1, her teacher was kind enough to stay behind at lunchtime every day in order to keep her up to date with what the other children were doing in class while she took remedial work. After several months of help, she was allowed to return to her regular reading class. Both these girls continue to have problems right up to the present, but they have learned to cope, and they are now enrolled in university.

The two of us met through the ACLD and Norma eventually contributed her handicraft skills to the Gym Club, to help the children develop their fine motor skills.

When the Gym Clubs were first started it was found that parents had no knowledge of the disabilities affecting their children. This was perhaps understandable twelve years ago, because not very much had been written on the subject except a few books aimed at teachers. Today there are many good books (see the back of this book for a list) that give in-depth information about learning disabilities. Our intention has not been to give a comprehensive overview of the theories surrounding learning disabilities. Rather, we have tried to offer practical advice and strategies for helping the learning-disabled child at home, based on the success of the one-to-one approach used in the Gym Clubs. Because this child can often be very disruptive within the family circle, we have also included methods you can use to modify his behavior and information on how other family members can support the child's struggle to fit in. This unhappy child who feels so "different" needs all the understanding he can get.

This book is designed primarily for the parents of children from nursery school to about age twelve. We have, however, included a chapter on the specific problems of the teenager with learning disabilities. By the time they reach this difficult stage, the chronic low self-esteem of these children can create serious social problems. For them the normal adolescent need to be part of their peer group is even more urgent, and they are more easily led into delinquency and drug abuse. Studies have indicated that a staggering proportion of young criminals suffer from learning disabilities that have probably never been diagnosed.

If you are the parent of a child with learning disabilities, you face an exceptional challenge. Confronted by jargon-laden psychologists' reports, impatient teachers, family conflict, insensitive comments by everyone from your best friend to the proprietor of the corner store, and your own exhaustion and frustration, you are repeatedly asking yourself, "What can *I* do to help my child? How can *I* keep him from feeling like a failure?" Although there are no easy answers, no all-encompassing solutions to the problem of learning disabilities, you the parent can do a great deal to improve both your child's capabilities and his self-esteem. The strategies, games, and activities we offer you here will take your time and energy, but you know that your child is worth it.

Your Child Can Win

PART ONE

Your Child at Home and at School

CHAPTER I

What Is a Learning Disability?

He is not blind, but he cannot seem to see.
He is not deaf, but he cannot seem to hear.
He is not retarded, but he cannot seem to learn.

Nancy's Story

Nancy's parents marvelled at her energy and curiosity and were thankful that their little girl was so full of bustle and good nature. She was into everything, eager to learn, and playing at going to school long before she was ready. Before she had even entered kindergarten she had prepared breakfast in bed for her parents with help from her younger sister. Friends of the family laughed and prophesied that she would be a brain surgeon or a leading scientist some day.

Everything looked rosy for Nancy until she entered school. Her boundless energy and amiability propelled her through kindergarten, but when Nancy reached Grade 1 it was as if she had hit a brick wall. Unfortunately her teacher had a nervous breakdown halfway through the year because of several hyperactive youngsters who were so disruptive that they had to be removed from school. Nancy and two or three of her friends developed severe tension headaches. Nancy's slow progress was put down to the difficult classroom atmosphere.

In Grade 2 she had a good teacher who tried to make up for the poor beginning in Grade 1 but confessed to Nancy's mother that she could not make much headway with Nancy despite her obvious intelligence. By Grade 3 her teacher was calling Nancy emotionally disturbed because she was lying about finishing her workbook and was becoming more and more withdrawn.

The emotional effects of her inability to learn to read were devastating for Nancy. From a bright, happy, good-natured, energetic child she became a whiny, withdrawn, unhappy little girl. She would sneak money out of her mother's purse to treat her classmates — trying to buy the friends she felt she didn't deserve. One day her mother missed four quarters from her purse and she knew exactly what had happened. Nancy had just left to return to school after lunch. She was accompanied by two other girls her own age who lived near by. When they had called for Nancy there had been much whispering and giggling in the hall as they left. Nancy's mother hurried over to the corner drugstore and confronted the three girls, about to buy chocolate bars.

"Nancy, I would like my four quarters back," she told her.

Nancy hesitated for a moment, then handed them over. The other two girls ran off in the direction of the school before Nancy's mother could say anything to them.

"Nancy, why on earth would you steal money from my purse?" her mother asked.

"The kids won't play with me if I don't have money," was Nancy's reply. "They keep telling me I'm stupid. Mummy, is that right? Am I really stupid?"

It was this conversation that convinced Nancy's mother to spend the money necessary for an independent psychological assessment of her daughter, a decision she never regretted.

Tests showed that Nancy was suffering from a reading problem called dyslexia. She reversed letters in words and had poor visual memory: she could not remember the "picture" of a word. Remedial reading over a period of many years has improved Nancy's skills and she is now doing well in university and is a happy and energetic girl.

Timmy's Story

From almost the moment he was born, Timmy appeared different from his brothers and sisters. He was never still. He cried a lot. Even at a very early age he was a whiny, disruptive child. He learned to walk early and was into everything. He had an explosive temper and was as likely to throw a glass of milk across the room as he was to drink it. He seemed to have constant colds, which contributed to his mother's frustration, because it was impossible to keep him in bed. Twice he was nearly hit by a car when he darted into the road without looking. By the time Timmy reached Grade 1, the local hospital's Emergency Department was used to seeing him; he was constantly getting cuts, bruises, and bangs from fighting or from not looking where he was going. In fact, it seemed as though he just didn't see things right in front of him.

Timmy was finally sent to an allergist after a series of colds which led his pediatrician to suspect he might have allergies. The results were surprising. Timmy had a long list of allergies that were undermining his health. It wasn't easy to begin the task of eliminating the sources, but for Timmy's sake it was essential. The allergist also suggested a series of allergy shots. By the time these tests were done, relations within the family group were very strained. Father was accusing Mother of spoiling Timmy and giving in to his every whim and demand. The other children maintained that Mother had no time for them any more. His school was complaining about his disruptive behavior in class.

When Timmy's allergy shots began and the household was organized to eliminate as many allergens as possible, amazing things began to happen. It soon became clear that Timmy's hyperactivity had been at least partly due to his many allergies. When most of these had been identified and treated, he began to be less hyperactive, to have much improved concentration, and above all, to be much easier to manage. From a supercharged little demon he settled down into a fairly normal little boy who could now profit from schooling because his attention span had lengthened considerably. It was found that he had a moderately severe visual perception problem, but this now proved amenable to remedial help.

Mark's Story

From birth, Mark did not seem to develop in the normal way. His had been a difficult birth and his parents couldn't help wondering if this had anything to do with Mark's multiple problems. He was not spastic, but he had obvious poor coordination. He was late rolling over, sitting up, holding a spoon, and walking. He couldn't talk until he was three years old and then only in short, stilted sentences. He seemed to bump into everything, fall over anything in his path, and generally be a walking accident looking for a place to happen. Mark's parents took him to several doctors and got nowhere. One doctor said he would probably grow out of it; another said he thought Mark was mentally retarded and his parents should just learn to accept him as he was. As he grew older, he could not fit into his peer group because he was so uncoordinated that he couldn't learn to ride a two-wheeler, skate, swim, or do any of the things other little boys his age could do.

It was not until his pediatrician suggested a complete psychological and physical assessment that a group of doctors working together found that this little boy was not mentally retarded but was a victim of severe learning disabilities, possibly due to his difficult birth. Mark had a visual-perception problem that prevented his brain from registering what he saw as quickly as it should, resulting in his tendency to trip over objects right in front of him. Also present was an auditory-perception problem that made it very difficult for him to tune out background noises. Both his gross and his fine motor development were much below average, but the doctors and the therapists felt that they would improve with the constant repetition of prescribed exercises.

Fortunately for Mark, his family never lost faith in his ability to master his problems. They worked with the Gym Club, doctors, therapists, educational specialists, and special schools, and Mark has made exceptional progress. He has accepted the limitations of his disabilities, and has developed skills in areas that are not affected by his problems. His determination and intelligence have made him a champion chess-player. Mark himself laughs when he says: "I may never make the Olympics, but I can play a helluva game of chess!"

What Is a Learning Disability?

The National Advisory Committee on Handicapped Children in the United States describes a learning disability as follows:

> Children with special learning disabilities exhibit disorders in one or more of the basic psychological processes involved in understanding or using spoken or written language. These may be manifested in disorders of listening, thinking, talking, reading, writing, spelling, or arithmetic. They include conditions which have been referred to as perceptual handicaps, brain injury, minimal brain dysfunction, dyslexia, developmental aphasia, and other terms. It does not include learning problems which are due primarily to visual, hearing, or motor handicaps, or environmental disadvantages.

Unlike the mentally retarded child, whose ability to learn is restricted in all areas, and who will never achieve average performance at any skill, the learning-disabled child may be performing well in math but be unable to read, or vice versa. While the mentally retarded child's problems are general, the child with learning disabilities usually demonstrates specific anomalies in learning, and extensive testing is needed to identify the individual areas affected.

What we are saying, then, is that children with learning disabilities have difficulties learning in the accepted way at the accepted rate for their age group. They do not follow the normal pattern of maturing. For some reason their channels for learning do not process input in the usual way. Experts estimate that learning disabilities affect as many as one out of four, which means that in the average-sized classroom, three or four children will have moderate to severe learning problems.

It can come as either a shock or a relief to parents when a child is first diagnosed as having a learning disability, depending on whether their child has exhibited severe symptoms previously or has appeared perfectly normal. When they finally hear the words "learning disability," parents are often left wondering what this means and what the future holds for their child. If the professional who writes the assessment couches it in a lot of technical verbiage, they may be almost as much in the dark as they were before they read it. Sometimes meetings with teachers, guidance counsellors, and psychologists only add to their confusion.

If you feel bewildered by your child's learning disability, you are not alone. It is important for you to understand as much as possible as soon as possible, but if it just seems too much to take in all at once, don't be dismayed. It is a complicated business that is constantly changing. New discoveries and new methods are constantly evolving and no one can keep abreast of all the new developments. If you have faith in your child's school and do your best to help at home, you can rest assured that your child has the best possible chance for a good future.

The Importance of Communicating

Most new babies are born with the inherent capacity to perceive and communicate, although at birth they are far too immature to comprehend their surroundings. Except for their innate need for warmth, security, and food, they are, for several weeks after birth, fairly oblivious of what goes on around them. However, once they do start to tune in, they do so very quickly. Even at three months most babies have become quite aware of their surroundings and adept at communicating their desires.

As a child matures, he develops more complex ways of relating to his environment and acquires necessary skills. As these skills become more coordinated, the child gradually becomes aware of the increasing importance of communicating with his world, of obtaining information from his environment and giving information in return. He perceives his world through his senses and interprets it according to the messages he receives, and correlates these with his limited experience. If his perception is faulty, or the processes used to relate to his world are deficient, he will receive incorrect impressions of his world. Unfortunately he will not be aware that his impressions are askew because he has no point of comparison.

Probably the most important form of communication, although by no means the only one, is language. A small child needs someone who will talk to him if he is to develop language skills. Deprived children often do not develop these skills until very late in childhood, not because they are unable to speak but because they rarely hear the spoken word. If we think about it, language skills form the basis for the largest part of our learning throughout our lives. The ability to understand the spoken word, to read, to write, to speak, and to interpret information correctly is basic to living in today's world.

Language skills are the result of coordinating millions of nerves, muscles, receptors, and brain cells into a working team. These skills take a surprisingly short time to develop, considering the complexity of the task. By three years of age the average child can understand what is said to him and can communicate in simple and effective language. By six or seven many have learned to read well enough to enjoy a simple book. They are on the road to a lifetime of learning based on their language skills.

How We Communicate

In the simplest terms, communication is the interchange of information between an individual and the external world. The information is received by us through our five senses: taste, touch, smell, sight, and hearing. It is then processed by our intelligence and stored in our memory. Taste, touch, and smell are used by very young babies to learn about their environment right from birth. Sight and hearing are slower to develop and are more dependent upon feedback from the environment. Although a baby can hear at birth, he cannot identify and discriminate between sounds. His sight is even less developed, since his eyes are not able to focus on an object for at least six to ten weeks after birth.

In his first year, a baby constantly tests the reality of his world with his senses, starting with those senses that are most highly developed. Haven't we all been amused or exasperated when a baby puts all sorts of objects into his mouth or explores their feel and texture with his hands? The sense of touch is very important to a baby because it gives him the feedback of information that creates feelings of comfort and security. He loves to explore new touch sensations, such as squeezing food through his fingers before he tastes it, but he will also pull his hand away quickly from something hot, cold, sharp, prickly, or unfamiliar as his environment communicates discomfort or possible danger.

A baby soon learns to recognize the face of his mother, then the faces of other family members, and finally the familiar things that make up his environment. When he begins to pay more attention to new things in his world, he will often fall back on taste, touch, and smell to investigate. While a newborn might turn his head toward a loud noise, it is weeks before he begins to separate sounds and identify them. First he recognizes his mother's voice as meaning food and comfort are on their way. Then he begins to associate the different sounds of his world with different objects. He will know that a telephone rings, a dog barks, and a cat meows, or that he can make a delightful noise all by himself just by waving a rattle in his chubby fist. He has learned his first lesson about controlling his environment. Soon he discovers his voice and begins to babble to himself as he discovers the methods of forming sounds with his vocal chords. Before long his delighted mother distinguishes what sounds to her like "Mama," and by showing her pleasure gives positive reinforcement to her baby's vocalizing efforts.

All these are average developmental patterns within the first year of a baby's life as he learns from his environment and begins to communicate with it. However, for the child with a learning disability, the pattern is entirely different. Although he is not aware of it, his world is giving him mixed messages.

These most often involve the two senses which develop more slowly, sight and hearing. For reasons which are not understood, some children appear to be born with an inherent defect in processing information received through their eyes or through their ears, much as another child might be born with a foot that turns in or a birthmark on his shoulder. While there may be nothing wrong with his sight or his hearing, his visual or auditory processes may not be giving him the same information that most children of his age are receiving. He comes to incorrect and confusing conclusions about his environment, although he has no way of knowing this. The result is usually a confused and frightened child to whom nothing is as it appears to him.

How Your Child Experiences His Disability

Visual Skills are described as the ability to receive patterns of light and interpret them correctly. We receive light through our eyes, which then deliver a picture to our brain, where we process the information, learning to distinguish among the pictures received and relate them to past experience. This accumulated knowledge is then stored in our memory for retrieval at some future time when it is needed. A baby learns to know the faces and objects of his confined little world quite quickly. The child whose learning disabilities involve visual skills is in a totally different position. While his eyes may see an object with complete accuracy, the message transmitted to his brain, or the processing of the information, may be incorrect, giving him a distorted or incomplete view of his world. Sometimes the problem is in committing visual data to long-term memory. A child with this problem can't remember the name of an object, or associate the "picture" of a word with the word itself. Norma's older daughter showed her poor visual memory when she was learning the names of the different colors. It took her much longer than average to remember that the name of the sky's color is blue and the name of the snow's color is white. When a child has a psycho-educational assessment, one of the first things tested is visual acuity; this often uncovers one or more problems, such as an inability to distinguish distances, difficulty seeing an approaching object, an inability to pick out a familiar object from a group of unfamiliar objects, and others.

If a child is having a problem in any visual area it cuts down on his ability to receive information from his environment. If he is receiving incorrect information which he does not know is incorrect, his response will be unintelligible to those who are not aware of his disability. This can be very frustrating to parents and teachers.

Bobby, a very bright seven-year-old, was constantly in trouble with his teacher because, when asked to bring an object from a nearby shelf, Bobby would return to report that he couldn't see it. The teacher and his parents put this down to laziness, inattentiveness, or perverseness on Bobby's part. Only after the results of an assessment were known did they understand Bobby's problem. He could not separate objects from their backgrounds. He could see scissors or a ruler on a shelf by themselves, but if there was a jumble of other objects as well, Bobby could not pick out the scissors or the ruler. All he could see was the jumble.

For Patty the problem was even more serious. She was just not aware of approaching traffic. Her eyes didn't convey a warning to her that a car was approaching, because her brain was unable to judge distance. She might wait for a car to pass which was two blocks away, or step off the curb and attempt to cross right in front of a car. It took a great deal of training for Patty to understand her difficulty and learn to cross only when she knew it was safe.

Auditory Skills involve the ability to receive sounds and interpret them correctly, and to utter spoken sounds which will be correctly interpreted by those hearing them. Again we are faced with many children who have no physiological problems with their hearing, but only with the processing of what is heard. The following story illustrates one type of auditory learning disability and how it can severely affect a child's school performance and his self-esteem.

Philip was a delightful, inquisitive youngster who appeared to be very intelligent when he entered Grade 1. His parents expected no problems at school and were very surprised when they received negative reports from Philip's teacher. Philip would not pay attention in class, he was constantly disrupting classroom activities, he would not answer when spoken to, and he appeared to be living in a world of daydreams all his own. By the end of first term, Philip's teacher was convinced this child had a severe emotional problem. Philip's parents were unable to shed any light on his behavior at school, because he was no trouble at all at home. His mother finally took the time to sit in on a few of Philip's classes and was surprised and upset by what she observed. Philip paid not the slightest attention to his teacher, and had not prepared any of the work he was asked to do. That night Philip's father decided to have a word with his son to see if he could come to any conclusions.

"Philip, I understand you aren't doing very well in school. What's the trouble? Don't you like your teacher?"

"She's O.K. I guess," Philip replied. After a thoughtful pause he continued, "Dad, why do I have to go to school?"

"You have to go to school to learn, just like everyone else. You know that, Philip."

"But, Dad, I'm too dumb to learn anything. Why can't I just stay home?"

"What do you mean you're too dumb? Where did you get that idea?" his father demanded.

"Well, that's what the other kids say, because I can't learn any of the stuff that dumb ol' Miss Johnson is teaching."

"Why can't you learn, Philip?"

"I dunno, but all she does is stand at my desk and yell at me."

This conversation disturbed Philip's father to the point that he requested an interview with Philip's teacher and the school principal. At the suggestion of the principal, the school psychologist was included.

"The boy is either mentally retarded or emotionally disturbed," was Miss Johnson's opinion.

"Nonsense," said Philip's father. "He was beginning to read even before he entered Grade 1."

Both the psychologist and the school principal listened

carefully, then talked to Philip himself. The child was subdued and cooperative, but did little to help them.

"I dunno what you want me to say," Philip told his principal. "I guess I'm just stupid and always will be."

The boy's defeatist attitude was very familiar to the psychologist, who immediately recommended a complete psychoeducational assessment. The results surprised everyone: on standard intelligence tests, Philip scored at a near-genius level. Nevertheless, he was not learning and had developed severe emotional problems. He saw himself as a failure and had given up trying. The psychologist soon discovered why. In kindergarten, Philip had progressed amazingly well because he was in a quiet, controlled setting. When he was moved into Grade 1, he was placed in an open-concept classroom containing both Grades 1 and 2. The children were allowed to wander at will with little or no discipline, so that there was always a good deal of background noise, coupled with traffic noise coming in from the outside. Further tests showed that Philip suffered from poor auditory discrimination. He found it impossible to separate his teacher's voice from the background noise unless she was standing right at his desk shouting at him. He had retreated into his own world, convinced that he couldn't learn. When his problem was discovered, Philip was moved into a more controlled, quieter classroom where the teacher fully understood his disability. By the end of Grade 2, he had caught up to and passed most of the classmates who had labelled him dumb, stupid, and retarded.

There are other learning disabilities, similar to Philip's, associated with the processing of what is heard. Some children have poor auditory memory. Others have difficulty learning to speak properly because they don't hear the sounds of words correctly. These children are often slow learning to talk. Other children need practice in listening because they tend to have problems understanding the spoken word, especially if the speaker has an accent with which they are unfamiliar. These children will often have problems answering verbal questions in class and yet have no trouble if they are written on the board.

Remember, all these children *hear* perfectly well. One of

the best ways to understand their dilemma is to think back to when you were studying a foreign language at school. Perhaps you were able to understand when a person spoke very slowly, separating each word so they didn't run together. An animated conversation between two or three people, however, was a frustrating cacophony. That is how human speech often sounds to a child with an auditory learning disability.

As well as with sight and hearing, a child might have problems with the control of large and small muscles: poor physical coordination. While this in itself can be troublesome, it is usually accompanied by either visual or auditory problems. We have found in the Gym Club that helping a child with gross and fine motor control, thus improving his self-esteem, almost always helps him in other areas where he is weak.

It is hard for the adults in a child's world to see his problems from his point of view. If they have never had a disability, how can they begin to understand the frustration of a child who sees or hears something incorrectly and then is criticized for acting on the information he has received? While a child may think he is communicating or receiving communications correctly, if the perception or processing is faulty he is not in touch with the reality of his world. No one has the ability to receive or impart all information perfectly. Some people are inarticulate, some are tone-deaf, some can't remember names, many find the language of numbers a complete mystery. As a general rule, these impediments are so slight that, though they cause frustration and embarrassment, they do not slow down the learning process or affect the ability to communicate effectively. Until his learning disability is discovered and assessed, the child has no idea why his world is different from other people's, why adults and his peers don't understand him, or why he can't learn as quickly as his friends. He is alone and afraid in a world he lacks the basic tools to understand.

What Causes a Learning Disability?

Anguished parents ask this question probably more than any other. We would like to be able to give a reassuring answer,

but none exists. In certain cases, the cause seems to be heredi-
tary; in others, allergies are sometimes involved; still others
show a pattern of difficult birth or maternal ill health during
pregnancy. Just as often there will be no apparent reason.

It is important that parents understand that the causes of
learning disabilities are almost impossible to pinpoint, because many of them are quick to try to assign blame. Parents
who are carrying a load of guilt cannot do their best for their
child. Many marriages have broken up because one or other
of the partners pointed a finger of blame when there was
absolutely no reason for doing so. Even if it were possible to
assign blame, what good would it do? With the possible
exception of fetal alcohol syndrome (heavy maternal drinking
during pregnancy), or one or two other prenatal influences
such as German measles or a very high fever during pregnancy,
there appears to be no prenatal reason for these disabilities. A
slight loss of oxygen during a difficult birth may cause minimal brain damage, yet there are just as many children who had
difficult births who show no apparent effects as there are
children who suffer from learning disabilities. Some hypothe-
size that a series of very high fevers or convulsions in infancy
may be responsible, but again this has yet to be proven to be
a causative factor.

It is surprising how often we hear one parent blame "bad
genes" or "bad blood" on the part of the other parent. They
will point an accusing finger at "Old Uncle Harry who was
never quite right in the head." Investigation might show that
Uncle Harry suffered from the aftereffects of a severe head
injury, not "bad genes" or "bad blood." It has not been proven
that heredity plays a role in learning disabilities. Another
parent will ask whether a chronic infection could be responsible.
The answer is no, although an infection might make a child
more tired at school so that he has difficulty concentrating,
which might lead a teacher to suspect a learning disability. A
professional assessment combined with a physical examination will reveal chronic infections and dispel worries about a
learning disability.

Parents who want the best for their learning-disabled child
will forget about trying to assign blame and will conserve

their energy and emotions for the task of helping their child in every way possible.

How Serious Is My Child's Problem?

No one can assess the seriousness of your child's disability except a group of experts working together. One of the most important outcomes of a good psycho-educational assessment combined with a thorough physical examination is that they will give both you and your child's school some idea of his potential. The assessment cannot offer absolute predictions: some disabilities seem to improve dramatically as a child matures; others remain for life. Only time will tell for many children, but almost all are left with at least a residual disability, even after years of remedial work. Your child must understand that he will get all the help possible, but he must also learn to cope with whatever disability is left. Norma's two daughters have battled moderately severe reading problems since early primary school and are now succeeding at university despite their problems, because they have learned to allow extra time for studying and to use other methods of reinforcement to aid their learning. Children with visual problems must learn to use their auditory senses to compensate, and vice versa.

For the child with a really severe disability, or a disability compounded by other problems, it is almost impossible to predict the future. Unfortunately a learning disability can be such a powerful psychological influence that a severely disabled child needs almost more help than any one system can provide. This child must have special schooling, special psychological help, and strong support in making social adjustments. If a child with severe problems but average intelligence can be encouraged to make his greatest efforts, seeming miracles can occur. There are case histories of children who appeared headed for an institution but who finally managed to get their behavior and their learning process on the right track, and have ended up as well-adjusted, productive members of the community. Success seems to depend on overall cooperation between schools, parents, psychologists, and doctors, all working as a team for the child's good. You, as a parent, are in the best position to coordinate and assess these efforts. This puts a real burden on you, but it is a worthwhile job whose end result is a happy, motivated child who matures into an effective adult.

Who Has Learning Disabilities?

Anyone can have a learning disability. Looking back to your own school days, you might recall one or two subjects that were much more difficult for you than other subjects. You might remember that you, or a friend, had low averages in the early grades but that these improved as you got older. You might also remember a child who was the class "dummy" who later edited a newspaper, or became president of a multi-million-dollar corporation. Learning-disabled children can be the offspring of doctors, lawyers, presidents of universities, farmhands, street sweepers, or factory workers. Winston Churchill was considered to be of dull-average intelligence in primary school. Albert Einstein's parents were so worried about his poor performance that they doubted his ability to make a living when he grew up. Leonardo da Vinci, not only a great artist but also one of the most inventive thinkers who ever lived, wrote everything in mirror writing.

It is interesting to note that there appear to be about four times as many boys as girls affected with learning disabilities. No one has been able to discover why, although recent studies have suggested that a boy is less likely to show symptoms of learning disabilities if his teachers in the early grades are men rather than women.

What Are the Effects of Learning Disability?

These are difficult to predict because there are so many variables, such as the degree and type of learning disability, available resources, family environment, and the child's overall personality, to mention only a few. The most noticeable effect is unevenness of learning. The typical pattern of a child with a moderate to severe problem is average or above-average learning in some areas, with below-average or very much below-average learning in others. This is such a common picture that it is usually the first indication of trouble at school. Such was the case with Sally, an obviously bright youngster who was full of bubbly fun, could read at Grade 7 level when she was only in Grade 4, but was unable to learn to tell time and couldn't pass Grade 1 math.

Many of these children also seem to have coordinational difficulties, although these are not always present. Some outstanding athletes have learning disabilities, and lots of people with poor coordination have no learning problems. When coordination problems accompany a learning disability, the combination can be devastating, especially for little boys who want desperately to be one of the gang. It is a terrible blow to the ego if all your friends can ride a two-wheeler or skate but you can't. Helping to train both small muscles for fine motor control and large muscles for gross motor control can improve a learning disability, but whether this is a direct effect or the result of improved self-esteem remains to be determined.

The effects that are most disturbing to parents are the emotional problems that usually result from a learning disability. Because your child is not like other children, at least in his own eyes, he will probably develop many coping devices and possibly moderate to serious psychological problems. Even a child with only a slight disability may see himself as "different." It is in this area that a parent can be of most help to a child, at least initially, by letting him know that *he is not a problem child, just a child with a problem.* It is often difficult, but patience and persistence usually pay off.

When there is a very severe psychological effect, and behavior is affected to the point where a child is not socially accepted and is a disrupting family influence, a wise parent will enlist the best psychological help available. A study done some years ago in the United States in a school for emotionally disturbed boys showed that close to ninety percent had a learning disability. Where at one time it was thought that the learning disability was a result of the emotional problems, it is now almost universally accepted that the emotional problems are a result of the learning disability. If the emotional problems alone are treated, then only the symptoms are being attacked instead of the problem itself. A concerted attack on the disability, coupled with emotional support, can work seeming miracles with these unfortunate children.

Occasionally the effects of a learning disability are first noticed in a child's social development, especially when a formerly easygoing child changes dramatically on entering school. It has often been found that the school bully and the school clown are really unhappy youngsters whose problems stem from a learning disability. These children may exhibit no symptoms until they enter school and find themselves not able to keep up to their friends, like Nancy in our opening story. One may resort to bullying his peers to establish his spot in the pecking order. Another becomes the class clown in an effort to get some positive attention. Some children will seek negative attention if they find it impossible to get positive attention.

There are many varied effects of a learning disability and therefore no firm rules that say, "If your child has this problem, he will behave in this way and show his disability in such and such a way." While the very unpredictability of this problem makes it so difficult to deal with, it also offers every parent hope that his child can overcome his disability to enjoy a satisfying, useful life.

What Help Is Available?

Where you live, more than any other factor, determines the amount and type of help available for your child. The larger the city, the better and more numerous the resources will be. If you live in the country, or in a small town, good help may not be as readily available. Your first source of professional help may be your family doctor if your child's problem is obvious before he begins school. Through your doctor you have access to medical and psychological personnel in your area who are specialists in learning disabilities. Your school is the next place to turn. The school's resources are likely to be geared mainly to those children with borderline to moderately severe problems, and they may or may not be equipped to assist with psychological difficulties. Any psychologist you consult, whether for administering tests or for assessing emotional problems, should be a specialist in learning disabilities. If such a specialist is not available in your area, it may be necessary for you to take your child to a larger center for proper assessment and even for follow-up treatment.

One of the most valuable supports for parents is the Association for Children with Learning Disabilities. The ACLD is represented in all large centers and in many small centers throughout most English-speaking countries. If there is not one in your area, it is worth considering getting together with other parents and starting a branch. The ACLD provides parents with information about local services and new discoveries, publishes an excellent newsletter, and offers an opportunity to get together with other parents and compare notes. For parents struggling with the worries and frustrations of raising an LD (learning-disabled) child, the encouragement and support of others who have been through the same difficult situation is invaluable. If you can't locate your nearest ACLD, ask your school. If they don't know, write to your national office, whose address is listed on page 243.

If your child has become too much of a burden for you and your family, or if his behavior is such that your local school can no longer cope with him, there are now many excellent special schools available. It should be noted that most Boards of Education are now required by law to provide specialized education for your child to enable him to reach his potential. If this means special classes, special teachers, or even a special school, the board will usually be required to pay the cost of any facilities that they are unable to provide. Consult your local Board of Education about this.

CHAPTER 2

Parenting the
Learning-Disabled Child

When you are raising a child with learning disabilities, you have a whole new set of rules to play by when it comes to such matters as discipline, structuring, sibling rivalry, confrontation, and all those other ingredients of day-to-day parenting. The trouble is, no one can tell you what the new rules are. As each child is an individual, each learning disability is individual as well. However, in the large majority of cases, you can assume that if your child has a learning disability, you will eventually run into behavioral problems that are the result of low self-esteem. This poses a delicate dilemma. Parents hesitate to deal too severely with any child who has a low opinion of himself already, and yet no one wants to spoil his child. Methods of handling the behavioral problems of learning-disabled children must be considered very carefully. That is where *positive parenting* comes in. If certain basic precepts are followed and great care is taken to bolster your child's self-esteem and help him in every way possible, he may ultimately pose no more problems than any average child. If he is also hyperactive, you may have a much more difficult time of it. A good deal will depend on the character and personality of the household members. A calm, well-organized family unit is better able to accept a hyperactive child and do the best for him.

It is safe to say that all children thrive on a structured life with known limits set by firm, loving parents. This structured life-style is doubly important for a child who is getting mixed messages through his faulty perception of his world. Continuity is of prime importance to an LD child, and it has been our experience that a disturbance in the established structure of his life can set back many of the gains he might have made. For example, the even, predictable quality of a deliberately structured day — when he gets up, what he wears, when he eats, when he goes to bed — can often help control the aimless, compulsive movements of a hyperactive child. A disruption in his normal routine can completely unsettle him and spark uncontrollable behavior. It is, therefore, worth the effort for everyone in the family to assist in keeping the life of this child on as even a keel as possible.

We are not suggesting that your child be wrapped in cotton wool and protected from the outside world. It is necessary for him to learn to live with other people, and to take the consequences of bad behavior. It doesn't do him a bit of good if the family condones his unacceptable behavior, because people outside of the household certainly won't accept antisocial actions. What you, and your whole family, are aiming for is a child who acts like any other child, except that he happens to have a learning disability.

Even the most severely afflicted child can be taught how to behave well enough so that he has a social life, which will give him the positive feedback he so desperately needs. If he is not taught how to get along with both adults and his peer group, he may suffer irreparable damage, which will become evident when he is an adolescent or a young adult. We know of one young lad who had near-normal intelligence, but severe and numerous learning disabilities. His parents did an amazing job of helping him adjust to his multiple problems, but they ignored the socialization problems of adolescence. His self-esteem in what he had accomplished at school was strong and he had pleasant manners towards adults, but he had never learned how to relate to his peers. When he began to develop sexually, he could not cope with this new drive. At nineteen, driven to frustration by his lack of social skills, he molested several girls. His was an exceptionally sad case, because he had almost won the battle against great odds.

It is never easy to know what is best for a young child, but there are certain guidelines which will help you make a more qualified judgment about the various factors which will influence the way you approach such problems as discipline.

Attack the Problem, Not the Child

Although this sounds like a truism, it is unfortunate that in our culture it is not widely accepted. However, we feel it is probably the most important point to remember in your day-to-day living with your learning-disabled child. Keep in mind that his need for positive feedback is much greater than that of the average child. Most parents at some time or other become angry with and critical of their children. Unfortunately it is much easier to do this with learning-disabled children, who are easy targets. It may be very hard to remember that this is a child with a problem, not a problem child.

If you call any child a "rotten kid," he feels devastated and all too often will take your words as being literally true. After all, you are his parent, you are older and presumably wiser, therefore you should know. If this criticism hurts the average well-behaved youngster, think how much harder it is for a child whose behavior is erratic and whose performance is often below that of his peers.

With any child, it is much better to criticize the unwanted behavior and then try to discover what is causing it. There is a distinct difference between telling a child in words or in effect, "You're a rotten kid," and telling him: "You're a great kid, but that was rotten behavior." It is essential that your child understand the difference, especially if he tends to be disruptive. However, you must also guard against giving your child's bad behavior too much attention, as this only serves to reinforce it.

With some children who have gross or fine motor problems, it is easy to fall into the trap of either saying or implying, "Can't you do anything right?" or taking over when he is trying but not succeeding. Often it will take many repetitions for even an eight- or nine-year-old with fine motor problems to learn something as seemingly simple as tying a knot or doing up buttons. It is too bad that parents, many of whom are working and/or single nowadays, lead such busy lives that it is hard to find either the time or the patience to allow this child to keep trying, or to give him subtle help and instruction so that he won't feel put down. If there are other children in the family, there are often added problems; however, when older children are able to understand the problems of their learning-disabled brother or sister, they too should be encouraged to help the youngster.

If a child has not been diagnosed as having a learning disability before he enters the school system, he is likely to develop emotional problems in the early grades, which may be the first signs that something is wrong. This is why we are strong supporters of the Early Identification Programs that are present in most school systems today, and that endeavor to pinpoint those children most at risk as early as nursery school or junior kindergarten. Unfortunately there is still a large number of children whose learning disabilities are not discovered until Grade 1 or later. One of the reasons for this is that their problems often masquerade as something else. A happy, confident, eager child can enter school and quickly become an emotional basket-case because of his sudden feelings of inadequacy. If criticism at home and at school tends to be aimed at him rather than at his problems, you will soon have a child who feels he is a loser. We have known far too many seven-year-olds who have given up on themselves and see their futures as hopeless.

Put yourself in your child's place. What could be more devastating to a child than to fail kindergarten when all his friends are going into Grade 1, or to seeing his friends all learning to read when he can't understand anything in his workbook? Even the most confident child feels shattered. He may be labelled emotionally disturbed because he tries to lie his way out of difficulties caused by his undiagnosed learning disabilities. He may be accused of laziness, disinterest, poor attitude, bad behavior, and so forth. He is actually trying his hardest but is getting nowhere — but no one will believe him.

When he finally succeeds in accomplishing a formerly impossible task, he will be blamed for not trying hard enough before. His is a classic no-win situation.

Often the worst damage to a child's self-esteem is done before either teachers or parents are aware of his disability. Sometimes it will take years before an astute teacher or concerned parent will finally suggest a complete psycho-educational assessment. During the intervening years, the child is attacked again and again for something over which he has no control. His coping devices are usually, first, to tune out, second, to drop out. Some drop out psychologically by just giving up and not trying to do anything; others will start to run away physically from situations that are no longer tolerable. One parent admitted that her son dropped out of the school system at ten, even though he was still there in body. Others just refuse to turn up at school, day after day. Some who are old enough leave home, if home is the source of more criticism and conflict.

There are too many of these unhappy, misdirected kids on our streets today. Not long ago one of the street vendors common to all large cities approached us to buy some jewelry she had made. It was beautifully made with exquisite, intricate workmanship. We were enchanted with her work and questioned her about it. It was obvious this girl did not value the quality of her work. At least twice in the first few minutes she made the statement that she was just a "dummy" doing this for fun. We both recognized that this girl, probably not more than sixteen, was a good example of a learning-disabled child who had never been diagnosed. Our suspicion was quickly confirmed. She was selling her wares for little more than the cost of materials. We suggested she show them to a friend of ours who had a boutique and offered to write down the name and address for her. "Better print it, then, 'cause I don't read writin' too good," she replied. Positive parenting and positive teaching skills that attack the problem and its symptoms without attacking the child can help prevent a lifelong battle with negative self-esteem. You'll need to engage the cooperation of all family members and the school system, but it is essential to your child's wellbeing. It is up to you to make sure that the positive way you treat your child at home is followed through at school. Don't, under any circumstances, allow anyone, anywhere, to belittle your child and add to his already heavy burden of problems.

The Dangers of Negative Parenting

Perhaps it is a hangover from Victorian or Puritan times, but there is a common method of dealing with children in our society that certainly does not bring out the best in them, whether or not they have a learning disability. This method is most often found in parents who were themselves brought up by strongly authoritarian parents who firmly decreed that children should be seen and not heard (and seen as little as possible). Although these parents themselves may have hated their repressive upbringing, they will almost always fall into the same pattern when they begin rearing their own children.

This style of raising children is sometimes referred to as parenting by confrontation or intimidation. Parents who hear themselves saying things like "Now if you don't pick up all your clothes I'm going to give you a spanking you'll never forget!" are practitioners of parenting by intimidation. If parents confront their children with accusations and inquisitions instead of asking questions and listening to answers, they are parenting by confrontation, a method that invariably leads to family arguments and dissension.

The "spare the rod and spoil the child" school of child-rearing might do little damage if the child is absolutely sure that he is loved and accepted by all members of his family. Some children are astute enough to "read between the lines" and assume correctly that Mother and Father aren't nearly as tough as they sound. However, many learning-disabled children are not as emotionally secure as their peers, and they are more sensitive to threats and criticisms — of which they hear more than their share. These children soon learn not to expect any positive feedback, to keep out of the way as much as possible, not to ask any questions, and to leave home as soon as they are legally able. Severe punishment is often their lot if they deviate from accepted behavior. They also seek attention outside the home and often find it in the form of negative attention at school. A boy may become a school bully; a girl will often become promiscuous at an early age. Occasionally children who have suffered either physical or psychological abuse at home will store this abuse in their subconscious and become, to the eyes of the community at least, good citizens. Unfortunately they will usually revert to this same destructive method of raising their own children. We can't help feeling that many children who are victims of parental mistreatment were victims first of a learning disability of which their parents were unaware or which they didn't understand.

Repression is not the only form of negative parenting. Because many parents rebelled against their own authoritarian upbringings, a new method became popular after the Second World War. As so often happens, the pendulum swung sharply in the other direction. Many of the baby-boom parents were determined not to make the same mistakes their parents had made, so they followed the gurus who told them to let their children learn from experience. Let them "do their own thing." No direction, no structuring, nothing positive in the way of values. While it is very important that children learn self-discipline and how to make decisions, they can't do it if they grow up in a void. If they have no structure, no rules, they are apt to grow into little savages. This "no parenting" method resulted in many spoiled and undisciplined petty tyrants whose parents couldn't stand to have them around. While all children need structure and limits, the learning-disabled child *must* have them to survive and learn, so this permissive method of parenting robs him of his chance to succeed.

Positive parenting is not easy, but it is worth the effort. It is all too easy to ignore a child who is behaving well and pay attention to him only when he is misbehaving. It is easier to say "don't" than to say "do." There will be many failures, no matter how hard you try, but don't be guilt-ridden if you are really trying and not always succeeding. It gets easier with practice and is certainly worth the effort when the end results are children of whom you can be proud.

Parenting the Difficult Child

Not all children with learning disabilities will be difficult to raise, but the great majority will have some problems not experienced by the average child. The most difficult to handle is the question of self-esteem, and the problem of building self-esteem without sacrificing discipline. It is never easy to keep tabs on a hyperactive child who darts from place to place, task to task, in an aimless display of high energy. These children are constantly at the mercy of their impulses, and it can be very wearing. It is hard to understand that a hyperactive child has little or no control over his behavior. It is also hard to cope with the child who seems unable to remember anything for more than a few seconds. You may ask him for a glass of water, but he will have forgotten what you said by the time he reaches the door.

Some children have such obvious behavioral problems that they are ostracized by their peer group, and even by the parents of children their own age. The mother of one clumsy little boy, who has both gross and fine motor problems, relates this story. Peter had been playing in a sandpile with a little friend from down the street. The little girl's mother came looking for her daughter just as one of Peter's awkward movements scattered some sand, some of which landed in his companion's eye. She started to cry. "Come, Susan," her mother said. "You know you aren't supposed to play with him. He isn't right in the head." In this case, the child's action was an inadvertent mishap; how much worse for the parent whose child deliberately throws sand in a friend's face.

The patience to deal with these children can only be learned by unrelenting practice and constantly biting your tongue to keep back that quick criticism. You also must ignore the insensitive remarks of others. You are bound to hear someone say, just loud enough for you to hear, "Let me have that kid for a few days and I'd get him into shape!"

Unless you were born with unlimited patience and the type of temperament that is always cool and collected, you will find yourself becoming angry and frustrated — with your child, with yourself, and with other people. You are apt to take it out on your unfortunate child and then feel terribly guilty. If you are like many other parents in a similar position, you will then have to battle with yourself not to overcompensate by being lavish with your attention (thus reinforcing the undesirable behavior) or overprotective (an emotionally destructive method of child-rearing).

Don't worry and feel guilty if you are less than perfect parenting a less than perfect child. You are not alone. This is one of the reasons we strongly advise parents to join a nearby ACLD group where they can air their troubles and difficulties among other parents with the same problems. This interchange of ideas will boost morale, relieve guilt, and provide lots of concrete suggestions.

Although thousands of books have been written by educators, physicians, teachers, psychologists, and parents concerning the care and nurturing of difficult-to-manage children, no one way is guaranteed to work with every child. We will endeavor to give you some guidelines. Try different methods that appeal to you, and if one works, use it. Read everything available which might help you with your problems; use those parts that work and discard the rest. Make up your own rules as you go along.

Winners and Losers

Psychologist Eric Berne (see Chapter 3, "What Is Transactional Analysis?", page 43) gives us a concept that can be very useful to parents who are faced with raising a difficult child. He suggests that children are programmed to become winners or losers in the business of living before they even enter school. If a child has a winning "life script," because he has been reared in a loving and accepting family, he will in all likelihood act out this built-in script all his life. He will see himself as a winner, as someone who is worth while, as someone who can overcome difficulties and land on top of the heap. If, on the other hand, he has been programmed to see himself as a loser by being put down (Dr. Berne calls it discounting) by family, peers, and teachers, and given only negative feedback, he will quite likely be a loser all his life. Negative parenting can undermine any child; it is almost guaranteed to do so to any child with a learning disability.

The child with a winner's outlook on life has a built-in mechanism to help him cope with the problems of a learning disability. With careful management by parents and teachers, he has a good chance of coming out on top and living a good life within the limits of his disability. He will learn to accept his problem, and will be willing to do the extra work necessary to improve his disability. He will learn to live with whatever disability remains when everything possible has been done.

The child with a loser's outlook on life already sees himself as a failure. When a learning disability distorts the picture even more, he will often use it as a crutch and an excuse. "What do you expect from someone with my problems?" will be his theme song, and he will tune out and drop out. This type of life script can be reversed, but it is very difficult. If very low self-esteem is evident, sometimes only professional help can turn things around.

Janet, a lonely girl with severe learning disabilities, was overprotected by one parent and severely criticized by the other. She developed such a low opinion of herself that at fifteen she became anorexic. When her weight dropped to the point where she was almost skeletal, her parents sought professional help. The psychiatrist told them that her anorexia was the result of such low self-esteem that she did not deem life worth living. It was a subconscious attempt at suicide. Janet's parents had tolerated taunts from other siblings, both younger and older, directed at their learning-disabled daughter; they had made no attempt to make her feel like an important member of the family. She knew she was a disruptive influence in the family and started running away at twelve. She constantly referred to herself as "the dummy." With years of psychiatric help, Janet gained confidence and made friends, yet how much easier her recovery would have been if her problems had been dealt with earlier, before so much harm had been done.

Making Your Child Feel Accepted

If your child has already been showing signs of being different from other siblings, a verdict of a learning disability may come, initially, as a relief: "Ah, now we know what the trouble is! Let's get down to doing something about it!" We have already mentioned time and again how important the cooperation of the whole family is in helping your child achieve his potential. Their overall attitude can often tip the balance between success and failure in helping a child realize his potential despite his disability.

However, we must now consider the sequence of emotions that will at some time or another affect the whole family: surprise, disbelief, anger directed at the child, themselves, or the person who breaks the news, or at the Fates, and a combination of guilt, shame, and disappointment. These emotions may be stronger in families where high hopes are held for all the children. If Mother and Father are both university graduates, the feelings of guilt and shame may be deeply felt, even while their intellects are telling them they shouldn't feel this way. On the other hand, there are those parents who reject the whole idea of a learning disability. They maintain either that there is no such thing as a learning disability or that it couldn't happen to their child. This denial often robs their child of needed assistance as well as implying to him such messages as "You could do it if you tried harder," "Learning was hard for me but I didn't get any special help," "If I made out, so can you," "Don't worry, you'll grow out of it like I did," "There's nothing wrong with that child that a good spanking won't cure."

All these emotions must be worked through by both parents if they are going to attack the problem of helping their child in the best possible way. Mothers traditionally accept the verdict of a learning disability more easily than fathers, possibly because they are with preschool children for most of their waking hours and so come to know them better. It may be, also, that Father is the parent who feels most ambitious for his child. Fathers also tend to blame mothers for being overprotective and too soft. The authoritarian father is often very hard to convince and may question whether there is any such thing as learning disabilities. "Where were they when I was growing up?" one father asked. "How come we never heard of such things until a few years ago?" another queried. This father was more understanding when he was reminded of the so-called "dummies" in his school who had succeeded despite the system.

Brothers and sisters will be strongly influenced by their parents' attitude toward a child with a learning disability. If Mother and Father accept the child with warmth and loving concern, the children will probably eventually do the same. They have a special problem, however, that is sometimes shared by one of the parents. Occasionally one parent, or both parents, will give so much attention to the child with the learning disability that the rest of the family feels neglected. One young girl was heard to remark, "Jason's lucky! He's dumb, but he gets all the attention. We don't get any!" Even one of the parents, usually the father, may feel this way if the mother spends so much time with her learning-disabled child she neglects her husband. Learning-disabled children have un-intentionally broken up many marriages, often leaving wounds of guilt and condemnation from which a family never recovers. It is important that parents and children work *together* to give support to the child who needs it so badly.

The first step to such cooperation is for all members of the family to acknowledge their negative feelings. Once all these emotions are out in the open — the guilt, anger, jealousy, shame, and disappointment — they can be dealt with, creating a healthier emotional atmosphere in the home. Parents, brothers, and sisters should understand that these feelings are perfectly normal, that everyone has them at some time or other. Once this is accomplished, the family can get on with the business of being helpful and supportive. It is also important that every member of the family understand that there might be social problems, as well as academic problems, and their aid should be enlisted to help wherever possible. All family members must avoid using this child as a scapegoat for everything that goes on in the household: "It was all Peter's fault! He's so clumsy he made me drop it!" "It's all Susie's fault that I don't have any friends! She's so awful they won't play with me!" "If you didn't spend so much time with Billy we could go out together once in a while and our marriage would be better!"

Parents must avoid placing blame, and they must not allow their other children to do so either. They must go out of their way to reassure their other children that they are loved equally, but that at the present time Johnny (or Janie) needs extra care and attention. Wise parents will try to set aside some time each day to be with each other and with their other children, free from all distractions. When the whole family is together, make sure that both parents aren't involved at the same time with the learning-disabled child. It is common for these children to seek negative attention at home, and to develop an insight into manipulative behavior. They can become experts very quickly!

When siblings are ashamed of their learning-disabled brother or sister, it will often help if you can sit down with them and explain what his or her problems are and what you hope to do about them. If your children are young, it is best to keep the explanations simple so that they can understand. Enlist their help. When Tim was discovered to have a problem with visual perception that affected his learning severely, his father explained to his older brother: "If Tim is playing ball, he doesn't see the ball the same way you do. It's as if by magic the ball disappeared and then reappeared somewhere else. Until we can help him see the ball properly, he won't be very good playing with the other kids." His brother came up with a good idea: "When the other kids don't want him around, I'll let him chase the ball for us. Then he'll feel like he is in on the game." So Tim happily became the local team's ball boy, doing a job that no one else wanted to do and feeling involved with other kids.

Why You Should Not Be Overprotective

Some well-meaning parents can ruin their child's chances for a normal, well-adjusted life because they are too solicitous and overprotective. It is part of the nurturing instinct to give every possible help to a child who is suffering, whether from a case of the flu, a twisted spine, a broken leg, or a learning disability. Unfortunately this can mean killing with kindness. If a child is shielded within his family and protected from all contact with the outside world, he can be devastated when the day comes that he must face the real world. People out there aren't going to make allowances for him. The worst thing you can do is feel sorry for your child and try to shield him from the consequences of his disability or his antisocial behavior.

One twelve-year-old with multiple problems was observed during a church service talking rather loudly and annoying the people who were seated near him. His mother shushed him gently, but made no move to correct this unseemly behavior. After the service, a friend mentioned that the parishioners hated to see this child come into a service because he almost always disrupted either the hymn-singing or the sermon. We had had this child in one of our Gym Clubs and we knew that he was quite capable of behaving himself, but we had also heard his mother say after some inexcusable behavior, "Please forgive him, he has a learning disability and doesn't know any better." This same mother had bought her son only slip-on shoes because "He'll never be able to learn to tie up laced shoes, poor dear!" One of our volunteers had him tying his shoes in three sessions.

There are several psychological reasons why parents become overprotective. If the LD child is the youngest child of several, mother will sometimes become overprotective in order to bind the child to her. She needs to be needed, here is a child who clearly needs her more than the others, and she subconsciously sets out to make him totally dependent on her. We watched one strapping ten-year-old demand that his mother, who was not much bigger than he was, give him a piggyback ride down two floors and out to the car!

Catering to their whims makes little dictators out of these children and can be even more of a disruptive influence than their initial difficult behavior. In these cases Father usually will become more severe with the child to try to compensate, and then there is a constant tug-of-war between the parents, which does nothing to improve the atmosphere at home. The child will often learn to manipulate both parents, playing one off against the other. Sometimes brothers and sisters are drawn in and end up taking sides, until the household becomes an armed camp. Finally, everyone suffers, no one benefits.

Sometimes overprotectiveness is a reaction to extreme feelings of guilt. A parent may feel that he or she is responsible for their child's problems and try to overcompensate. Nine times out of ten, there is no truth to this assumption, but the damage has been done. Some do not see that their overprotectiveness is a reaction to anger. They deny their anger at this child for being as he is, deny their feelings of shame and frustration, and cover the whole mess with a blanket of overprotectiveness that ruins their child's chance of adjusting.

One mother we knew would not let her daughter start with a new teacher unless she first saw the teacher, to let her know what her daughter could and could not do and what to expect in the way of bad behavior, and to beg the teacher not to be too hard on her child because "After all, she has a learning disability." This teacher's unsympathetic reply was, "So does more than half of this class. Sorry, no special favors for your child. She'll have to take her lumps with the rest of the children." Mother then arranged to have her daughter transferred to another class. She was not doing her any favor. She was robbing her of the opportunity of fighting her own battles and working out her own methods of getting along with her peers and her teacher.

If you feel sorry for your child, you can be sure that he'll soon start feeling sorry for himself. This self-pity can result in antisocial behavior, laziness, and a refusal to try to cope with even normal problems. The disability becomes an excuse for not trying. In cases such as this, parents lose sight of the fact that what they have is a child with normal or above-normal intelligence but a learning disability. All they see is the disability and they allow it to rule their every waking hour. This attitude is guaranteed to cause major psychological and educational problems throughout their child's school years. They will probably end up with a young adult who can't cope with life because all he can see, all he can think of, is his learning disability. Even in those cases where a child has many major problems, it is up to parents and teacher and his peer group to encourage and help the child hidden under the weight of disabilities. By emphasizing and encouraging those aspects that are not disabled, they can help him come to terms with his disabilities and learn to live independently.

A learning disability can be a *cause*, but it should never be used as an *excuse*. The reason Johnny is two grades behind in his reading is because he has poor visual memory. The reason Billy has to sit at the front of the class is because he cannot eliminate background sounds and can't hear his teacher if he sits farther back. If Johnny says he hasn't done his homework because he knows he can't do it, if he won't even try to succeed, he is using his reading problems as an excuse to goof off. If Billy sits in the front seat and daydreams instead of paying attention to his teacher because "I never know what she says anyway," he is using his auditory problem as an excuse.

Overprotected children become very adept at dodging anything unpleasant or difficult by hiding behind their learning disability. It can become the scapegoat for any situation they find unpleasant, and unfortunately they usually manage to manipulate their parents to the point that they get away with it. One mother became impatient with her eleven-year-old daughter who refused to go to the corner store for her. "I can't read your list and you know I can't remember anything" was Karen's excuse. A few days later, when it was time to shop for her birthday party, Karen suddenly discovered how to read and how to remember. A sixteen-year-old who consistently failed anything in school which required reading managed quite nicely to read the manuals and pamphlets necessary in order to obtain a driver's licence.

Parents Must Look After Themselves, Too

It is a matter of survival that parents make sure they have time for their own lives and each other. Overprotective parents probably suffer more than any others when it comes to having a life of their own. Many parents become so busy living their learning-disabled child's life that they have no life of their own, to the detriment of both parent and child. Marriages can't take the pressure when one or the other parent is so totally immersed in the life of their child that they lose their own sense of identity.

Mothers and fathers tend to take different methods of coping with the crisis of discovering one of their children has a learning disability. Sometimes the coping devices which help parents deal with the problem can themselves become a problem, adding additional burdens to both marital and family dynamics.

As we have mentioned before, fathers are most likely to take an "I don't believe it" attitude toward both the idea of learning disabilities and the fact that they have a learning-disabled child. He does not want to admit that any child of his could be less than perfect, and he preserves this illusion by shutting out the reality of the situation. He sees any disability in one of his children as a reflection on himself. So much emphasis has been placed on higher education over the years that many men are ashamed to admit that one of their children will probably not be able to make it into university. If a son has coordination problems, father may deal with the situation by completely rejecting the child. One father was amazed to discover from someone else that his poorly coordinated eight-year-old son was very interested in and very knowledgeable about hockey, the father's favorite sport. Father had never taken the time to find out anything about his son; he'd just written him off as a "klutz." Sometimes a father will use the troubles at home as an excuse to spend more and more time at the office, or at any rate away from home. When he is at home, he tends to be either cold and aloof or a stern disciplinarian. Fortunately, not all fathers react this way. Most are warm, understanding, cooperative, and supportive, especially when there are already good lines of communication between husband and wife.

Our advice to any father with a learning-disabled child is to *get involved*. Don't leave all the parenting to the child's mother. Read about learning disabilities; discuss your child's progress with his teacher; get involved with the activities of your local ACLD or help start a branch in your community. Above all, get to know your child as a person. Remember that he is an intelligent child who very much wants attention and love from his father. Give him all the help and understanding you can.

A mother's attitude often differs widely from that of the father. Mother is much more likely to overprotect her learning-disabled child if she is a strong nurturer. Occasionally you will find a mother who will reject her child, either overtly or covertly. A strong, authoritarian mother, who has not much self-esteem herself, will often become very domineering and sometimes physically abusive, probably at least in part to compensate for a lack of understanding. Sometimes these mothers will develop coping devices which say, in effect, that there really isn't anything wrong. This is a covert rejection of their child.

Many mothers are blind to the fact that they are letting their learning-disabled child monopolize more and more of their time and are allowing themselves to be manipulated by a child who can sometimes be more demanding than a small infant. Don't allow yourself to fall into this trap. Take a firm stand with yourself, your husband, and the other family members so that they will not allow themselves to be manipulated. This takes a good deal of patience and insight, but it can prevent the situation where the whole household revolves around the mother and her problem child.

Of prime importance in helping to keep the situation in perspective is the absolute necessity of having time to yourself every day. Both mother and father need moments of complete privacy. One mother admitted that the only time she was really alone was when she went to the bathroom, and only then if she locked the door. If you can enlist the help of older children, relatives, or friends to give you the chance to get away from the house once in a while, your problems won't seem so insurmountable. Some couples take turns baby-sitting for each other; usually they have met at an ACLD parents' gathering. This is an excellent idea, because each understands the other's problems. If you work, and then have to come home to a pile of problems, try to keep the two sections of your life separate. It can be disastrous to both career and home if problems get mixed. If you are working, you may experience difficulty finding suitable daytime help. Some day-care centers are equipped to help children with learning disabilities, and some schools in larger centers make arrangements to keep children after school until they can be picked up. If you must have help in the house, you may find it through your doctor or your local ACLD.

One of the best escapes from day-to-day problems is involvement outside the home. If you are not working, try volunteer work, especially helping someone even worse off than yourself. Work as a hospital volunteer, with a church group, or with the ACLD. Take classes while your children are at school or in the evening. If you go to evening classes, try to organize it so that both husband and wife can attend. If this isn't possible, be sure that both of you get an evening out — at a movie, playing cards, doing anything that takes your mind off your problems.

No marriage can survive without mutual understanding, cooperation, and lots of communication. If their attitudes are different toward their special child, the parents must strive to make compromises on decisions affecting the child. Above all, they must work together to build a stable family life, allowing time for them to be by themselves. Parents owe it to themselves and to each other to get their priorities straight and to put the success of their marriage at the top of the list. If they can give each other support, coping with family problems will be much easier. When communication has broken down, mother is often unaware of how difficult life has become for father with problems at work and at home. Father, on the other hand, does not realize how hard it is for mother to deal with a difficult child. They should each undertake to understand the other's point of view. Sometimes a father is the first one to spot a new problem arising because he is away during the day and not as close to the situation. Mothers should at least listen to what the other parent has to say, even if they feel they know more about the difficulty.

The amount of time husband and wife can find to be alone together usually depends on the severity of their problems at home. As we have said, do try to get out for dinner or to a movie as often as possible. Don't think that it is money wasted. It is money invested in mental health and a good marriage. We realize how difficult this can be, but it is really worth heroic efforts because you will feel refreshed, have an improved outlook, and be much more tolerant of your learning-disabled child if you can get away from him once in a while.

A word about your own health, both mental and physical. Don't neglect it. Caring for a difficult child who is hyperactive or who has behavioral problems can be very taxing. Even living in the same house can be difficult. One father of an especially hyperactive young son has come up with his own solution. His son never sleeps through the night, although he is nearly eight years old. In fact, Jimmy doesn't appear to need much sleep, and can't understand why the rest of the family shouldn't get up when he wants to get up. So Jimmy's father just moves to a hotel for a few days when he is under heavy pressure at the office.

Many parents have sleeping difficulties, either because they are constantly overtired, or because they have a child who never seems to sleep. They end up worn to a frazzle.

If you find your health is being seriously impaired, discuss the situation with your doctor. It may be that you just have to have a rest from your child. If you can't get away from him, it may be possible for him to get away from you. Many cities now have day camps or residential camps especially for children with learning disabilities. They are usually supervised by either the ACLD or a school which specializes in learning disabilities. This can give parents a summer break without any feelings of guilt, since they know their child is getting proper care. If the problems show no signs of improvement, we strongly suggest you consider a private residential school which will give your child the maximum amount of help and give you a chance to recuperate.

CHAPTER 3

Using Transactional Analysis
To Improve
Your Child's Self-Esteem

No one likes living with a child who is chronically badly behaved. Not only is putting up with such a situation wearing for all family members, but it also does not help your child learn how to get along in the world. The impulsive child must be made to think before he acts; the bad-tempered child needs to gain supremacy over his outbursts; the hyperactive child needs to learn some control of his aimless movements. Above all, your child must learn that to be accepted by his peers, teachers, and family friends, he has to understand and practise the niceties of everyday social interaction.

How do you teach these lessons to a girl with an attention span of sixty seconds at the outside? Or a boy who never remains in the same place long enough for you to complete a sentence? How do you instil social graces and the essentials of good behavior into any child who is convinced he is a dummy whom no one could possibly like? It's not easy.

The first step is to establish a healthy self-esteem for both yourself and your child. Make sure you value both yourself and your child as worthwhile people. Don't be embarrassed to state your child's problem to someone if you feel it will help, but don't go out of your way to make long explanations to people who really aren't interested. There will be far less rejection of even a very difficult child if his parents accept him first, and help him improve both self-image and behavior, especially outside of his own home.

What Is Transactional Analysis?

Many family and marital counsellors use a method of helping an individual realize his potential that has proven very effective. Transactional Analysis, or TA, can work wonders with a troubled child and radically improve a troubled family dynamic. TA is the brainchild of the late Dr. Eric Berne, whom we mentioned earlier when we talked about the concept of Winners and Losers. His ideas for self-actualization can also be applied to the exchanges or transactions between people in the normal course of daily living. An understanding of the principles of TA could be the key to helping your learning-disabled child and your family.

Dr. Berne defines a Winner as a person who is true to himself. He presents this true picture of himself to the world without apology and does not play games to try to persuade or manipulate people. There is a basic honesty about a Winner that cannot be mistaken, and it's very appealing. A Loser, on the other hand, spends much of his time in role-playing, acting out, pretending, manipulating, and generally being less than honest to himself and about himself. His brittle self-esteem makes it impossible for him to face the facts of who he really is, and he expends most of his energy playing games with other people. No one is all Winner or all Loser, but those who have been programmed to be Losers develop a life script that is negative and difficult to change.

Losers are often the victims of labels which they carry all their life. They come to identify with these labels and will subconsciously go out of their way to make sure that they live up to their label. Sometimes these Losers are labelled in childhood, sometimes not until later in life, but once they have accepted their label, it is very difficult to change their thinking. We must be very careful how we use the label "learning-disabled." This could be the label your child wears for life, his excuse for being a Loser. We feel that it is better to *describe* the problem than to label it, if an explanation must be used. Say "Johnny has had trouble learning to read," or "Janie reads well but is not very good at math," rather than saying that Johnny or Janie has a learning disability. If labels are avoided both at home and at school, they are not nearly as likely to stick as a life script.

The basics of Transactional Analysis are intended to help you change your own life script, if you feel it could be changed for the better, and to help you communicate effectively with others with a minimum of manipulation and game-playing. TA has often been combined with Gestalt Therapy in a group setting where constant feedback from the group can help a person overcome personality problems and self-defeating game-playing. For our use, we will consider TA as an easy-to-understand, useful means of helping you deal with your learning-disabled child.

The Ego States

Berne declared that everyone has three ego states which he described as "a consistent pattern of feeling and experiences directly related to a corresponding consistent pattern of behavior." These patterns of feelings and behaviors are described as the Parent ego state, the Adult ego state, and the Child ego state, each representing a real person within a person. Each is spelled with a capital to distinguish it from the actual parent, adult, or child.

The *Parent* ego state is composed of behavior and attitudes learned from our own parents and other adult sources when we are small children. It is quite firmly established before a child even enters school. It can be in turn nurturing and caring, or stern and critical, depending on the type of parenting the person had in his earliest years.

The *Adult* ego state is that part of a person which is in constant touch with reality. It is organized, adaptable, and intelligent, and it functions by testing reality in a logical way, gathering information and making objective conclusions. Our Adult ego state functions much as a computer does, processing and assessing input in a logical way, and making conclusions based on logic. It begins to develop in an infant around ten months of age.

The *Child* ego state contains all the basic impulses found in young children. Here are recorded our early experiences, feelings, and emotions, and how we felt about ourselves when we were very young. It is our Child ego state that first establishes our self-esteem. It can be carefree and fun-loving, or bad-tempered, self-centered, unreasonable, and emotional.

An anecdote will illustrate how these three ego states can co-exist and show themselves within a short conversation. A father and mother had gone to investigate a summer camp for their son who had learning disabilities. The father's comments to the mother revealed the three ego states: "I don't think that young man we talked to will be strict enough with Jeff (Parent ego state), but there seems to be structure and a real attempt to help the children understand their problems (Adult ego state). Boy, won't Jeff enjoy that water slide (Child ego state)?"

To give a few further illustrations:

Parent: That accident probably served the driver right!
Adult: I'll call the police and an ambulance.
Child: Oh, boy! this is exciting!

Parent: You probably wouldn't have needed an operation if you had looked after your health.
Adult: I understand he is a very good doctor.
Child: Poor me! I'll have to look after the house while you're sick!

Parent: Oh, you poor dear, how did you skin your knee?
Adult: There appears to be dirt in the scrape.
Child: Oh, I hate the sight of blood!

A newborn can broadcast his needs only by a lusty cry, but when he learns to communicate better and investigate his world, he absorbs the basics of all three ego states from those with whom he is associated and the world around him. He can pretend to be a Parent while playing with dolls or other children, he can be objective and Adult when solving a problem, and then he can quickly revert to his self-centered emotional Child ego state. Peter, aged three, had received a toy garage for his cars. He was pretending to be Daddy coming home from work (Parent ego state) when he found he couldn't open the garage door to put his car away. He took time out from his game to figure out how the catch worked (Adult ego state). Once that was accomplished, he started to put his car away but threw it across the room when one of the wheels came off (Child ego state).

How You Relate to Your Child

In Transactional Analysis, transactions refer to the exchanges which take place between people every day. A complementary transaction is one in which the message sent is responded to in the expected way. If the Parent ego state speaks to the Child ego state, and the Child responds, this is a complementary transaction. If, however, the wrong ego state answers, you will have a crossed transaction. The transaction might also be complicated by facial gestures, tone of voice, body posture, or other things which might convey a different message than is actually spoken.

These simple transactions between two people are from similar ego states and therefore are complementary:

1. *First Speaker:* Can you come to dinner on Saturday?
   Second Speaker: Yes, we'd love to. What time? (*This is an Adult-to-Adult exchange.*)
2. *First Speaker:* Let's go swimming!
   Second Speaker: That would be fun! (*This is a Child-to-Child transaction.*)
3. *First Speaker:* I feel Joannie needs a new coat for winter.
   Second Speaker: Be sure to get her one tomorrow. (*This is a Parent-to-Parent exchange.*)
4. *First Speaker:* Be sure to put on your rubbers; it's wet outside.

Second Speaker: O.K. I will. (*This is a Parent-to-Child exchange.*)

These can become crossed transactions if inappropriate or unexpected responses are given such as these:

1. *First Speaker:*   Can you come to dinner on Saturday? (*Adult*)
   Second Speaker: Now, you know it's too much trouble for you. (*Parent*)
2. *First Speaker:*   Let's go swimming! (*Child*)
   Second Speaker: You'll catch cold if you do. (*Parent*)
3. *First Speaker:*   I feel Joannie needs a new coat for winter. (*Parent*)
   Second Speaker: You know I'm not made of money! (*Child*)
4. *First Speaker:*   Be sure to put on your rubbers; it's wet outside. (*Parent*)
   Second Speaker: I'm quite aware it's raining out. (*Adult*)

Transactions can also be identified as Indirect, Diluted, or Weak. An Indirect Transaction takes place when one person speaks to another hoping a third will overhear. A Diluted Transaction can carry a hidden meaning. A Weak Transaction is a chatty time-passer.

The most complex type of transaction Dr. Berne called the Ulterior Transaction. This type of transaction is socially acceptable on the surface but conveys a hidden meaning, often barbed, delivered from a different ego state: Husband to Wife: "Why do you want to read that? It's just for people who understand business." This is a statement of fact, but it is also a putdown of his wife. Or, a salesclerk says to you: "You probably won't like this blouse. It's very expensive." This is another statement of fact, but intended to imply the customer hasn't enough money to buy the article.

Children are quick to pick up the hidden meaning in an Ulterior Transaction, especially if there is an implied putdown or discount. If you say "Do you think *you* could do that?" with enthusiasm and confidence in your voice, you will convey something quite different from "Do you think you can *do* that?" spoken with hesitation that clearly expresses your feeling that he can't do that.

Children who expect criticism will often unconsciously invite it, and parents often comply, also unconsciously. They will not be aware of their Ulterior Transactions until someone points them out. A twelve-year-old girl might say, "All my friends are reading Nancy Drew. I don't suppose there's any use me buying one." Mother answers, "Wait until you can read one. Better stick to Dr. Seuss books." On the surface, this all seems innocent, but the girl is asking for a putdown and Mother is obliging with an implicit criticism of her daughter's reading ability. Children will also invite discounts in other ways. While they may turn a school assignment in on time, it may be so full of errors or so sloppily done that there is no doubt that criticism will follow. Losers will often unwittingly indulge in Ulterior Transactions to strengthen their belief that they are Losers. The Adult ego state might be saying, "See how good I am!" while the hidden Child is saying, "Kick me, I'm no good."

A variation of "Kick Me" is often played as a manipulative game by children with learning disabilities. It is as if they wear a sign saying, "Please don't kick me, I have a learning disability," and then go out of their way to provoke a "kick" from someone by deliberately inappropriate behavior, or an obviously incorrect or silly reply to a question. The purpose of the game is to try the patience of the other player(s) until the child gets "kicked," whereupon he will vigorously protest "But what do you expect from someone with a learning disability?" In the terms of TA, the only antidote (called an "antithesis") to "Kick Me" games is to refuse to play. If a parent or a teacher spots the game in time, he can divert the child and prevent reinforcement of his low self-esteem.

A variation of what is usually a marital game between husband and wife often shows up with LD children. It is called "Look How Hard I've Tried!" A child will make a half-hearted stab at accomplishing something and then convey either "I'm helpless, I can't do it," or "I'm blameless, you can see I tried." The parent is then put in the position of doing it for him, or not blaming him for not doing it because he "really tried." This can be a ploy to get out of an unwanted task and to solicit sympathy. It is worthwhile investigating where a child learned how to play this game, as it is frequently learned from other members of the family who use it to get out of unwanted tasks or to get attention.

Strokes, Trading Stamps, and Discounting

The need to be touched is essential to the well-being of a newborn baby. Children who are not cuddled and loved wither and die. This hunger to be touched is also present in a psychological sense. Just as an infant needs the reassurance of physical stroking, we all need the reassurance of psychological stroking. If we do not receive this positive attention from those around us, we are likely to seek negative attention. These strokes are an integral part of TA and are especially important for those children who are not as likely as others to win approval. Positive feedback, or stroking, needs to be incorporated in your day-to-day dealing with your child to help him develop good feelings about himself.

As a child develops, he learns to recognize a favorite comfortable feeling and will consistently, throughout his life, try to return to that feeling as someone might return to an old pair of slippers. If he has good self-esteem, he will seek situations that reinforce it, but if he is used to guilt, shame, or a feeling of inadequacy he will create situations that arouse these negative feelings.

There is a current expression: "I know where you're coming from." With some learning-disabled children, they are constantly "coming from" their Child ego state, feeling more comfortable with a destructive Child emotion than with a more positive Adult emotion. In order to bolster this chosen position, your child might set out to collect what Dr. Berne calls Trading Stamps. These can be collected over a period of time and then "redeemed" when the time seems right. By manipulating those around him, any person can force another person into belittling him, frightening him, arousing his guilt, and so forth. Usually this is done by playing psychological games, but sometimes it is done just by taking the wrong meaning out of a simple statement. You might say to Johnny, "Will you please feed the dog at nine o'clock?" and Billie, who has a learning disability, might come back with "Why didn't you ask me? I suppose you think I can't do it!" Billie is collecting stamps. When he has collected enough he will cash them in by throwing a temper tantrum or indulging himself in some other way until he is reassured by his parents' anger that he is right to put himself down.

If a child feels guilty about something and learns from his mistake, that is a positive feeling. If he does not learn from his mistake and repeats the same mistake again and again, making excuses for himself each time, then he likes the feeling of guilt and is being self-indulgent.

Johnny and Billie were both notorious for keeping their parents waiting when they were going somewhere in the car. Finally, their father sat them down and explained that this behavior could not go on. They were no longer willing to wait up to an hour while the two boys dawdled. Johnny apologized and made determined efforts to be on time. Billie continued to be late but always had an excuse: "I forgot to feed the fish," "I have to go to the bathroom again," "You said I had to tidy my room and I forgot till now." Finally, in exasperation, Father and Mother decided to leave Billie behind with a baby-sitter when another outing was planned. Now Billie could trade in all those stamps and cry and carry on that nobody cared about him.

I'm O.K. — You're O.K.

Parents with no understanding of Transactional Analysis are frequently mystified by statements from some school psychologists, or from counsellors in family dynamics, like "Your son is coming from a Not O.K. position." The concept of O.K. and Not O.K. were originated by Dr. Thomas Harris in his book entitled *I'm O.K. — You're O.K.* Briefly, Dr. Harris describes how we take a position on our worth early in life and work hard to keep this position throughout life. It is an adaptation of the Winner and Loser concept that is in wide use among family therapists.

I'm O.K. — You're O.K. refers to someone thinking well of himself and his fellow man.

I'm O.K. — You're Not O.K. is a position which says, "I like myself, but I don't like you." It is a position often taken by abused children.

I'm Not O.K. — You're O.K. is a position taken by most learning-disabled children.

I'm Not O.K. — You're Not O.K. is a position taken by people with low self-esteem who see the rest of the world as being out to get them.

Therapists say that in any of the life scripts other than the I'm O.K. — You're O.K. position, a child will grow into a potential Loser. Since these scripts are developed in the first few years of life, it is very important that a child feel secure, loved, and accepted.

CHAPTER 4

Using Contracts and Conditioning To Improve Behavior

Learning disabilities are often characterized as a "dis-order" or a "dis-ability" to cast aside immature thinking and perception and replace it with a more orderly and mature method of organizing thought. What might be acceptable behavior in a two-year-old, such as running around endlessly to investigate his environment, lack of perception, and disorganized thought, is entirely inappropriate in a child of ten. This apparent immaturity, caused by perceptual or other problems, is a feature in many of the children who have serious behavioral difficulties.

What do you do if your child's behavior is inappropriate for his age? Bringing up this type of child is a matter of trial and error. What works with one child will often be useless with another. Not every child with a learning disability is a behavioral problem, however. Some hypoactive (underactive) children are models of good behavior, but they are also timid, withdrawn, and lethargic. It is almost always true, though, that most LD children will pose some behavioral problems, not just because of their apparent immature behavior, but also because they see themselves as different and their perception of their world is distorted. Children who hear sounds incorrectly may appear to be disobedient when they actually heard a different message from the one sent. It can be very confusing when you say "stop" and your child hears "pop" or "bop" or "top." Children with visual perception problems may walk into things or appear to knock things over deliberately, because while their eyes see an object, their brains don't register the fact. Probably the only common denominator is that all of these children need help in ordering and structuring their lives and their behavior, and an extra amount of tender loving care.

It is essential to try to gain some control over a child's inappropriate behavior as early as possible, because the day comes all too soon when it will be almost impossible to correct a poor, but deeply ingrained, behavioral pattern. Once children enter their teen years, changing behavior becomes more and more difficult, as they try to establish their own sense of identity and pull away from family and home. If we can change those aspects of a behavioral pattern which need changing and help the child with internal organization so that he can continue his improved behavior on his own, we can be sure that the teen years will be much less traumatic.

None of the methods used for altering unwanted behavior and reinforcing good behavior is guaranteed to work under all circumstances. All are useful some of the time under certain conditions; all of them have also failed on occasion. There are many good books available which can go into greater detail than we can about behavioral management, but please don't expect miracles. If you can control your temper and at the same time exercise a maximum degree of patience, you will stand a good chance of making at least some of it work.

Remember, too, that many outside circumstances can influence how your child behaves at home, at school, or in the community. Norma had the experience of hating to see a beloved daughter come through the door from school because she exploded into a temper tantrum the instant the door closed behind her. It took some detective work to track down the reasons behind these outbursts. In this case Norma had been over-zealous in emphasizing that you absolutely did not show your temper at school under any circumstances. Frustrated because she couldn't read her workbook and unhappy because she was being ignored by her teacher, the child blew up at whoever was in the way as soon as she arrived inside the safety of her own home. This aggravating situation was helped by modifying her overreaction to a difficult school situation.

Lack of sleep can also cause poor behavior. LD children are often erratic sleepers, and occasionally even a ten-year-old can profit from a snooze when he arrives home from school. Think of how irritable anyone can feel after a busy and frustrating day and you can better understand how these children feel in the late afternoon or early evening. Often they need help to wind down and relax, and any technique you can develop to aid this process will improve this difficult time of day immensely. Naps, warm baths, a quiet story, an enjoyable play-and-learn session, relaxation exercises, a hot drink and cookie are just a few ways you can help your child unwind and gain control over erratic late-day behavior.

Sometimes an infection of which you are unaware can be at the bottom of sudden difficult behavior. So can teething, even in an older child. Before you put all aberrant behavior down to low self-esteem, frustration, and other reasons connected with his learning disability, check for the more obvious reasons to make sure you aren't being unfair to your child.

Making a Contract with Your Child

In the previous chapter we described the use of Transactional Analysis. We left one of the central themes of TA, making contracts, until now because it seemed to be more fitting to explain its use as a method of changing behavior. In law and business, a contract is arranged between two people for their mutual benefit. For example, I agree to paint your house and you agree to pay me a certain sum. You might contract with your child to set the table each day for a week, refrain from losing his temper all day, maintain a tidy room for a specified length of time, or for any other behavior you want to establish. In exchange, you promise a certain reward such as an outing, or staying up for a favorite TV show.

Contracts can be used either to break old, bad behavioral patterns or to establish new, desired behavior. The important thing is to discuss, and preferably write down, your contract with your child — what is to be done by you, and what your child is to do. If your child does not fulfil his part of the contract, you are under no obligation to reward him. The advantage of a contract is that it depersonalizes the situation: your child knows that he is being denied his reward not because he is a bad kid but because he has failed to live up to his part of the bargain. The contract encourages him to behave like a responsible, mature individual, to act from his Adult ego state. Once desirable behavior is established or poor behavior amended by contract, the change usually lasts, because the child sees the clear connection between his behavior and how he is treated, and he learns to like feeling good about himself.

The contract method of changing behavior can be used with any child old enough to understand how it works. Please do not think of it as a bribe. A bribe is offered to encourage someone to do something against his principles or against his better judgment, and usually against the interests of a third party or society in general. You bribe a juror to hold out for the acquittal of an obviously guilty person. You bribe a judge to give a lighter than usual sentence. You bribe a child to lie to one of your friends and say you aren't at home. By contrast a *reward* is given for doing something right and mutually beneficial.

In this type of contract it is important to keep in mind what your child can and cannot do. Obviously you can't contract with a child to do calculus when he is just beginning his multiplication tables. If the contract is too difficult, the ensuing frustration will just make changing behavior more difficult. You want your child to have the experience of succeeding. A child of eight who is having trouble printing might make a contract to do a whole line of A's within the lines by next Thursday, but he certainly cannot contract to learn and write the whole alphabet in the same length of time.

Choosing the Right Reward

Choosing the right reward for your contract is critical. It is not necessary that the reward be very large, or even very tangible, but it must be something your child values. It can be something he really wants, or something he really wants to do. It could be an extra half-hour of television because he sat all through dinner and didn't throw anything. He may be taken to a movie if he has shown that he can sit quietly through the church service. If there are constant repetitions of a contract, it may be necessary to introduce new rewards. The old ones can then be reintroduced at a later time. (Food is not a desirable reinforcement because using it will encourage your child to equate food with reward. This attitude can become one of the harmful emotional contributors to obesity.)

Your child will often suggest reinforcers himself, and these should be used whenever possible. After all, he has a pretty good idea of what is most likely to help him change unwanted behavior. The rewards themselves can be used as learning tools: small coins help an understanding of money, marbles help an understanding of colors, and so on.

How To Use Conditioning

Conditioning is a word coined by psychologists to describe the use of rewards or reinforcers to encourage the repetition of some desired behavior or performance. Suppose you have been teaching a child to tie his shoelaces and he hasn't yet managed to get the lace through the eyelet. You can reinforce each improvement with praise or some small treat as a method of conditioning the behavior. Just being pleased is often reinforcement enough, because this helps your child internalize a feeling of satisfaction at his accomplishment.

Be sure to express your appreciation at the time the event happens, not a long time later when the child has forgotten. Immediate reinforcement works much better. Strokes help your child become aware of the satisfaction of doing something well. If the performance falls short of expectation, don't be critical, but don't reward, either.

When you are using this method of changing behavior, it is wise to break the behavior down into small, manageable steps so your child won't be frustrated by failure. Often repetition will help him improve the behavior before he moves along to the next step.

Poor Uses of Conditioning

Both consciously and unconsciously, many people reinforce behavior incorrectly. If your child is behaving badly, you might question whether he is seeking negative attention. If he is not getting positive attention, he will sooner or later seek negative attention. If he gets that attention — after a temper tantrum or after tying a can to the cat's tail — he will have won that particular game. He will have received attention and will also be confirmed in his I'm Not O.K. position.

Another poor use of conditioning is the use of punishment, especially inappropriate or severe punishment, for behavior of which you disapprove. Either psychological or physical punishment that is inappropriate to the severity of the offence can cause a child to be justifiably resentful. Obviously Junior has to be stopped from beating up his little sister, but beating him in turn is not going to teach him not to use violence. All he will learn from that type of behavior on your part is that what he can't do, you can do, and it's probably because you're bigger than he is. A great way to create a bully!

We are all guilty of using inappropriate and excessive punishment at times. With a child who is harder than average to handle, it can sometimes be quite catastrophic. Again, this is negative parenting: punishing (often too severely) wrong-doing but never reinforcing good behavior. If punishment is indeed necessary (after all, Junior must learn that he is not allowed to beat up his sister or anyone else), let the punishment fit the crime. In this case, it would be much more appropriate to remove Junior from the scene of the crime and forbid him playing with anyone until he is willing to behave himself. If there is a group of children, he might be allowed to play on the far side of the yard (or the room) by himself, but not allowed to participate in their games. If he appears ready to mend his ways, he can be allowed to join them under strict supervision. If he again gets violent, he must be removed immediately and firmly and for a longer period of time. If the other children are having fun, it won't take him long to get the message that he can have more fun if he behaves himself.

We had one little boy, George, who threw horrendous

temper tantrums in Gym Club. His volunteer just couldn't control him and he became a real tyrant. His mother had been conditioned by George to come running if he lost his temper because he could be very destructive. When George tried this on Joan, she just isolated him at one side of the room and ignored him. There was nothing he could destroy but a sheet of newspaper, which he tore into little pieces. When he realized that he was being ignored, he gradually quieted down and began edging closer and closer to hear a story Joan was reading to a circle of the children. When he realized that he was not going to get the attention he usually got with this behavior, he moved so that he was in a position where Joan couldn't help seeing him. Joan smiled at him, and finally invited him to join the group to hear the finish of the story. It was the first time he had consented to sit in the circle with the other children. When the story was over, George edged closer to Joan and said, "I'm sorry, Joan!" "George, we were so happy to have you join us for our story," was Joan's reply. "Come on, suppose I help you clean up those bits of paper."

George rarely posed a problem after this, but it took us some time to convince his mother that she could change George's behavior at home using the same method. We suggested that when he threw a tantrum she just remove everything breakable from his vicinity, especially his toys. If he broke any of his belongings, they were to be removed and not replaced. It took a lot of doing, but finally George's mother got some control over his temper.

Sometimes psychological punishment can be devastating for a child. If a child has misbehaved and is discounted in front of other people as a result, he will usually withdraw or overreact. Teachers are often guilty of belittling children whose performance is below the expected average if they are not aware of a learning disability. Parents can sometimes be guilty if they are embarrassed by poor behavior where others have witnessed the episode. They tend to overreact because they don't want onlookers to feel they are being too permissive.

Unfortunately some children become so conditioned to expect harsh punishment that they will go out of their way to attract it. A ten-year-old boy in a special section for children with learning disabilities had carefully conditioned his teacher to give him discounts he felt were his due. David had been quite well-behaved and really no trouble at all until one day when he was making an obvious mess of an assignment his teacher had given him. The teacher called him down in front of his school chums, and David answered back in rather colorful language. The teacher sent him out of the room. The next day, David's bad language continued. He interrupted his teacher, threw his lunch across the room, and ended up being chastised again. This continued until his teacher finally decided to look into the reasons for this sudden escalation in undesirable behavior. It turned out that David's behavioral change coincided with his parents' decision to separate. David secretly blamed himself and his learning disability for his parents' marital troubles and was deliberately seeking punishment from his teacher to reinforce his image of himself as a Not O.K. person. To change his behavior, his teacher began to withhold attention from David when he misbehaved, and to give him lots of positive attention when he had acceptable behavior. Along with outside therapy, which showed David that he was not the cause of his parents' separation, this proved to be all that was needed to turn David back into a reasonably well-behaved child.

In Chapters 3 and 4 we have tried to give you some basic psychological tools to improve your child's self-esteem and to modify unwanted behavior. We repeat: these are not foolproof and they will have varying degrees of success from child to child. Your patience will often be stretched to the limit and you'll ask yourself almost daily whether your efforts are having the smallest impact. You must have faith that they are.

Along with creating the best possible psychological environment for your child, you are also responsible for providing a physical environment that helps him concentrate his energies. This is a very rewarding pursuit for parents of LD children; you will be able to see tangible results for your efforts in a more directed, peaceful child. We tell you how to structure your child's physical world in the following chapter.

CHAPTER 5

Structuring
Your Child at Home

Until your learning-disabled child can learn to cope with changes in his environment, it is essential that you structure every possible aspect of his home and his life. As we said, so many things that we take for granted are major problems for him. While most seven- or eight-year-olds have learned to cope with small day-to-day changes not only in their homes but also in the neighborhood outside their homes, a learning-disabled child often feels as though he was suddenly stranded on a strange planet when things change.

Because his disability and his immaturity do not allow him to process information from his environment in the same way as we would process it and to predict and adapt to change, the LD child needs reassurance that his world is not going to change suddenly and unexpectedly. If you don't see something in a familiar place, you just look around until you find it. Your LD child can be terrified by and throw a temper tantrum about something as simple as a misplaced teddy bear. If his socks aren't where his socks are supposed to be, he can become panicky and disoriented. To understand how he experiences disorder, think of when you were learning to dance. You had to listen to the music, concentrate on the rhythm, think of how to move your feet, and be aware of your partner. It was very hard to do at first, wasn't it? If someone spoke to you, or if the rhythm shifted suddenly, you would be thrown into confusion. Your child's world throws him into confusion when the unexpected happens or when things are not as they usually are. It takes him much longer than most children to internalize these everyday happenings and routines and to accept small structural changes in his environment.

Why Your Child Needs Structure

Time is often a total mystery to an LD child. Five minutes and an hour are all the same to him. Space, too, may confound him. He may lack an awareness of himself in space which he may try to overcome by touching things or by looking for a familiar item in a familiar place. He may hate to go to bed and hate to get up, be slow to leave a toy to come to dinner and then not want to leave the table. Only carefully structured routines can help him shift from one activity to another, because these routines become comfortable and familiar. He is much more likely to be able to control himself if his environment is controlled for him.

This child may also have a great deal of trouble dealing with choices. It may be quite easy for you to decide whether you want white or brown bread, chicken or hamburger, pink or purple socks. This may not be true for your LD child. At least while he is still young and until he has learned to cope with his environment, he should be given few opportunities to choose and never more than two alternatives at a time. Choices produce anxiety. Don't ask him whether he wants to play ball, read a book, or go to the shore. Help him by simplifying choices ahead of time.

Be sure to advise your child of predictable change in his life, then keep reminding him or he is likely to forget. Don't say to him, "But I told you last week that we were going on a trip." Last week has no meaning for him. Sudden and unexpected happenings, which are bound to occur, are certain to upset him. Be prepared for anxiety and overreaction. He may scream and yell, use foul language, throw a temper tantrum, or hide in his closet. He may regress to being a baby if he feels he can't deal with a situation. This is when you must treat him with understanding and kindness and allow him to retreat into his carefully structured world. It will help if you let him know that the suddenness of events has upset you, too. You might say, "I'm very disappointed that Daddy won't be home for your birthday, too, but Daddy sometimes has to go away on a trip suddenly. He can't help it and he would really rather be here with you." Don't bark: "Stop acting like a baby! You're a big boy now!" The immaturity of his thought processes will often make his reaction to unexpected happenings much different from the reactions of the average child of his age.

It is hard for us to realize, too, that these children often have no real understanding of simple words such as up, down, in front of, behind, and so forth. Your child might indicate he knows what you mean, then do just the opposite. Be sure that he really does understand what you mean when you are talking about his world. It helps to rehearse constantly these opposites with him so that he can internalize their meaning to help him understand his environment. Don't be surprised, however, if you ask him to brush his teeth after dinner and find that he is delighted to oblige by brushing his teeth *before* dinner.

Your learning-disabled child is in desperate need of your help in ordering his life so that he can cope with all the unexpected sensations that are constantly invading his world like creatures from outer space. They may be familiar to us but they really scare him.

Structure Yourself First

Before you can do an effective job of structuring your child's life, you have to be sure that you have structured your own. Positive interaction with your environment and the people in it depends on using thought and imagination in organizing your world. Putting a learning-disabled child into a household is a little like putting a wrench into a running motor. If it is well planned and executed, it can be done smoothly and may even help the motor run better. If it is done carelessly, it can lead to disaster.

First, it is important that your whole household understand

the structure and routine you are setting up for yourself and your learning-disabled child. They must understand how it will affect their lives. You can plan your routine to adjust to your child's, or plan his to fit comfortably into yours, but your household as a whole must also be considered. If your husband must be up at a certain time, plan for your child to be up earlier, or later, whichever is easier to manage, then stick to this schedule. If your child arrives home from school at three o'clock, plan your day so that you will be there to greet him. If you must be absent, be sure he knows ahead of time. Try not to schedule anything that will cut into the time you allow for your child, remembering all the time how important consistency is to him.

Structuring yourself also means structuring your method of dealing with your child. His home, his family, and especially his parents are the rocks upon which he must build his life. Consistency and constancy are a must. If you use the same tone of voice for the same type of instructions, you are being consistent. If you yell one time and speak quietly another, you are giving your child a mixed message which he will find confusing. Even such small things as seeing you in pants most mornings and then finding you in a dress can throw him. Obviously you can't structure yourself into rigidity, nor can you always be consistent, but be prepared for a reaction when there is change in the usual pattern.

If you tell your child you are going to do something, make every possible effort to do it as you have said, or explain why you can't. Don't promise him that you will take him to the park in his free time after school and then refuse because the book you are reading is too interesting to put down. On the other hand, if the minister drops in that afternoon, you should take your child aside and explain that it is rude to leave a guest but that you haven't forgotten your promise and you will fulfil it when your guest has left or the next day.

It is really important to mean what you say and stick to it. Think before you speak, not afterwards. This often means that you are stuck with something you have said on impulse or in anger, but it is important for your child to be able to depend on what you say. It is probably more harmful to him if you are inconsistent than for you to have to follow through on something that you later regret.

One of the most frequent reasons for dissension within the family is the inability of parents to agree on what is best for a child. All children learn at a very early age to manipulate their parents when they differ. Learning-disabled children often become masters at manipulating their parents and their environment when they spot inconsistencies and differences. This is usually avoidable by discussing any decision well ahead of time and coming to a mutually satisfactory conclusion before you say anything to your child. If you haven't had an opportunity to discuss an issue, tell your child you will give your answer in a few minutes rather than committing yourself to something you haven't had time to discuss.

Structuring Your Child's Room

Your child's room is his castle. It is his private place where he can feel secure and comfortable. In order for it to be the best possible retreat for him, forethought and imagination are necessary. It must be organized according to his needs, but he should have at least some say in how it is done. Let him put some of his own ingenuity into his environment.

Your decorating scheme should be kept simple, with an emphasis on plain or very simply printed fabrics. Large or very colorful prints can be very distracting and tend to disturb an easily distracted child. Choose colors that are soft and relaxing rather than bright and stimulating. You often see children's rooms, especially boys' rooms, done in reds, bright blues, brilliant yellows, and other bright colors. These can overstimulate a susceptible child, while the more harmonious colors have the opposite effect. This appears to be especially true for hyperactive children, but it is common sense for any child when you consider that this is where he is expected to relax and rest. A hypoactive child, on the other hand, might profit from bright colors.

Because many children with learning disabilities tend to be allergic to various inhalants, it is good sense to eliminate as many dust-catchers as possible and to substitute non-allergenic fabrics for wool and feathers. Wall-to-wall broadloom can sometimes be a great comfort to a small child. It is pleasant to put his feet on in the morning, it is quiet, it is warm to sit on if he is playing on the floor. A synthetic fibre can fill all these qualifications as well as being non-allergenic and usually easier to keep clean than wool. It should be vacuumed frequently so that it doesn't become a collector of dust, and should have a relatively thin pile. Be sure the rug is large enough and heavy enough that it doesn't slip when stepped on. Rugs that are too small tend to be skid-prone and can cause nasty falls.

Your child's room should be as light and airy as possible. Avoid using heavy drapes, especially in a room that is already short of natural light. Sheer glass curtains are easy to wash and let in the maximum amount of light and air. A blackout blind (the type with a dark core and light exterior) added to a window can help to shut out early morning light.

When you are arranging furniture, your child should be consulted if it is at all practicable. He may not want his bed in a certain position because the shadow from a window scares him when he lies down. If his ideas can be incorporated in the furniture arrangement, it will give him a sense of controlling his own environment. Once a satisfactory furniture arrangement has been found, it is well to stick to it if at all possible. Rearranged furniture can throw your LD child into confusion.

It is a good idea to help your child make a simple map of his floor plan. You can draw an outline of his room on a piece of paper and then help him place his furniture on it, either with line drawings, or with cutouts from colored cardboard. This not only will help him understand where everything is in relation to other things in the room and in relation to himself, but will also give him a concept of how a map works in its simplest form. If he is going to work in his room, his uncluttered desk should face a blank wall so that there won't be any distractions. Ornaments and bric-a-brac should be kept to a minimum, and preferably be unbreakable. Some children like to have a corner devoted to a roly-poly punching bag (the kind that returns to the upright position after being hit). It is a great way for a child to get rid of his frustrations and aggressive feelings. Others love to have a rocking chair where you can rock him to soothe him or where he can retreat and rock himself when he is upset.

Lighting is very important. Think of how stimulated you are by brilliant or brightly colored lights and you can understand how important it is to have appropriate lighting. For most LD children, you will want soft and relaxing lighting in the room proper, with a brighter light on his desk or in other work areas. On the other hand, if you have a child who needs stimulating, you might like to try much brighter lights in his room. You should arrange the lighting so that a lamp is within easy reach of the bed and the door; your child can turn it on if he wakes up at night or on entering a darkened room.

It is a help if your child has a clock in his room. Although he may be experiencing trouble learning to tell time, it will be easier for him to learn if he has a clock of his very own. If he has trouble relating to time on a regular clock, try a digital clock. They are sometimes easier for LD children to understand. A timer, the kind you would use in your kitchen, is also a good idea to help your child understand the concept of the passage of time. It is useful when you are establishing routines, as well. It is more understandable if you say, "You should have your socks on when the timer goes off," than if you say, "You should have your socks on in five minutes."

Often a small, sturdy, low stool, enables you child to reach such things as wall light switches and out-of-reach objects. If he tends to be clumsy or to fall easily, either eliminate the need for a stool, or make sure that it is large enough and secure enough for him to climb and stand on with ease. Help him practise while you are present so that he will feel secure.

In the arranging of such things as clothing or precious belongings, a good maxim is "A place for everything and everything in its place." Not only will it help establish habits of tidiness, but it will also cut down on the confusion and uncertainty of a disorganized room. Help your child return things to their proper place when he has finished using them, and make sure that you do the same with both his clothes and his belongings. Shelves are easier for him than drawers because many LD children have trouble visualizing what is at the bottom of a drawer. Clothes can be organized and arranged by category (socks, underwear, sweaters, etc.) or by outfits. It simplifies things if you try to arrange clothing color schemes so that everything automatically harmonizes or matches, such as all one color of socks, one color of underwear, neutral-colored sweaters, etc. This helps your child if he has problems matching colors, but it also speeds things up for him while he is dressing. An additional advantage with socks, especially, is that it is faster when you are sorting laundry, and you never have any odd socks. If there are other children about the same size, assign them a different color of underwear and/or socks so there is never any argument about whose is whose.

If your child's chief play area is to be his room, his toys should be kept out of sight of his desk or other work area. If his room is small, this can be done by having a small cupboard with shelves and a door. When he is finished playing, every-thing can be put back in its place and the door closed. This will help avoid distraction when he is trying to work or rest. A multitude of toys is not a good idea for a learning-disabled child, who won't know what to play with next if he has too many choices. Keep a few of those toys he appears to be tired of in another part of the house and bring them out later. Allow him to keep his current favorites in his toy cupboard. If he is being destructive with his toys, remove them for a while and leave him only soft or indestructible toys.

A child's clothes cupboard should be accessible to him without his having to use his stool. Many stores carry an apparatus which hooks over an existing rod to hold another rod at a lower level where your child can reach his clothes readily. One father used two pieces of wood, one for each side of the closet, with holes at about six-inch intervals. A rod was fitted into the holes at the appropriate level and raised as his daughter grew.

Structuring Your Child's Day

Establishing a routine that is workable for both you and your child will help you to keep the patience you need to deal with him throughout the day. While a haphazard life-style may be relaxing for some adults, it is demoralizing for a child with a learning disability. He needs to know his limits, to understand what is expected of him and when, and to know how long he is allowed for different activities and pastimes. He doesn't like surprises and will show an unexpected intolerance of them. While the average child might squeal with delight if you announced in the morning that the whole family was going to the zoo that day, your LD child might dissolve into tears or be in an absolute frenzy of anxiety at this unexpected happening.

When planning your child's routine, remember to allow him adequate time for activities. Starting in the morning when he gets up, be sure he has time to do those things for himself that he is capable of doing. It does nothing to improve a child's self-image if you take over dressing him just to get him down to breakfast on time. As soon as he has learned a new skill, such as doing up his own buttons or tying his shoes, allow him to do it for himself, with extra time allotted so he won't be rushed. This helps to eliminate early-morning hassles that get both your days off to a bad start.

First thing in the morning, any small child can try your patience. If you arrange your LD child's routine in such a way that you will not be tempted to explode in anger or do something for him out of sheer frustration, you are on the right track. It often helps to consult your child when a routine is obviously not working the way you had planned. He may be able to come up with good suggestions, and if his suggestions are adopted, he is more likely to follow through without protest.

A little trial and error and a sense of humor will help you organize a morning routine that will not be traumatic for you, your child, and your whole household. It may be necessary for you to guide him through this routine many times in the beginning, but the time will be well spent if it can mean a more peaceful beginning for your day. Initially, it will help a great deal if you use a strong, positive reinforcement such as "That was really great!" or "I knew you could do it!" As the routine becomes better established, the reinforcement can gradually be eased so that he can follow his routine and get positive feedback from his satisfaction at doing something well all by himself.

Even when a child is fully responsible for getting himself dressed and down to breakfast, clothing choice can prove to be a stumbling-block. He may try on six outfits before making a decision, and miss breakfast as a result. Try to help your child develop the habit of deciding the night before what to put on next morning. If there is some reason for a change, such as a change in the weather, don't allow him a choice between more than two similar items: "Do you want to wear your blue or your beige sweater?" Careful planning can prevent temper tantrums at not finding clean socks or his favorite pair of jeans. Try to keep abreast of washing and mending, and if something he wants is not available, warn him in lots of time.

While your child needs routine, his day should not be over-scheduled. Every child needs free time to do what he wants to do. We all know how demanding it can be to have to live by a tight schedule day in and day out. Some flexibility can be built into a routine, such as allowing a later bedtime on weekends, and possibly a morning to sleep an extra hour. More free time can be allowed on weekends, and a whole new schedule will have to be worked out for holiday periods. Special holidays such as Christmas require special planning, and this should always be done well in advance. When necessary changes occur, such as houseguests or a visit to relatives, you should try to stick to your child's routine as closely as possible.

Play activities or remedial activities which are scheduled in your child's daily routine should be given a specific time limit. Allow him enough time to finish a project when you are doing remedial work with him. If he dawdles, let him know that he will still have to finish his task next day. If he is enjoying a game, be firm about putting it away when his time for that game is over. Shut off the TV firmly when his TV time is over. If all this sounds heartless, remember that what you are trying to do for your child is more important than a few moments of frustration on his part.

No matter how much you structure, your child will set up his own routines within the routine you establish for his everyday living. He will, for instance, establish a favorite way of walking to school — maybe not the fastest, but his very own. He may have discovered a beautiful black dog around the block and want to pat its head — never mind that it takes nearly twice as long to get to school. Respect his freedom here, and incorporate the extra time into his time allowed to get to school. One mother described a routine that her son had established for reasons of his own which could have caused a great deal of frustration if she hadn't viewed it with a lively sense of humor. Her seven-year-old would dress himself in underwear, socks, and shoes every morning, and then try to put on his jeans over his shoes. Of course they wouldn't go on, so he would take off his shoes, put on his jeans, then put his shoes back on. When she tried to explain that putting on his shoes twice was a waste of time, he replied quite calmly that he *liked* doing it that way. She decided to let him have his way and it was several weeks before he himself broke the habit.

Because your child is likely to have problems with left and right, front and back, and so on, it helps to mark his clothing so that he knows immediately how to put it on. The marks can be red for left and green for right, or X for left and O for right, or any other method that your child can understand. Eventually he won't need this marking, but it is fast and easy for him when he first begins dressing himself. His teacher will bless you, and you are much more likely to find the clothes he wore to school come back with him. Shoes seem to be especially difficult for most children, even those without learning disabilities. Because there doesn't appear to be a great deal of difference to their eyes between a left shoe and a right shoe, marking them on the inside helps a great deal. Norma's younger daughter appeared in the kitchen one morning with tears streaming down her face, exclaiming, "These shoes are hurting my feet!" When Mom explained, "You've got them on the wrong feet!" her answer was a classic: "But they're the only feet I've got!"

While you are planning routines for your LD child, it is well to remember that you can't take anything for granted. He must be constantly reminded of what went before and what comes next. If he has an auditory problem, it will help if you get him to repeat instructions so that you can be sure that he understood them correctly. It takes constant reminders and repetitions to establish his routine and to help him internalize all those little things we take for granted. Often a chart can be of great help to both you and your child. You are ordering the lives of the whole household, so you may be forgiven if you forget what comes next in your child's day. A chart on the wall of his room is a handy reference for both of you. Sometimes it works well to have this chart in the kitchen or the family room where the whole family can see it. If they understand how much better the quality of their own lives will be if they don't upset this routine, they will be more receptive to consulting the chart before making demands on your time or interrupting you. When your daughter yells that Johnny has overstayed his time in the bathroom, you should know immediately if she really has cause for complaint. Has Johnny overstayed the time allotted to him? If he has, get him out. If he hasn't, tell sister she'll get her turn in a few minutes. It helps to know where you stand!

If you have a clumsy or destructive child, it is a good idea for all the family to put away anything breakable for a little while. We hate to suggest locks on doors, but sometimes this is the lesser of two evils. It is better to establish for everyone in your household that a closed door is sacred, that you *never* open a closed door without knocking. The same is true of closed drawers and cupboards. They are *never* opened without permission. It will take an LD child a long time to appreciate that this is as much for his own protection as anyone else's, but eventually he will understand.

Avoiding Mealtime Hassles

Along with the multiplicity of other problems, your LD child may have poor eating habits that date from infancy. Food allergies and hypoglycemia (low blood sugar) often accompany a learning disability. One mother reported the problems she was having with her small daughter in late afternoon. When she mentioned her yawning and her cranky behavior, she expected to be told to put her daughter to bed. Instead, she was advised that the cause might be a drop in blood sugar in the late afternoon. Her doctor suggested increasing the proteins eaten at breakfast time so there wouldn't be such a drastic behavioral change late in the day. The yawns disappeared and with them the cranky before-dinner behavior pattern.

If your child shows no inclination to eat at regular mealtimes, it is often wise to feed him separately at a different time. A poor eater will often eat more if he is not constantly distracted. If he is fussy about what he eats, it can often take a good deal of ingenuity on your part to make sure he gets the necessary nourishment. Eating by himself is a good idea if your child is a disruptive factor at meals, as well. After all, there is no reason why the whole family should suffer from indigestion.

Some children with poor manual dexterity have trouble with utensils. Give him every opportunity to practise by himself so that when he does join the family for meals he won't be embarrassed by his disability. It is likely that he will eventually improve both his behavior and his eating patterns so that he can be a part of the family group at meals as soon as possible.

Many children develop tastes for favorite foods that they will eat so much of and so often that you wonder if they can survive the experience. Sometimes you can circumvent the consequences of food fads yourself; sometimes you might be advised to consult your doctor or a nutritionist. Psychologists are usually adept at getting Johnny or Janie off Teeny Toastums and onto the four food groups needed for good health. You might try using a contract to encourage a child to eat a disliked food by rewarding him with one he likes, but beware of using this tool too often because it might encourage your child to invest it with too much emotional value.

It isn't often that food poses a really serious problem, but if you feel that it has become more than you can handle, consult your doctor.

There is one problem which should always be discussed with your doctor. Some LD children develop a craving for something unusual which they will eat whenever they have the opportunity. They might eat dirt, cement dust, paint, ink, paper, fabric, or something else totally inappropriate. This is called *pica* and is usually short-lived. Your doctor can advise you whether your child is harming himself with his strange diet.

Points To Remember

- Always prepare your child for a change.
- Keep his choices to a minimum.
- Keep your promises to your child.
- Establish family routines and stick to them.
- Organize your child's room so that it is peaceful and neat, and things are easy to reach.
- Be patient when your child creates his own inexplicable but harmless routines. They may be temporarily necessary to make him feel in control, but he'll likely soon outgrow them.

CHAPTER 6

Helping Your Child Adjust to the World

While we can order a child's world within the confines of his own home, we can do little about the world outside. No matter how well your learning-disabled child adjusts to his disability at home and at school, he still has to face a world that will not make an exception for his problems. He must face strange situations and learn not to be thrown by callous remarks and unexpected happenings. He is going to be misunderstood and often called names. He will be labelled as "retard," or "stupid," or "not right in the head." His self-esteem, which you have tried so hard to bolster, will suffer constant onslaughts from unthinking people with no understanding of his problems.

Trying to help your child adjust to everyday life can be difficult, distressing, and exhausting, but it is vitally important. The extent of his adjustment problems will be in direct proportion to the severity and complexity of his learning disabilities. Some children manage well, especially if their disability is largely an educational problem. If a child has not been overprotected and understands his own disability, he will learn to fight his own battles and make his own way in the world. However, children with many serious disabilities have an almost insurmountable problem, and there will always be some who will have to live in a sheltered situation because they can never learn the skills necessary for everyday living.

If you live in a city, especially a large, fast-moving city, the problem is greater than if you live in a small community or in the country. Away from the larger metropolitan centers life is lived at a more leisurely pace and your learning-disabled child is better able to cope with a slower life-style. These children often thrive on a farm, where routine is an established part of their world both outside and inside the home. Learning-disabled children usually form firm bonds with animals, with whom they seem to have a special empathy. They seem to have an innate understanding of the order of nature, so that even severely disabled children flourish in this less demanding atmosphere.

If you are a city dweller and your child is unable to cope with the complications of city living, it might be worth your time and energy to see if there is some way he can become a part of country living, even temporarily. Some residential schools and camps for learning-disabled children are located in the country or in small towns where the slower pace gives a child a chance to mature at his own speed without being buffeted by the frantic rush of city life. If he can be given the chance to experience life in the country with people who understand his problems, he will feel a sense of satisfaction that is difficult for him to attain in a world he cannot understand.

How Your Child Feels in Unfamiliar Environments

If you were somehow transported to the center of a large foreign city where you had trouble communicating and whose inhabitants were impatient with your failure to adapt to their customs, you might feel as frightened and vulnerable as your child does in an unfamiliar environment. An LD child must be introduced to the world outside his home very carefully or he may never recover from his initial experience. He will need all the help and support he can get from family and friends because he will be frightened and confused. He will receive mixed signals from busy surroundings and will not be sure how to translate them. His perception may make it difficult for him to understand the dangers of cars on a busy street and he may attempt to walk in front of them. Going a single block to a friend's house all by himself could be like a jungle adventure to someone else.

This child must be made to understand that the world is different from the way he perceives it and he must be helped to understand it as it really is, because the world is not going to wait for him to learn. If he sees a fluffy kitten on the far side of a busy street, no car is going to stop to let him cross, and yet he is quite capable of forgetting traffic and darting into the street without thought of consequences. He often appears unable to differentiate between various aspects of reality. He might think a shadow is solid, or he might walk into what is obviously a brick wall. If someone tries to help him, he may take it as criticism and respond in an inappropriate manner, doing or saying the wrong thing. He will feel dumb, stupid, and inadequate because he doesn't understand a world in which others of his age are perfectly at home. He is embarrassed if he is poorly coordinated and often feels that people are picking on him, which they sometimes are. He is aware that he is "different" and will often just stop trying, because if he doesn't try he can't fail.

How Others See Your Child

Unfortunately, the world we live in is often a cruel place — sometimes through ignorance and misunderstanding, sometimes for no apparent reason. People who see an LD child with severe problems away from his home or his school may mistake him for a child who is mentally retarded and will make cruel and unthinking remarks within his hearing. This is unpardonable, but not unusual. Children his own age will call him names like "air head" or "dummy," or something equally demeaning and deflating. Even a child with a minimal difficulty can suffer because in some area or another he fails to fall within that charmed circle called "average" or "the norm."

Most people will not take the time to try to understand this "different" child. They might have sympathy for a child who is blind, or crippled, but because your child has a "hidden disability" he receives little understanding or sympathy. He is often labelled spoiled and undisciplined when he is only frightened. His behavior will often be unacceptable even if he is trying, because he hasn't understood what is expected of him. While people might be tolerant of a two-year-old's erratic behavior, they will not tolerate the same behavior in an eight-year-old.

If your child is poorly coordinated, he will suffer agonies any time he tries to participate in team sports. He knows he will be the last to be chosen and that he will be at the end of the line for anything requiring coordinational skills. Every bit of training you can give him that will help him improve his skills will increase his self-confidence in sports so that others won't see him as a klutz and a total loser.

Bolstering Self-Confidence and Self-Esteem

No child is just a mass of quivering disabilities. He has strengths as well as weaknesses. Some parents tend to overemphasize his weaknesses when they should be building up his strengths. If carefully nurtured, his strengths can often be used to alleviate problems caused by his weaknesses. Discovering his strengths may take some searching, but persevere. Think back to Mark's story at the beginning of Chapter 1. He had many problems to overcome, but he had a keen mind and loved the challenge of chess. He was given every opportunity to play chess and learn to excel, until he became locally famous for his mastery of this difficult game. He used this as a focal point upon which to build his social life and his sense of being an O.K. person. Today he is a very well adjusted young man, even with his many disabilities.

In our Gym Club our motto and our philosophy have been "one step at a time." It is a good motto for any parent who is faced with bringing up a child with learning disabilities. Once you have established his strengths, help your child develop them, one step at a time. Keep emphasizing your child's innate intelligence and help him achieve success in whatever way he can.

We had one little girl in our Gym Club who felt completely defeated by her learning disabilities. Sally had fairly severe reading problems, and she was also very poorly coordinated. Her mother had brought her to the Gym Club because she had no friends and had become a very solitary child. The psychologist at school had suggested the Gym Club because he felt Sally might profit from eye-tracking training and from the various activities which would help her gross-motor coordination. She was very timid about trying anything new, but we gradually coaxed her into some of our simpler games. As she began to succeed, she became more confident of her ability. Her greatest success was learning to stand on her head. One evening she arrived at Gym Club so bubbling with excitement that she could hardly talk. Her mother finally told us the story. In Sally's physical education class at school, her teacher had attempted to teach her pupils how to stand on their heads. Everyone who tried had failed, except Sally. The whole class made a fuss over her and admired her ability to accomplish this feat, not once but several times. They wanted to know how she had learned and asked her to help them do it. She had more positive attention from the other children in her class in one hour than she had had since she started to school four years before, and even received her first invitation to a birthday party.

Success for your child might be learning to swim well, learning to ride a two-wheel bike or a horse, learning to care for a garden or a pet, taking music lessons. Success is learning to do something well that will make your child feel that he can succeed when he has known so many failures in the past. One mother allowed her eleven-year-old son to take riding lessons, although it was an expense the family could ill afford. The experience paid handsome dividends in increased confidence for her son and helped him feel more equal to his brother and two sisters who had no problems at school. After all, he could ride and take care of a horse; they couldn't. Early in his teens he began to teach riding in his spare time to earn a little pocket money and he was the envy of many of his peers who didn't have a marketable skill.

When children fail too often, they tend to stop trying. They take the attitude "If I don't try, I can't fail," or "I didn't really want to do that, anyway." By allowing your child to succeed wherever he can and however he can, one step at a time, you can help him overcome the feeling that he will always fail, so why try. It might help him to realize that many great men and women have tried and failed many times because of learning disabilities and then have gone on to succeed. Among these famous people are Sir Winston Churchill, physicist Albert Einstein, brain surgeon Harvey Cushing, General George Patton, psychologist William James, and many others. Tell their stories to your child in simple language he can understand. It will encourage him immensely if he knows that others have had his problems and have been able to overcome them and succeed.

Teaching Social Skills

While poor behavior may be tolerated at home, it will not be accepted by those outside. One of the greatest favors you can do your child is to teach him how to play with others and how to behave when he is away from home.

Your child will respond in ways that are different from those of other children of his age. For him to understand his limits, they must be firmly established and frequently repeated. First, he must understand the necessity of acceptable behavior within his own home; then this can be extended to include his behavior outside his home. It is important to develop a method of speaking to your child that he understands easily. Usually simple language, short sentences, and one-step-at-a-time instructions are the most effective. Be sure you are specific when you are giving instructions. It is much easier for your child to structure his behavior if you say, "Now it is time to get undressed," then "Now wash your face," then "Now clean your teeth," and so on, rather than giving a blanket instruction such as "Go and get ready for bed." He will probably be confused by this vague request and unable to sequence in his mind the logical events leading up to getting into bed.

As the average child matures, he moves from solitary play to parallel play, to playing with one friend, and finally to group play. Most children move toward their role as social beings in a fairly predictable way without having to "learn" their changing role as they grow. With many learning-disabled children, their immaturity makes it difficult for them to take the next logical step in becoming socially adept. They may need to be taught social skills and be given many chances to practise so that they can develop new social skills without feeling defeated by an inability to cope. If your child is having problems of this sort, you should plan carefully how you can best help him succeed in social situations, even setting up situations ahead of time where he can succeed. Parents must also be ready to intervene if they find their child being humiliated or if they realize he is unable to cope. If this is done with diplomacy, he will not feel the sting of defeat. At least at the beginning it may be necessary to keep these social contacts very simple and very short if his attention span is limited and his behavior tends to deteriorate.

Parents almost need to develop second sight with a learning-disabled child. You need to be aware ahead of time that certain situations might be disastrous and try to circumvent them. You need to know when your child has taken all the emotional pressure he can take, and remove him from the scene. Suppose you are having a family gathering to celebrate a grandparent's birthday with a good deal of chattering, laughing, present-opening, and so on. Your learning-disabled child can participate and enjoy only up to that point when the pressure of this social event begins to break down his carefully coached social graces. You might take him to the kitchen with you to help with refreshments, or suggest he show an understanding guest the garden, his room, the new television set, or something similar. If you can diplomatically remove him from the scene of all the excitement for a while, he is much more likely to be able to survive the celebration with his social skills and his self-esteem intact.

You need to be aware constantly that your child is likely to be unpredictable, and yet you have to try to guess what he might do next. You must try to foresee social emergencies, yet all the while encourage him, stimulate his enthusiasm, remain uncritical, and give him as much praise and encouragement as possible. It's a tall order, and you may feel unequal to the task without some professional help to guide you along the way. Other parents at the ACLD will be of great help, too. They will have many suggestions that are worth trying, because they have tried them and found they worked.

When equipping your child for a social role, it is well to remember that all of his disabilities will carry over into his social skills. If he is a clumsy, poorly coordinated child, he will be even worse in the insecurity of a social situation. This will sometimes give people an entirely wrong impression. We remember one mother who said her delightful little boy was known as the Walking Disaster Area. Wherever Paul went he left a trail of chaos behind him. If he went into a restaurant, something would be broken, or he would knock over a chair. At home, someone would rush to run interference for him so that he wouldn't fall over the furniture or knock something off a table. He was full of high spirits and enthusiasm and his mother hated to curtail him, but the disasters had reached a point where no one wanted to see him coming. Over the course of several months at the Gym Club, Paul was taught to slow down and to actually "see" where he was going. His visual perception was such that it couldn't keep up with the speed at which he moved. Added to this were clumsy gestures and a rather shuffling walk which were helped a good deal by various remedial games. The disasters lessened and Paul became a more welcome visitor and playmate.

The types of social skills which should be taught to children with learning disabilities are often the little things which are only noticeable if they are absent, such as how to shake hands with a firm grip, the importance of smiling when spoken to or introduced, the value of please and thank you, the importance of eye contact when talking to someone, how to modulate the voice, how to interpret facial expressions and other body language. These small social skills can make a great difference in the child's feeling of self-assurance in social situations.

Teaching Decision-Making Skills

It is never too soon to begin teaching your child how to

make decisions. If a child has never been given the opportunity to think for himself, make up his own mind about anything, or take the responsibility for his actions, he can never become an effective adult, whether or not he has a learning disability.

It has been our observation that a great many parents overprotect their children unintentionally by not allowing them any chance to take charge of their own lives. We recall one child we had in Gym Club who was having no problems whatsoever at school but was having moderately severe coordination problems. He was coddled and babied by his mother because "he falls over his own shadow." His father was a very well coordinated man who had been a professional football player at one time. He tended to ignore his only son, who was, as he put it, "a real klutz." This child is now a young man in his twenties. When he graduated from secondary school with an average of over eighty percent, both his mother and his father decided it was time for him to start making his own decisions. His decision was not to make a single decision. He has said for five years that he is going to university. He has never gone because he can't decide what to take. He was offered a full-time job with a good future, but he couldn't decide whether or not to take it, so the job was given to someone else. He is still working at a part-time job he took the summer he finished secondary school, and waiting for someone to tell him what to do.

Making decisions takes training and experience just like every other life skill we learn. It is an integral part of the process of maturing into an effective adult. It is not something that can be learned overnight just by someone saying, "You are old enough to make your own decisions, now. So go ahead and do it."

It is obvious that a three- or four-year-old can't be expected to make important decisions that could have serious consequences. No very small child can be allowed to decide to cross a busy road by himself until he full understands the consequences if he is hit by a car. The very young child has a very limited amount of experience upon which to base a decision, but he does learn with time, and consequences can be carefully explained to him. Even some decisions which could have serious consequences can be allowed without a fuss if parents take the time and trouble to circumvent any real dangers.

Norma's younger daughter refused to eat anything but breakfast three times a day shortly after she was a year old. This lovely blonde baby had a will of iron and apparently no appetite at all. She never seemed to be hungry. Her pediatrician told Norma to stop fussing and let her child eat what she wanted as long as it was moderately well-balanced, and to make sure she got her daily vitamin supplement. For three years she lived on milk, fruit and vegetable juices, whole-grain cereals, bacon, whole-grain toast, and biscuits. She was as healthy as possible and never had a cold or any other illness. She was full of energy all the time. At age four she decided to try some new foods and over the years has added to the list. She still has food dislikes, but she eats a well-balanced variety of foods and almost no "junk" food of any kind.

Sometimes forcing a child to comply with a decision you force upon him can be more detrimental than the consequences of a decision he makes himself. Psychologists have repeatedly stated that forcing a child to eat when he is not hungry or to eat food he doesn't like will result in eating problems that will last a lifetime. Making a child eat every last bite on his plate will sometimes result in a guilt complex about eating everything on his plate later in life, so that as an adult he eats long past the point when he is full and ends up with a weight problem. Many parents aren't aware that a child's appetite falls off sharply just after one year of age, so they try to force more and more food into a child when he doesn't want it. This is just one case where mother doesn't know best and a child's instincts are better than mother's nurturing.

One thing you might start allowing your LD child to make a conscious decision about is clothing. When you are helping him lay out his clothing in the evening for the next day, allow him to choose what he would like to wear, keeping in mind that a choice between two things is easier for your child. Even at three years old it is possible to learn that you don't wear a favorite sweater when it is hot outside or you'll be very, very uncomfortable. An older child might profit from being allowed to decide how to spend his free time, how to spend his allowance, and so on.

By the time a child reaches school age, he can be given many opportunities to make small decisions which will give him the feeling that all decisions have certain consequences. He will learn that some consequences are good and some are bad. An LD child may take longer than average to relate bad consequences to his previous decision, and you may have a good deal of trouble convincing him that the consequences he doesn't like are, like it or not, his own fault. Suppose, despite your schedule for him, he decides that he is not going to do his homework as soon as he arrives home from school because he is "too tired." You allow him to drift around the house or watch a little TV for the hour he would normally have been spending on remedial work. Then he is back on schedule, but his remedial work is still to be done. This means that while his brothers and sisters are watching a favorite family TV program after dinner, he has to do the work which should have been done earlier.

There is a difference between giving advice and giving information. If your child appears to be headed toward a decision which will cause him trouble, be sure he has all the necessary information. Under some circumstances you must obviously forbid a decision which might have irreparable consequences, such as jumping into deep water before learning how to swim. It is the skill of decision-making that is important, so that your child can internalize this ability and think things through before making a decision. By the time he is an adult he will have had enough practice to be able to take charge of his life without hesitation and fear of the consequences. He will develop foresight, so that if he chooses a certain path he will have a very good idea of what lies at the end of the path. He is much more likely to have a good idea of what he wants to do with his life when he finishes school, rather than drifting and waiting for someone to tell him what to do next.

Strategies To Prepare Your Child for New Situations

Sometimes it is more difficult for a parent to adjust to an LD child's growing awareness of the world around him than it is for the child. Anxiety is an ever-present emotion that all parents must try to control. With a learning-disabled child this anxiety is much more likely to come to the fore, and unfortunately it is as catching as measles. If your child senses your anxiety, he will feel it too. He might feel quite comfortable about going to the corner for a loaf of bread, but if you stress the problems he might meet on the way ("Don't get lost"; "Make sure you get the right change"; "Look both ways before you cross the street"; and so on) he will feel threatened and anxious.

Suppose you allow your ten-year-old to go to the store with a short list of things to buy and the money to buy them. He arrives at the store but is unable to read all the items on the list or has trouble figuring out the money. The clerk is sharp with him and makes the comment: "What's the matter, can't you read?" or "Can't a big boy like you figure out change?" He comes home hurt and in tears. You can storm out to the store and tell the clerk what you think of her, or you can decide that your child isn't ready to go to the store yet, but neither of these strategies helps your child learn this new task. It is better if you explain to him that the clerk was probably in a bad mood that day, help him understand what he couldn't figure out at the store, and send him back once he has calmed down. Your child then will understand that sometimes people are just crabby and that it's not his fault, and he gets another chance to try and to succeed. You must not under any circumstances lecture your child: "Now tears won't help. You should have been able to read that list. You know perfectly well how to figure out how much it would cost." You will just add to his sense of defeat if you blame him for the incident.

If your child's disabilities are severe, or if they include behavioral problems, more preparation may be needed. With any child who has a learning disability, it is important and necessary to repeat over and over to him that he is not "dumb" or "stupid," that he is an intelligent child with a learning problem. This cannot be repeated too often, because he is apt to take his peers' assessment of him at face value, and that can be uncomplimentary in the extreme. Try to ensure that he understands what his learning disabilities are, how they affect him, and how you intend to help him. If he is anxious to do something that his peers are doing, such as go to a movie or to a restaurant, and if his behavior has been such that it might just be possible that he is ready for such an outing, you might make a contract with him to give him the desired outing in return for continued improved behavior. If the desire is strong enough, he will live up to his side of the bargain. Don't try too soon, however. Some children, especially hyperactive children, have to wait for a certain stage of maturation before they are able to undertake such an outing.

Let us suppose that you have decided to take a child with rather severe problems, including behavioral difficulties, to a nearby restaurant for lunch. In the past he has been quite unable to handle this type of situation because he is as likely as not to heave a plate across the room or dump a bowl on the floor. Now, however, he has shown sufficient improvement that you feel it is time for him to try an outside social occasion. It might be as well to choose a quiet place that is relaxing rather than stimulating, and to choose a time when the restaurant will not be very busy. Be sure ahead of time that the menu contains something he likes. If you explain your problems to the management ahead of time, you are likely to have the fullest cooperation. People are usually very kind and helpful when they understand the situation.

Playing a game of "restaurant" several times with your child will help him to get an idea of what it is going to be like and how he is expected to behave. Use a menu and have someone act as waiter or waitress. If the first rehearsal isn't very successful, keep at it until your child feels quite comfortable in the role of restaurant patron. He might even like to play the part of waiter some time.

If possible, walk past the restaurant ahead of time. Allow him to look inside and see people enjoying themselves.

Make him want to behave so that he can be one of those people. Remember, there is nothing in the world your child wants more than to be thought an average child, rather than "different." It will help if you can be very relaxed about the outing and help your child think about it as being fun. Your first efforts may not be an unqualified success, but with careful preparation ahead of time, the expedition will probably come off well enough that it will reinforce your child's desire to think of himself as an O.K. person.

If he can't read a menu, but is able to go into a restaurant on his own, advise him what is most likely to be on a menu. Even adults have this problem in ethnic restaurants, so you can sympathize with his trouble. Help him choose food for which a menu isn't necessary. He can't go wrong ordering eggs for breakfast, a ham or peanut-butter sandwich for lunch, or steak or chicken for dinner. These are the basic foods that lots of adults order as a matter of course.

It is often a good idea to enlist the aid of family and friends in helping to prepare your child for social experiences outside of his immediate environment. Many children with behavioral problems are not welcome guests, but if you can enlist the sympathetic help of someone who understands your child's problems, you can convey to your child how he should behave as a guest in someone else's home much better than you can within the familiar walls of his own home.

There are many books available which will help you ease your child into the social world, but if your child's problems are really severe, you may need to seek professional help before you feel secure about allowing him out on his own.

Basic Skills To Rehearse with Your Child

- Teach your child to use buses, streetcars, subway systems.
- Make sure he learns how to use money and make change.
- Rehearse telling time and the "feel" of time intervals.
- Drill him in the use of a telephone and basic telephone etiquette.

- Help him to read and find things in a newspaper.
- Allow him to help you with a shopping list and go shopping with you.
- Show him how to make a bed, cook a simple meal, set a table, and do other simple tasks around the house.

Providing Additional Learning Experiences

If your child has trouble reading, he is likely to fall further and further behind his peers in general knowledge as well as in school-related subjects. Other than by television and radio, almost all our knowledge of the world reaches us via print. If a child is unable to read, we must make every effort to make sure he learns about the world and gathers as much information and general knowledge as possible in other ways.

There are many opportunities to provide your child with educational experiences, such as touring a police station or a fire hall, visiting a radio or television studio, watching how automobiles or some other item are made. Take advantage of any tours of this type within your area. Allow him to see ships in a seaport, planes in an airport, buses, and trains, and explain how their schedules work. Take him to zoos, botanical gardens, museums, sporting events, or anywhere else where you feel he can learn something about the world around him. Use these outings occasionally (but not always) as the reward in a contract.

The single most important item to a child with a reading problem is a television set. It is his friend, his escape, his teachers, and his window on the world. If parents use a TV wisely, it can contribute immensely to the total knowledge of your child. We are not advocating indiscriminate viewing. Watch programs with your child so that you will know what the content is, look for educational programs that will enlarge his general knowledge, and be firm in forbidding TV shows that violate the sense of values you are attempting to instil in your child. Fortunately, the airwaves are filled with programs that can bring joy, adventure, laughter, insight, and knowledge to a child whose learning disabilities make it hard for him to have these experiences in other ways.

Through your school or your local ACLD you can find out

whether any of your local TV stations are broadcasting actual lessons which your child might find interesting and valuable. In addition, you might watch for such things as programs to help a child care for a pet, learn to cook, learn the basics of carpentry, and so on. Watching news and public affairs programs with your child will give him information about what is going on in the world at large. Help him to locate cities, countries, and other places mentioned on a large map of the world. Discuss distances to places seen on television and plan a route that would take you there. Estimate how long it would take to get to a distant destination, and what time it would be there in comparison to the time where you are at that minute.

Try to make your child's television-watching an active rather than a passive experience. Ask him to repeat the story, the names of the characters, where the story happened, and other details he remembers in order to help his memory, both auditory and visual. Ask what color a character's costume was, what your child noticed about the character's appearance. Try turning off the sound to see if your child can follow the story line without sounds, and then try it without the picture. Get him to repeat back to you rhyming jingles from commercials. Learn to use every aspect of television as a creative learning medium.

Both your ACLD and your school will have some idea of the resources available to you to help your LD child learn about the world around him and experience social occasions so that he can improve his life skills. It is important that he learn to feel comfortable in these situations without parents to lean on. Eventually he will have to step out on his own. Your child may be ready for Scouts or Guides, church-sponsored social groups, or other similar groups which have some supervision. It is an excellent way for your child to polish up on newly acquired social skills. If your area doesn't have a resource list for parents of children with learning disabilities, it might be worth while suggesting to your ACLD that it would be a very valuable project for the future. Such a list changes all the time and must be kept up to date, but it can be an invaluable aid to parents trying in every way possible to help their child learn about and adjust to the world.

CHAPTER 7

Your Child's Psycho-Educational Assessment

We have chosen to discuss your child's psycho-educational assessment before considering his experience at school, because this assessment is the foundation upon which your child's whole educational future depends. We cannot stress too strongly how important it is. In some small centers there will be little or no attempt made by a school to have a proper assessment done by a competent psychologist or psychometrist. If this is the case, if your child has been judged to have a learning disability because he is not functioning as well in some subject areas as he is in others, we strongly suggest you approach your school principal about having a proper assessment done. Only then will you, and your child's school, have an authoritative guide to how he learns and where his problems lie.

When a youngster starts to school, it is expected that he will proceed through the various stages of learning at an average rate. If he fails to do this, the first reaction most parents have is "Could my child be mentally retarded?" While it is true that some slow learners are not diagnosed until they enter school, as a general rule parents are aware of mental retardation or dull-normal intelligence before a child enters Grade 1, usually because he has been below, perhaps much below, average in all areas of development. If a child has appeared quick, eager, and curious before he enters school and then begins to fail, the reason is most often a learning disability.

Early Identification Programs often pinpoint those children most at risk, and some parents are aware before their child enters Grade 1 that there is a good chance he might have learning disabilities of one sort or another. Some children will already have had Reading Readiness classes in preparation for Grade 1. However, most parents first become aware that their child might have learning disabilities when they are informed by the school that he should have a psycho-educational assessment. This is usually requested by a child's teacher, who will have discussed the problem with other school officials. These will usually include the school principal and a school psychologist or psychometrist, guidance counsellor, or other educational specialist. Teachers are usually required to make written application explaining why they are requesting an assessment. They will indicate problem areas and what materials and strategies they have already tried and with what success. You may ask to see this report if you wish.

In some cases, a child may be well beyond Grade 1 before his school suggests a complete assessment. Quite often children with learning disabilities can keep up with their schoolwork for the early grades but fall further and further behind as the work becomes progressively more difficult. While they may zoom ahead in math, they may experience serious problems in some other area such as reading. A good school will then question why an obviously bright child appears to be failing in one area.

What Is a Psycho-Educational Assessment?

Each Board of Education has its own way of assessing a child, and indeed may even call the process by another name, but in general the assessment consists of a series of tests given to a student in a standardized situation where conditions, timing, and instructions are as much the same as possible for each child tested. The results are used to assess a child's present levels of performance and to indicate his potential for learning.

Some assessments are primarily diagnostic and show a child's strengths and weaknesses in such areas of learning as mathematics, reading, and so on. Others will supply information concerning present ability and achievement and will measure how quickly a child acquires knowledge and skills. Individual tests of ability are administered by a psychologist or psychometrist who is experienced in learning disabilities. This person will try to examine a child's background before the assessment is done, so that it can be taken into account when the final recommendations are made. This background information will come from your child's school file, from discussions with his current teacher and any remedial teacher he has been seeing, and from his parents. It is important that you, as a parent, give as much and as factual information as possible. You are likely to be asked questions about your child's early development — when he walked, talked, and so forth — as well as information about pregnancy, delivery, past illnesses, allergies, siblings and how he gets along with them, and general behavior outside of school.

Test scores are based on English-speaking children. If another language is also spoken in your home, or if your child's first language was a language other than English, be sure to mention it. Even if a child speaks a second language only occasionally, it may have a bearing on test results. One little girl in Toronto came from a home where only English was spoken, but she lived in an area where all her playmates were Italian. Her learning disability centered around language problems because she was mixing the Italian she picked up from her friends and the English she learned at home. When she began Grade 1 it became necessary for her to have intensive help from a speech therapist to help her straighten out a polyglot language of her own invention.

When Is an Assessment Indicated?

Besides uneven learning patterns, there are many other clues that suggest why an otherwise bright child is not succeeding in school and that will indicate to an interested and informed observer that the problem might be a learning disability.

Some children might exhibit a short attention span, an inability to follow verbal instructions, a difficulty processing information into long-term memory, or problems with memory retrieval. There might be difficulties in expressive language, poor coordination, or problems in performing simple motor tasks. Concerned teachers will evaluate your child's problems against the way the majority of the class performs and decide whether or not an assessment could provide the information necessary to help your child. The final decision might be made after the psychologist has an opportunity to observe your child in his classroom.

Occasionally you may feel the need for an assessment yourself, and wish to request one. Your child may not be doing as well at school as you expected. You may have noticed changes in behavior, headaches, or other unusual happenings, coupled with a failure to proceed at the expected rate. If you already have one child with a learning disability, you may be the first person to notice that a subsequent child is running into problems at school. If you query your child's teacher, she will discuss your fears with you, and if she agrees that there is cause for concern, she will consult the school principal and/or psychologist.

What usually happens then is that samples of math and written work will be studied for errors of spelling, grammar, mechanical math skills, and problem-solving ability. If any area appears to be appreciably below the class average, while the rest of the work appears to be average or above average, then it is likely that your request for an assessment will be undertaken. In most cases the tests administered will be based on what your child's teacher and the psychologist have discovered when reviewing your child's current classroom work.

When Should the Tests Be Given?

No child should be allowed to take the series of tests which comprise an assessment without some prior preparation. It is therefore very important that you be informed ahead of time so that you can meet with your child's teacher and discuss how you can help to prepare him for the assessment. At the same time you will have a opportunity to assure yourself that the person giving the tests is a psychologist or a psychometrist with experience in the field of learning disabilities.

A child who suddenly must undertake a series of strange tests is bound to be a bit apprehensive and bewildered, even though many of the tests are put into a game form that children enjoy. Reassure your child ahead of time that the tests are just a way to find out how his teacher can help him in whatever area he appears to need help. Be sure he is well rested. If he feels comfortable and assured about taking the tests, the results are much more likely to be a representation of his best efforts. If, on the other hand, the tests are sprung on an unsuspecting child without warning, we feel you might be justified in questioning the results. Psychologists report that children who are relaxed about the assessment will usually be enthusiastic when they are finished and want to know when they can come back and play some more games.

If, by any chance, your child has a heavy cold or some other physical problem that makes him feel miserable on the day the tests are to be administered, we advise you to discuss with the school the advisability of postponing them to a later date. They may suggest that his condition can be taken into account when grading his tests, or they may choose to move the assessment to a better time.

What Tests Will Be Used?

The most commonly used individual tests are the WISC-R (Wechsler Intelligence Scale for Children — Revised) and the WAIS (the Wechsler Adult Intelligence Scale); the WPPSI (Wechsler Pre-School and Primary Scale of Intelligence); the Stanford-Binet (popularly called the I.Q. Test); and the Slosson Intelligence Test (a short test designed for rapid administration). The advantage of having your child individually tested with one of these is that you will gain more information about his strengths and weaknesses than could be obtained from a group test. Many children also feel more comfortable working by themselves than taking a group test with their peers in which they often feel too much competitive pressure to do their best work. The time involved in individual testing and scoring is an expense to the school board, and they will arrange for individual testing only if they are convinced it is necessary. Understandably, there will be a delay of perhaps several weeks between a request for testing, the administration of the test, and the subsequent report.

A learning-disabled child will often exhibit delayed and/or uneven development in many areas. The Wechsler tests provide two separate scores, one measuring verbal skills and one measuring performance skills. Discrepancies between the two scores are diagnostic of learning disabilities. The Wechsler test uses various sub-tests. The Information sub-test measures associative thinking and general comprehension of facts acquired both in the home and in the school, and the child's alertness to the world around him. The Comprehension sub-test measures the child's use of common sense, judgment, and reasoning. Poor verbalizers often have a low score. The Arithmetic sub-test measures the child's ability to apply basic arithmetic processes to problem-solving. Abstract concepts of number and numerical operations, and overall numerical reasoning and abilities, are also involved. The Block Design sub-test is the best single non-language sub-test. Analysis and reproduction of abstract designs are included. It indicates whether a youngster can recall a design and relate a part of the design to the whole shape or form. These are just a few of the sub-tests which might be used when your child is tested. Make sure that the psychologist explains these sub-tests to you in terms you can understand.

The use of specific learning-disability testing is another important type of evaluation that gives prescriptive teaching information. It indicates a pattern of errors or miscues which will help a teacher focus in on your child's specific educational problems and will assist in the development of an appropriate educational program. These tests point out how a child performs in specific academic tasks: for example, copying information from the blackboard or a book; finding words or designs that are the same or different; identifying and remembering words that he sees; remembering and being able to reproduce designs that he has seen for a few seconds; identifying initial sounds or final sounds in a word; remembering what he hears and writing it down; understanding and writing what he hears; answering comprehension questions.

These diagnostic assessments may include other tests, perhaps including some related to personality and emotional development, depending on the choice of the individual psychologist in your school. Always ask to have any tests your child takes explained to you.

How Should the Test Be Administered?

Your child should be well rested, physically well, and in a good mood. This will provide a much more accurate picture of his learning abilities than if he is apprehensive or not feeling well. If parents feel disturbed by their child's assessment, their anxiety will also communicate itself to the child.

Testing should be done in the morning, with the WISC-R being done before recess in a quiet place with good sound insulation, no visual distractions, no big windows, and no other children around. Your child should be allowed a break for recess. The tester should stop when your child seems tired and continue at another time. Ideally, during the testing the tester will be making notes on your child's distractibility, how long it took him to respond, if he seemed relaxed or apprehensive, and if he appeared to be trying — in other words, all of your child's reactions. These should be included in the report.

The Importance of a Good Physical Examination

It is very important that a complete physical examination be a part of your child's assessment in order to rule out the possibility of any physical reason for your child's learning problems. We recommend that your own doctor be consulted, rather than leaving a physical examination to a doctor who doesn't know your child. Obviously it is essential to rule out any possibility of either physical or neurological problems, and a doctor who is familiar with your child's previous medical history and has an open mind about learning disabilities is the best person to coordinate the necessary examinations.

Some doctors still tend to reassure parents with a pat on the back and put all learning disabilities down to heredity or slow maturation. Please, don't accept this approach. If you have a doctor who says there is no such thing as a learning disability, find another doctor. We know of one eye specialist who said that learning disabilities were all hogwash until his own child turned out to have a problem. Then he took the time to study learning disabilities and became one of the best-informed doctors around. If you must find a new doctor, look for one who has an open mind, who looks at the whole child in all situations, and who is willing to take the time to search for any physical or neurological clues which might help pinpoint your child's learning problems.

Your doctor's physical examination will eliminate basic physical problems as possible causes and he will probably also suggest tests of vision and hearing. You may find your child needs glasses, or has a slight hearing deficit, but unless the disability is severe it is unlikely that it is the reason for an uneven performance in school. It is also important to rule out any neurological impairment, although if there were any serious impairment it is likely it would have been diagnosed long before your child entered school. To be on the safe side, your doctor may order an electro-encephalogram (EEG) to establish your child's brain-wave pattern. If there is any indication of a convulsive pattern, he may suggest an anti-spasmodic drug.

If hyperactive behavior is a contributing factor, your doctor may suggest Ritalin or some other stimulant drug. These drugs are not addicting and have been used successfully by many children. In other cases they have proved useless. You should discuss the pros and cons of drug use with your doctor and then decide for yourself what you feel is best for your child. Before drugs are tried, or if they prove to be useless in your child's case, your doctor may suggest allergy tests. Food allergies, in particular, seem to be involved in some behavioral difficulties that contribute to learning problems in school. If there is a history of allergies in your family, but there is no specialist in your area, it is possible to test your child for food allergies yourself. Under the guidance of your own doctor, a dietitian, or a nutritionist, you can withdraw a food or a group of foods from your child's diet for a two-week period, then gradually reintroduce them. By keeping a daily chart of your child's health and behavior and having it interpreted by whoever is guiding you, you will have a good indication of whether or not a food allergy might be a contributing factor. Other allergies are a little more difficult to diagnose, but some of the commonest are feathers, dust, mold, wool, and pollens. If your child is subject to colds, asthma, or other bronchial distress, it would be worth discussing with your doctor the possibility of taking your child to your nearest hospital or allergist for extensive tests.

How Reliable Are the Test Results?

The bias of a tester sometimes influences the interpretation of results of an assessment. If you, as a parent, do not agree with the findings or if you feel the investigation is incomplete, then you should definitely get a second assessment. If the school has reported its concern to you and the problems described do not sound like the child you know at home, by all means follow your own intuition. After all, you know your own child better than anyone.

It is important that you report your doubts and the reasons for them to your child's tester immediately. In some cases the picture presented by a teacher is completely different from what you have observed at home. Moira was a case in point. When she was eight years old, this bright, eager, curious little girl was labelled a liar and a cheat by her teacher, who thought she was probably emotionally disturbed. Moira was copying from other students and lying about having her workbook completed. In this particular case, the school stood behind the teacher's opinion despite the fact that Moira's mother assured them that her daughter was anything but emotionally disturbed away from school. It was necessary to have a full assessment done outside the school. This showed a child with a reading ability at Grade 1 level although she was in Grade 3. She was unable to read her workbook and was too ashamed to admit it. If Moira's teacher had had her way, she would have had the label "emotionally disturbed" attached to the child's school file, which would have followed her for the rest of her school years. This case is not unusual. Like every child, Moira really wanted to succeed and has since proved that she can. If your child is not able to do this, it is important for you and his teacher to work together to discover the reason.

As a general rule, you will be able to tell if a tester is operating on the same wavelength as you are because his description of your child will ring true to your own experience with him at home. You should then put your complete confidence in that person, knowing that your child's best interests will be served.

Understanding Your Child's Assessment

You should expect to meet with the psychologist, your child's teacher, your school principal, and any other concerned persons so that the results of the assessment can be discussed. Again we stress that explanations must be in language that everyone can understand. The psychologist will review your child's background information, his academic success or lack of it, his behavior (distractibility in group situations, hyperactivity, etc.), his home conditions, physiological conditions which might have been uncovered by a medical examination, and finally his chief problem areas and his intellectual potential for learning. You should receive specific, clearly stated information about the types of mistakes your child is making; for example, "When he reads aloud he makes a lot of mistakes but is able to answer the comprehension questions," or "He is unable to use phonic skills to attack new words." You should *not* hear such remarks as "The child scored 5.2 on the Spache reading test," which gives you, as a parent, no useful information whatsoever.

The conclusions drawn by the psychologist after weaving together all these bits and pieces should be recognizable to you as a picture of your child. The tester will then make recommendations for

- *Placement* — This will indicate whether your child should be in a special class or remain in a regular class setting. It might question whether it would be to your child's advantage to be withdrawn from his classroom for special help.

- *Educational programming* — This will include materials, strategies, recommendations for follow-up, outside referral for further testing if necessary, and other resources available within the school system and in the community. There should be specific suggestions for parents to follow at home.

It is essential that you *take notes* and ask for explanations for any statement you do not understand. These notes should then be put into a file that should be kept at home and should include all the information you accumulate about your child.

The Language of an Assessment

You may hear many words that are unfamiliar to you during your meeting with the psychologist. All the sciences have their own vocabularies, but a good teacher, guidance counsellor, or psychologist will be able to give you a concise report in words you can understand. To help you, we have included a Glossary at the back of the book with some of the words you are most likely to hear. Do not hesitate to question any person included in a school conference if you do not understand their terminology. On occasion, some of these professionals may appear patronizing and arrogant without really meaning to give that impression. Many of these highly educated specialists find it difficult to translate the language of their specialty into everyday English. Don't be embarrassed about bringing it to their attention that you are not a specialist in education, psychology, or sociology. Most are only too happy to take the time necessary to make sure you understand fully the problems your child is encountering. What is most important is that the psychologist and the teacher give you a full report and explanation of why the assessment was done, what was discovered, and what they propose to do about it. That is your right.

Questions Parents Should Ask

- What is the school prepared to do? How soon? Are the resources available there or will the child need outside help? For how long?
- When will there be a follow-up meeting (end of the year? Christmas?) to report on the appropriateness of the program and your child's response to remediation?
- If the school cannot give your child the assistance he requires through its present structure, what modifications are planned to meet his needs?
- How do they think your child feels about himself? Was he upset? Worried? What can be done about his feelings?
- What outside help will be needed? Who will pay for it?
- Are there parent organizations in the community to provide support?

It is well to remember that the program must be made to fit the child, not the child to fit the program. This is the beginning of a partnership between you and the school, working together to ensure that your child reaches his fullest potential.

The Individualized Educational Program

Once an assessment has been done and the results have been analyzed, it is up to the school to produce an Individualized Educational Program (IEP) specifically designed for your child. You may or may not hear all the details when you hear about your child's assessment. Sometimes the details have not yet been worked out in time for the initial meeting. When you do get this further information, the school should offer a prognosis on the short term and on the long term. Their remedial plan for your child should spell out for you where they perceive his problems and his strengths to lie, and how they intend to go about helping him. They should have studied his learning style and adapted his individualized program to the way in which he learns with greatest ease, or at least with the smallest amount of difficulty. It is very important that you understand these plans so that you can assess whether or not they are being effective.

It is well to keep in mind at all times that any school has hundreds of pupils with whom they must deal every day. You have only your own family. It is therefore important that you be informed about the proposed program and kept up to date about your child's progress, and whether or not the remedial help that has been recommended is working. All children can learn at some level. If, despite remedial work, your child still doesn't seem to be learning, it is up to you to insist that new methods be tried until the school finds the method that will work. Unfortunately, if you put off discussing this with your child's school hoping that things will improve, irreparable harm can be done. No plan is any good on paper; it's only good if it works.

If the school insists that your child's learning problems are improving but no evidence of the improvement has shown in the work you are doing with your child at home, do go and see your child's teacher. If the remedial program is not working properly, your child can get lost in the school system. Almost all schools have a policy of passing children along from grade to grade, knowing they are really not prepared to be advanced, yet reluctant to keep them back because they get too far behind their peer group. This is one of the reasons for the constant reports we read about illiterate high school graduates. It is all too easy to become complacent once an assessment has been done and the school seems to be doing something about your child's problems. If you get report cards which seem fairly hopeful, it is very easy to ignore the fact that the promised progress is really not materializing. The final responsibility lies with you. It has been our experience that the parents who are actively involved in helping their child by keeping up to date on their progress at school, as well as helping them in positive ways at home, are the parents who will have well-adjusted teenagers, no matter how serious their initial disabilities.

If Your Child Is Not Making Progress

If a change in academic programming is not resulting in progress after a reasonable length of time, we recommend you arrange a meeting with your child's teacher to inquire what further efforts are planned on his behalf. It goes without saying that no program is any good if it doesn't work. Sometimes the school doesn't have the facilities necessary for the remedial work your child needs. Sometimes a new approach may be needed. If you are still unhappy about your child's progress, you might ask about additional help outside the school system. This may be all that is needed to bring your child up to the point where he can profit from the academic plan the school has provided for him.

There are many excellent special-education teachers who understand the various methods needed to teach children with specific disabilities in certain areas. Those that take pupils on an individual one-to-one basis are usually known to your nearest ACLD, and the school will also probably have a list of those who live close to the school. If you can afford this special help and the school thinks it is a good idea, by all means try it. If, however, the school doesn't feel that it is needed or if the cost is prohibitively high, you can do a great deal to help your child by including games and strategies as part of his daily activities around the house. You will find these aids in Part II.

We would also like to point out that almost every school system is now required by law to provide whatever teaching requirements are needed to help your child learn, so it may be that you will be able to get this outside help at no cost to you. This law includes special schools, special instruction, and any other teaching aids that will do the job. If you are in any doubt about whether or not your child qualifies for special consideration under this law and you can't get any satisfaction from talks with your child's school, get in touch with your local Board of Education.

When Should You Seek a Second Opinion?

Some school boards have an excellent system for diagnosing and helping children with learning disabilities; others do not. It is often hard to tell the difference. If, for any reason at all, you feel unhappy about the assessment of your child — if you think it is not a true picture, is inaccurate or incomplete or biased — we suggest you seek an assessment independent of your school system. Even if it is just an intuitive feeling that something is amiss, you will rest easier if you seek a second opinion. Although it is an expense (in some cases medical insurance may cover the cost), it is well worth it because you will feel more secure about your child's future. Your school might suggest an independent psychologist experienced in learning disabilities who could do additional testing. If they can offer no suggestions, try your local or a nearby ACLD, a children's hospital, your doctor, a local university (the psychology department), or if all else fails, your community social agencies.

Sometimes just speaking to other parents of children with learning disabilities can lead to the name of a psychologist who has experience. It is very important that you double-check credentials of anyone you select. If this second assessment coincides with the school assessment, then you will be reassured that the best is being done for your child. If the assessments do not coincide, ask the independent psychologist to meet with you to discuss the assessment and to exchange information with your child's school. Sometimes it is not easy to interpret the results of some tests. At other times some outside factors might have influenced the outcome of tests. Because your child's future is very dependent on this first vital assessment, we urge you to be sure that it represents a fair picture of your child as you know him.

How Often Should Your Child Be Assessed?

This is a question we are often asked and there just isn't a simple answer. If your child appears to be making good progress with the program laid out by his school, then frequent assessments are probably not necessary. However, appearances can be deceiving. Monica was experiencing difficulties finishing exams on time at university. Since it had been known from early grade school that she had a reading problem, it was decided to have her assessed again. Surprisingly, she was found to be reading at less than a quarter normal speed despite extensive remedial work throughout her school years, and despite the fact that she had always managed to get fairly good marks at school. Monica had compensated for her disability by working very hard and using her ears to best advantage, but the disability was still present and showed up when she was under time pressure, such as in a university examination. She has since had further remedial work aimed at increasing her reading comprehension. This has helped a great deal at exam time and has introduced her to the thrilling experience of actually reading for pleasure. At the time of writing, Monica has just finished, with a B mark, a course in the nineteenth-century English novel. If anyone had suggested to any of Monica's family, during those early years, that she would ever be able to take — and enjoy — a university credit course of this type, they would have been hard-pressed to believe it!

This is just one instance when follow-up assessments would have caught a problem much earlier. We feel that assessments are a good idea at least every two or three years, depending on a child's progress in school. As we are all aware, school boards are cutting costs wherever possible and the school may not have the funds to do a reassessment as often as they would like. However, if your child is not progressing, you may be sure that a good teacher will recommend a new assessment. One fact is interesting to note: If children are tested too often, they will score higher and higher with each passing test because they become so familiar with the tests. Practice may not make perfect but it certainly does make for improvement!

Each year new discoveries are coming to light in the field of learning disabilities, new studies are being made, and new advances are promising greater benefits for children with problems at school. If your child's school is on top of all the new work being done in the field, they will undoubtedly suggest a new assessment when they feel it is necessary.

Keeping a File on Your Child

Keeping an up-to-date file on your child's progress is very important. No person's memory is perfect and it is often hard to remember exact details. Your child has a complete file at school to which you have free access. If that file contains anything you consider inappropriate, inaccurate, or detrimental to your child's future, you have every right to question its inclusion in his file. Your own file can be kept up to date with an ongoing record of all educational data, report cards, assessments, physical examinations, dated notes from meetings, or any other information which might prove useful in the future. It is better to include too much than too little. If you should move to a new school system or if you become discontented with your child's progress in his present school, you will have your own file to back you up. One mother told us that she never went to a meeting with teachers, principal, guidance counsellor, or psychologist without her loose-leaf file. In many cases she was able to prove a point, and remind people of promises or plans that had not been followed through. Again, remember that these experts see dozens of children with problems every week, while you have only your own.

Questions and Comments

We would like to mention here that *The Exceptional Parent* magazine is an outstanding source of information for any parent with a learning-disabled child. Not only is it full of information to help you help your child, but it also is interested in your questions and comments. They would like to share the experiences of readers with others. Please mail your questions or comments to:

Psychological Testing
The Exceptional Parent Magazine
296 Boylston Street
Third Floor
Boston, MA 02116

CHAPTER 8

Your Child in the Classroom

There is no doubt that the child with learning disabilities has a harder time at school than his peers who have no problems. However, the difficulties he may encounter can be minimized if he gets all the help possible and develops a good self-image. So much will depend on how severe his disabilities are and whether or not he can remain in a regular classroom. A lot will also depend on his own attitude toward his learning disabilities. He will certainly need constant encouragement and help, and assurance that he is an intelligent, worthwhile person.

Children learn in different ways. If your child's disabilities conflict with the method currently in use in your school system, a good assessment will pinpoint this difficulty and allow the school to channel your child into a method of learning that is right for him. Reading through the "see-say" method is an example in point. It was decided some years ago that most children learned to read more easily using this method, which stresses learning the picture of a word or group of words at one time, then proceeding to new words. This method cannot be used effectively by children with poor visual memory. They need to be taught by a method which stresses an auditory approach, such as one using phonics. Many schools now test all Grade 1 pupils to ascertain whether they learn more readily through the visual or the auditory process, and take this into account when the pupil is introduced into the educational stream. This testing alone has helped solve many of the less severe reading problems.

Your Child's Classroom

Depending on the severity of his disability, your child may be placed in a special-education classroom, or in a classroom where he is withdrawn at certain times for special help, or he may be allowed to remain in the regular stream with additional help within the classroom. This last alternative is used as often as possible so your child will not feel "different" from his school peers. This is especially true if your child's disability doesn't include behavioral problems that make it difficult for him to fit into a regular classroom.

Most regular classrooms have at least one or two children with moderate disabilities. Many school boards are now trying to arrange for volunteer teaching assistants to help these children in the areas where they are experiencing difficulty. It is a comparatively new concept that is still being assessed, but it shows great promise because it allows many children to remain in the regular classroom while releasing the special-education teacher to help more severely learning-disabled students. In withdrawal classrooms, all children who need more help than can be provided by teaching assistants get intensive special help for designated periods each day, or several times a week.

The special-education classroom is always under the direction of a teacher qualified in special education. These dedicated teachers spend a great deal of time on their specialty, and cooperation and communication between home and classroom are very important. If your child is placed in a special-education class, it is because the school feels that he cannot learn properly in a regular classroom, that he needs the extra resources available to a special-education setting. If his disabilities are severe, he may remain in this type of classroom for most of his school years. More often, he is placed in this setting until the teacher feels he can manage on his own in a regular classroom. He will then be returned to the normal school stream.

Each school board has its own system for dealing with children with learning disabilities, which makes it difficult to give anything but the most general information. Because his primary schooling is so important to your child, we strongly advise you to consult your principal about the system used in your district. If it doesn't appear to be working for your child, you might be well advised to seek schooling outside your system or in a private school. Only do this if the system has proved wrong for the problems your child is experiencing, but we mention it as an alternative if you are not satisfied that his present school is doing its best for your child.

Why Your Child Needs a Structured Classroom

The open-classroom concept has become more and more prevalent in recent years. Many teachers feel that the structure in a traditional classroom is no longer a valid teaching tool. They like to stimulate a child's curiosity, rather than sitting him down and feeding him a lot of facts. For the average well-motivated student this works surprisingly well. They grow and blossom in this enriched atmosphere where they can learn at their own speed, inquire into what interests them, and satisfy their curiosity about the world around them.

A child with a learning disability is almost always lost in this type of classroom. Structure is the foundation of his life and he needs it to function. If he is allowed to wander at will, he will never light long enough to do any work. If he is hyperactive, he will be very disruptive. If he does not have explicit instructions, given one step at a time, he will not be able to function at all.

A structured classroom will give your child an opportunity to know his own space, and to adjust to rules which will make it easier for him to learn. He needs to know exactly what is expected of him in order to reduce his feelings of anxiety and frustration. While many learning-disabled children will run away from an open classroom, either physically or psychologically, most can be successfully integrated into a regular or special-education classroom that is structured, organized, quiet, and familiar. When your child knows where he is, where everything in a room belongs, he is much more able to focus his attention on his work. If your child is placed in an open-concept classroom, and you see that it is increasing his problems — at home or at school — speak to your principal about having him transferred.

Knowing Your Child's Teacher

Whether your child is in a special class for learning-disabled children or has been allowed to stay in a regular classroom, you should be his teacher's staunchest ally and biggest booster. After all, you are both trying to help your child in every way possible. It is a fact of life that this close liaison is not always feasible. If both parents work, it is very difficult to set up interviews or even to talk at any length on the telephone. There could also be personality differences that impede understanding. The way each of you views your child might be quite different. It is definitely to your advantage, though, to make every effort to get to know your child's teacher early in the school year and to offer your fullest cooperation in helping her in any way you can.

Of course, no one knows your child as well as you do, and it is up to his teacher to listen to what you have to say. Conversely, your child's teacher may be able to give you some good pointers on how to help your child at home and how she handles any behavioral problems.

If you have the opportunity to observe your child working with his teacher, please do so if at all possible. This will give you an excellent idea of the classroom atmosphere and of how your child functions, academically and socially, in this environment. A good teacher is adept at handling disruptive children and it is worth your while to watch how it is done. If your child's teacher feels that your presence in the classroom might upset him, don't press the point. It may be that later in the year he will feel more comfortable and you will be able to observe his progress. Leave the decision to his teacher.

If your child is in a regular classroom, he may present an exceptional challenge to his teacher, especially if he has behavioral problems. Some teachers are able to handle a large class of average learners plus one or more children with learning disabilities; some are not. Some teachers are exceptionally good at helping LD children organize their space, their time, and their thinking, and training them to filter out distractions.

Although parents are often discouraged, disheartened, and upset because of their child's behavior, lack of organization, and learning difficulties, many forget that a teacher can feel the same, or even greater, frustrations. These teachers are supposed to be the experts, and yet they will often try in vain to reach hard-to-teach children. They may think they have succeeded, only to realize later that they have actually failed. Teaching a class with only learning-disabled children compounds the frustration and anxiety, although the rewards for success are great. A good teacher at any time needs to be knowledgeable, adult, and firmly committed to the science of teaching. This is particularly true of teachers who spend all their professional lives teaching children who are defensive, disruptive, unhappy, or low in self-esteem, or who have any of the other problems which go with learning disorders. Remember to let your child's teacher know that you think she is doing a good job; she needs to feel appreciated too.

Do try to keep the lines of communication open and co-operative at all times. Some parents have a book that goes back and forth to school with comments from teacher and parents (if your child can be trusted to take it in both directions). If parents aren't available during the day, it is a good method of keeping track of what is going on at school and at home. Whatever method you work out, just remember not to take too seriously those terrible things Johnny or Janie might have to say about the teacher.

Sam was new to his teacher in Grade 3 and his mother had not had an opportunity to meet her when Sam began bringing home stories that had his mother really worried. "Do you know what that ol' teacher did to me?" he reported. "She made me stay in the corner all afternoon all by myself!" Another time he told his mother, "She made me leave the room for no reason at all!" Then came the final announcement that sent Sam's mother to see his teacher: "She made me wash the whole floor! It took me hours!"

On meeting her, Sam's mother was surprised to find the teacher to be an attractive, quiet-spoken woman who wasn't anything like what she expected. She reported what Sam had told her. The teacher laughed and explained: "When Sam had to stay in the corner, it was in his own little office," she said, indicating a desk against the wall. "It helps his concentration. As for making him leave the room — that was to go to a remedial-reading class. He will be doing that every afternoon for one period. And, yes, I did make him clean up the floor around his desk when he spilled a whole jar of dirty water during art class." Sam's teacher paused, then went on, "I was about to phone you because Sam tells me that the reason he is so tired in class is because he has to help you with the housework when he gets home. He said he washed the bathroom floor the other day." Now it was Sam's mother's turn to laugh: "He certainly did — after using the bathroom floor as a background for artwork created with a whole tube of toothpaste!" Finally mother and teacher agreed: "I won't believe everything he tells me about you if you won't believe everything he tells you about me!"

If Your Child and His Teacher Don't Get Along

Some time during your child's school years you may be faced with the situation that he and his teacher just don't get along, or that his teacher appears incompetent and unable to handle a child with learning disabilities.

Things are not always as they appear at first glance, so do a lot of quiet investigating before you form an opinion. If it is obvious that there is something drastically wrong with the way things are going at school, the first thing to do is to arrange a meeting with your child's teacher. If you already know each other from previous meetings, you will have had a chance to form some opinion. If you have not, this first meeting will give you an opportunity to discuss the problems you have encountered and will suggest the best way to approach them. If at all possible, try to arrange an opportunity for you to watch your child in class. This will often give a clue to where the trouble lies.

Not everyone likes everybody, so it is certainly likely to happen that your child at some time or other will not be his teacher's favorite pupil. This is usually just a matter of personality, and a good teacher will bend over backwards to make sure your child is not aware of her feelings. If he poses a particular discipline problem, a teacher is at a distinct disadvantage. While trying to curb unruly behavior, it is all too easy for the teacher to impart to a child the feeling that she doesn't like him, when it is actually his behavior she dislikes.

If, after investigation, you find that in your opinion your child's teacher is not doing the job you have a right to expect, discuss the situation with your school principal and/or guidance counsellor. It can happen that a teacher who appears incompetent to one parent will seem to be doing a terrific job to another. But there are also teachers who just can't seem to cope with children with learning disabilities. If this appears to be the case, request someone in authority to look into the matter and make recommendations designed to rectify the problem as quickly as possible.

Diplomacy in a situation like this is a must, and will ensure that you will get prompt attention from school officials. You must also be careful to let the child know that it is on your judgment — not his — that you are asking that he be transferred from a classroom, if such a step is finally necessary.

Teachers', Students', and Parents' Rights

Any good school system will ensure certain rights to the members of their teaching staff, backing them up on most decisions and doing whatever possible to make their teaching job easier and more efficient. However, students and parents also have rights, of which you should be aware.

A teacher's rights:
- Support from the principal, and other staff members who can be of help when needed, especially through assistance in student evaluation, program evaluation,

program resources, alternative educational forms, and assistance with pupil and parental guidance.

- Support from the parents, both in positive psychological support and with specific help for their child as he needs it.

- The best possible effort from students with a minimum of behavioral difficulties.

A student's rights:
- A teacher who is supportive, who believes that the student is a person worth knowing, and that he will achieve. This teacher will get to know all the pupils by name, and what each one is like; will make it worth the student's while to come to school; will use a variety of teaching approaches until one really works; will have a sense of humor.

- A school system which will support the student, and try to help his parents understand him.

- A principal, guidance counsellor, and psychologist who are willing to listen to him.

- A program for him that will work, whatever his learning disabilities.

Parents' rights:
- To have their child taught by a teacher who knows and can explain in understandable, simple words what is happening when, where, why, how, and with what results.

- To be kept informed of their child's progress and program.

- To be an integral part of the team planning their child's educational program.

- An alternative educational structure for their child if the school's program is not effective.

While there are other rights of teachers, students, and parents, these are the fundamentals upon which a good educational program is built. If each acknowledges that the other has rights and all try to work together, it will be a happier association all around.

Beginning a New School Year

By the end of each school year, your child is likely to have set up a rapport with his teacher which is automatically broken if he is moved to a new class with a different teacher. This is most likely to happen if your child is in the regular school stream, and can sometimes be rather traumatic. He may or may not have the same children in his class as he had the year before. If he doesn't, he is faced with making friends with an entirely new group, which is not always easy for a learning-disabled child. If he is starting in a new school, he may be very anxious about what lies ahead of him. Anything that you can do to help alleviate this anxiety will make his school year much easier.

When your child makes a major change within a school he is already attending (such as moving to a different wing or up or down a floor), or if he is beginning a new school, it might be well for you to take him on a trip of exploration before his first day in class. Most children with learning disabilities have trouble locating new things and remembering where they are. If the school is a large building, help him make a simple map of it, marking places he should know. If he requires a new route to get to school, be absolutely sure he knows how to get there and back to his home.

A walk-through of the school itself, one or more times, will help your child familiarize himself with his new surroundings. Help him to locate the washrooms and other rooms he will be using such as the science, art, industrial arts, and home economics rooms, the gymnasium, and also the office of the principal. Once school has started, make sure he knows the names of his teacher and the school principal (if it is a new school). After school has started, you might help him to remember the names of new children in his classes and the names of other school personnel he will be seeing frequently. With the help of his teacher you might like to drill him in the location of his desk, where he hangs his coat, and where games, puzzles, and books are kept.

Not all learning-disabled children will need this type of briefing, but it will help overcome the nervousness — almost akin to panic in some cases — that LD children experience when faced with a new situation. Anything that you can do to alleviate that "new kid" anxiety will help both your child and his teacher.

If the beginning of a new school year means your child is being moved into a regular classroom from a special-education class, he might need help in adjusting to this different situation. There will probably be a much higher ratio of children to teacher, so that your child may feel that he is in the middle of a mob scene. These may also be all new classmates, some of whom won't be at all sympathetic to your child's learning disabilities. If he has been in a special-education class, he will probably have had to learn to cope with name-calling at some time or another. Anything you can do to reassure him and bridge the transition will help ease him into this terrifying new situation. On the other hand, if your child has been moved from a regular classroom to a special-education class, his self-esteem is going to be badly bruised. He will feel anxious, threatened, frustrated, and defensive. It will take a good deal of reassurance and diplomacy on the part of both you and his new teacher to help him come to terms with his new environment.

The Importance of an Accurate Report Card

Most schools issue report cards of some type. Not all schools approve of formal report cards that assign letter gradings: A, B, C, D, or F. Many feel that this is not a true representation of a child's progress, since these marks often reflect only the results of tests and examinations. We agree with this point of view, feeling that a report card should reflect a student's day-to-day progress as well as the results of tests and examinations.

More and more report cards now carry a grading with

room for a comment from the teacher. This is often where trouble begins. Just how much can be said in the space left on the average report card! The usual comment that arrives home is something like "A delightful student to have in my class," "Performance could be improved with further work," "Not working up to potential," "One of my best pupils," or something equally vague. While parents may be pleased to note that "Sally is a happy little girl," or that "Johnny is working harder and doing better work this year," these remarks are not specific enough to be useful.

There are three main points that should be included in all report cards for a parent to find them really useful:

- Is your child working at his potential? If not, why not?
- Is the teacher following the program outlined for your child after his assessment? If not, why not?
- If, for some reason or another, you had to move your child to another school, would your child's new school be able to tell from his report card at what level he is functioning and where his strengths and weaknesses are?

A report card should indicate skills in reading and math your child has mastered, what still needs reinforcement, what materials and strategies the teacher had used and why, and whether or not the teacher felt they had worked sufficiently well to continue their use. There should also be some indication if your child has either gross or fine motor difficulties and if any remedial work has been undertaken to strengthen weak skills. This type of report card is also valuable to you for your own information and to add to your child's file at the end of each school year. A report card is a signed statement of what the school feels your child has achieved and should always be kept for future reference in case there is any question about what he did or did not accomplish.

The types of comments you should expect to see on a good report card, along with your child's grade in a subject, are as follows:

- "Johnny is reading at Mid-3 level using the Ginn series. He reads for pleasure and enjoys books on hockey and animals."

- "Janie has excellent sight vocabulary and uses her phonic skills to attack unfamiliar words. She needs additional help with (specific areas should be defined) . . ."

These are some of the other areas which should be dealt with in detail in a report card:

- *Oral Language* The teacher should be able to describe the child's oral language with special comments if there is any speech problem. The teacher should also indicate whether your child's vocabulary level is high or low for his age and whether or not he uses language fluently.

- *Written Language* This should be indicated by a grade level as well as showing progress in spelling, whether it is good, bad, or average, and if the teacher feels your child would profit from enrichment or remediation.

- *Writing and Printing* These skills should be analyzed as being good, bad, adequate, or possibly in need of remedial work.

- *Syntax* Where he is currently and what is going to be worked on next.

- *Vocabulary* His written vocabulary level and whether or not poor spelling keeps him from writing words he uses orally.

- *Reading* What your child's level of reading comprehension is. This is usually broken down into reading aloud and reading to himself. Is your child able to read words but not comprehend their meaning? The teacher should also mention whether or not your child comprehends well when someone is reading to him; whether or not he is finding reading enjoyable; and the types of books he prefers (if the teacher knows).

- *Mathematics*   There should be some indication of his computational skills, what level he has reached, and whether or not his problem-solving skills are good, bad, or average.

- *Environmental Studies*   Sciences and social studies are included in this group. Your child's teacher should indicate what is being studied, how class work is being handled, what assignments have been given and how your child handled them. She might also mention whether he was good at organizing his work.

- *Music*   If your child has particular music skills, it should be mentioned, as well as any method of using musical skills to help other areas.

- *Art*   This will consist mostly of how your child handles various art materials, whether he has creativity in this area, and whether or not he might need fine motor training.

- *Industrial Arts and Home Economics*   These are usually the most unstructured classes your child has, so a report on these areas should indicate your child's interpersonal skills, his work habits, his ability to organize his work space, his level of cooperation with peers and instructor, his ability to work with little or no supervision.

At the end of a good report card, your child's teacher should have a Summary which indicates how the school sees your child's future education. This should recommend where he would best be placed the following year: in a special-education class, in the mainstream of classroom learning, or in a classroom setting where he can be withdrawn for special help. The Summary should also tell whether or not your child made the expected progress for the year. At parent-interview time, these comments should be discussed, so that parents can clarify any questions which come to mind.

Strategies To Help Your Child at School

There are many points that you can pass on to your child's teacher that will help her understand and work with your child to his greatest advantage. Since you are the person who understands him best, it is worth your time to brief any new teacher on anything about your child that might make the teaching job easier and more effective, such as:

- Ways that you have found effective in handling your child.
- Situations to which you know he will react badly.
- Any allergies or fears that might be pertinent to a classroom setting, such as food allergies, fear of cats or dogs, fear of heights, etc.
- A warning of upcoming events which might be upsetting.
- A warning if something has happened away from school which might affect behavior at school.
- Any special interest or talent that you feel might be useful for his teacher to know. These can often be used as a teaching tool for an area that needs remediation.

For your part, we advise you to keep up to date on what your child is studying currently, what books he is reading, and where he is in math. Your child's teacher might like you to reinforce his school work at home by drilling him in math tables, borrowing books from the school library for additional reading at home, or helping him to locate places on a map from his social studies course. Discuss with his teacher any other ideas which would help your child by reinforcing remedial work.

If you meet resistance from the teacher when you offer your help, remember that there are some teachers who are reticent about communicating fully with parents for fear of interference. Reassure your child's teacher at every opportunity that you just want to do anything you can to help, and that you appreciate her efforts on your child's behalf.

What You Think About School Affects Your Child

Unfortunately some parents have a negative attitude toward school that they communicate to their child. This may be the result of their own unhappy experiences, or they may simply not see education as one of the top priorities in their children's lives. We had one father of an exceptionally bright youngster with coordination and reading problems who couldn't understand what all the fuss was about. He had dropped out of school in Grade 8 and started to work in a factory. Because he was a hard worker and bright himself, he made a very good living for his family. His attitude was that what he had done his son could do, too. He refused to recognize that success without education is a lot more difficult today than it was in his youth.

If either parent expresses this negative attitude toward school, their child will soon become aware of it. If a child already has had some unfortunate experiences of his own because of his learning disabilities, all these feelings will be reinforced. It is essential that parents make a real effort, no matter what their private opinion, to convey that learning is enjoyable and worthwhile.

Once a child sees school as a prison, and his years as a sentence to be served, it is very difficult to change his attitude. It is often these children who drift into delinquency. On the other hand, if you have been consistently enthusiastic about school, he is likely to take this positive attitude into every new learning situation, making it easier for both him and his teachers.

When Is a Special School Necessary?

We have been speaking about those children whose problems, both learning and behavioral, allow them to attend a regular school either in the regular classroom or in a special-education class. There are some learning-disabled children who just can't fit into this situation for one reason or another. If your child is not profiting from a regular primary school, or if his behavioral problems are such that he needs special help, a special school for learning-disabled children may be the answer.

A school specializing in learning disabilities may be a day school or a residential school. A day school is preferable if your child is not being too disruptive at home but is not learning in the regular school system. These schools are only available in large cities, as a general rule. A residential school may be the answer if your child is disruptive at school and at home and seems to be making little headway.

If you and your family are at your wits' end dealing with your LD child at home, a residential school might be the answer either for a short period, or possibly for all his school years. The experts at the best of these schools are adept at dealing with the behavioral and emotional problems which so often accompany a learning disability. They know how to build self-esteem, and they have the expertise to know the best methods of teaching your child. As he begins to achieve, you will find it is quite a different child who returns home for weekends and holidays. He will profit not only from the specialized teaching at the school, but also from being with children with problems as severe as his own. He will no longer feel as isolated and alone. As he gains self-assurance, he will be less of a threat to family well-being.

It is important that parents not feel guilty if they find it necessary to send their child to a residential school. Sometimes keeping a child at home can result in family breakdown, which benefits no one and deprives the learning-disabled child of his most important source of stability. If everyone concerned with the child agrees, then do what is best for your child and the family as a whole.

Unfortunately, no matter how much the experts and parents feel a child might benefit from a good residential school, the really good ones are few and far between, with a long waiting-list. If you feel that such a school might be the best possible solution for your child, be sure to get information and applications at the earliest opportunity. Go and see the school yourself. Talk to the people in charge, and if possible talk with some of the children. This will give you an idea of whether or not your child would benefit from that particular environment. Then put in your application to several schools you feel might be suitable. Information about these residential schools can be obtained from your nearest ACLD, from your local board of education, and sometimes through doctors or psychologists. Occasionally you will hear about them from other parents who are in a position to evaluate the program for you before you send in an application. Investigate carefully, then choose the best one available.

CHAPTER 9

The Learning-Disabled Teenager

Many parents think that once their learning-disabled child enters the teen years, the worst of their problems will be over. We wish that were true, but it seldom is. While many have overcome their initial difficulties at school, they may still possess that feeling of being "different." They may still have residual auditory or visual problems which make it difficult for them to understand lectures or organize notes or essays competently. They may find they have to work much harder than less intelligent peers who have no learning disabilities. They tend to believe the labels put on them by themselves and others and see themselves as "dummies," "stupid," "retards," or "freaks." No matter how hard parents have tried to work at bolstering self-esteem and self-confidence, the impact of the teen years can be devastating. In the words of one expert:

> All adolescents, whether learning handicapped or not, are in a confused and confusing state as they enter high school. They are struggling to achieve some independence from their families. They are attempting to develop an identity and a set of personal values. They are adjusting to the physiological changes that accompany the teenage years and trying to understand and control the emerging, sometimes frightening, feelings of sexuality. They are

working to establish and maintain relationships with the same sex and opposite sex peers, and to be accepted into a peer group. And they are beginning to consider what they will do after high school and for the rest of their lives.*

Good Parents Should Often Be Seen and Not Heard

All children are oversensitive to criticism during their teen years. This is especially true of LD children. They can seldom handle even the gentle joshing and teasing that is readily accepted by their peers, because they will look for the "hidden meaning" and take offence when none was intended.

When parents have nothing good to say, they are better to keep quiet. It is hard for us to realize that these learning-disabled children are all too aware of their own faults and limitations. What they need is support, not criticism. They are already full of self-criticism. So throw away critical comments and shower your child with encouragement and praise whenever praise is due. Reinforce his extra efforts by letting him know you realize how hard it is for him. Help him wherever you can and comment favorably on all behavior and efforts that please you. Refrain from criticizing those things you find it difficult to accept. This is conditioning at its best and can have very positive results.

If School Still Poses a Problem

Secondary school students face crucial decisions which will affect their whole future. If your child has gone into secondary school with less than perfect preparation for this advanced work, he may well be in real trouble. This is often a good time for a new assessment to be done, which may zero in on a fundamental lack of basic training from his years in primary school that could make it doubly hard for him to make op-

*Conger, 1977, as quoted by Rita Silverman, Naomi Zigmond, and Jan Sansone in "Teaching Coping Skills in Adolescents with Learning Problems," *Focus on Exceptional Children,* Volume 3, No. 6, February 1981.

timal use of his secondary school years. Because of his poor performance, he may be channelled into a vocational-industrial orientation when this isn't necessarily the best for him.

Because so many learning-disabled teens are often still far short of acquiring the skills necessary to succeed in a regular school, your child may have to be channelled into a different school from the one his friends will be attending. This will add to his feeling of being "different." Be sympathetic if your child must go to a secondary school with special facilities, but don't pity him, or he will start feeling even more sorry for himself. Try to provide a supportive but non-threatening environment at home. For those children who are trying to make it in the mainstream of learning, obtain extra help if it is needed, and give all the help you can yourself.

Norma used to circle her daughters' spelling errors in essays and English compositions because neither of the girls could recognize their mistakes. They could then go to a dictionary and look up the correct spelling. This not only reinforced spelling, but also cut down on marks lost because of errors. Joan taught her son the special tricks and devices she had learned as a child from her father to help process information into long-term memory and facilitate its retrieval.

Teaching your child how to use a tape recorder effectively by reading textbook or notes aloud into it, then playing the tape back over and over again, gives auditory reinforcement to children who have visual reading difficulties. There are many good books on memory development which emphasize mnemonics (special systems for aiding memory). Often, a course in speed-reading will be beneficial.

If you are arranging for special help, be sure the person you select understands your child's problems. If the deficit is minimal, you may be able to enlist the efforts of a bright senior secondary school student, but if there is still a serious problem, you would be well advised to seek a teacher who will give specialized help after school or in the early evening. You may find it necessary to discuss with your child's guidance counsellor the possibility of special classes within the school. Unfortunately, this often leads to a credit in a watered-down version of the mainstream course, which does not provide an adequate basis for future learning. We have found it much better to allow a child to remain in the mainstream if at all possible, and look for competent extra help for him outside of school hours. If your child is just not succeeding at all, you may have to consider special schools which will allow him to progress at his own rate.

Learning from Doing

Give your child the benefit of every opportunity to learn outside the school system. Make sure he is knowledgeable in all the small life skills which will smooth the way for him in the future. Help him develop self-assurance and good manners when meeting strangers. If your child wants to get a part-time job to make some money, allow him to do so. Make sure that he understands banking — a surprising number of teenagers have no idea of how to make a deposit or withdrawal or write out a check. Working, either at a paying job or as a volunteer, is excellent experience, and offers the additional bonus of a sense of self-worth, independence, and accomplishment that is hard to obtain in any other way.

Dropping Out of School

If your child is feeling defeated at school and wants to drop out, do not rush into a decision one way or the other. Consider all the options. Talk the situation over with his school and get all the information possible. Discuss the possibilities offered by specialized schools which either allow a child to progress at his own rate, or offer training in some specific area. Help your child assess his assets and his liabilities. What would he like to do in the future? Does he see himself in a profession? Has he a special talent he would like to develop? Would dropping out of school jeopardize his chances in the future? Could he return if he wanted to?

One of our volunteers informed us that she was dropping out of school at the end of her first semester in Grade 9. She had a serious reading disability which made it very difficult for her to handle any other language or to study any subject requiring a lot of reading. She was fifteen years old and would require special permission to drop out of school. Her teachers conferred with her parents (both well-educated and well-to-do) and they agreed that the type of formal education offered in a regular secondary school was useless for their daughter. She was bright, quite mature for her age, and very definite about what she saw in her future. Today, in her twenties, she is a well-known photographer. Had she been forced to remain within the school system, experiencing nothing but a succession of failures, her present success certainly would have been placed in jeopardy.

On the other hand, sometimes schools and teachers underestimate the determination of a student. Norma's two daughters were both told that they could not possibly achieve high enough marks to obtain admission to university or to succeed even if they did gain admission. Today, one is in her final year in Applied Human Nutrition, the other has just entered her second year of engineering. Both are achievers and work very hard. One admits that if she hadn't been told so often by so many people that she couldn't do it, she probably wouldn't have tried as hard as she has, because it *has* been difficult. But she was determined to prove a lot of people wrong, and to justify the faith of those few teachers who had believed her capable.

If your child shows any desire to go on to higher education, point out to him that the chances of success are almost zip if he doesn't get the necessary foundation at secondary school. Tell him that although mature students are allowed in to university courses in many places with a reduced prerequisite, it will do no good if he is incapable of learning in a university setting. If he appears merely to be fantasizing about his prospects, the chances are he won't even be admitted to a university, so you are not faced with the decision about supporting or discouraging his desire. On the other hand, these children are often capable of using their strengths, plus learned strategies, to overcome their learning disability and succeed when everyone expected them to fail.

The Dangers of Being Overindulgent

Don't fall into the trap of giving your teenager too much, because you will rob him of incentive and promote a "the world owes me a living" attitude. Many parents, because they feel sorry for their learning-disabled child, try to make it up to him by showering him with every possible material advantage. This can also hide a feeling of guilt if a parent feels he hasn't helped an LD child as much as he might have.

One of our former Gym Club pupils dropped out of school, refused to get a job, pawned some of his mother's jewelry, and generally made himself so obnoxious that his father finally kicked him out of the house. We had been trying to get his parents to realize for some time how much they were spoiling their son, but their feelings of guilt and pity seemed assuaged only by giving Jason anything he wanted. His weekly allowance was three times what most of his peers received. He had free use of a car, his own telephone, his own TV, his own charge cards — all at sixteen years of age, when he was by no means able to handle all these possessions. When his father gradually started cutting back, Jason felt he was being deprived of what was his right. At eighteen, he moved into a furnished apartment with his girlfriend and another couple. They all live on welfare and work only occasionally at odd jobs for a little extra money. All are school dropouts, all had learning disabilities. They enjoy their way of life and apparently have no desire to stand on their own feet and pay their own way.

Keeping Communication Open

You may not always agree with how your child sees things, but he has a right to his opinions. In the terms of Transactional Analysis, try to keep your conversations with your child on an Adult-to-Adult basis. If you come on as the stern Parent, you are likely to elicit a childish response. If you treat your child with respect and speak to him as you would to another adult who has the ability to think for himself, you are much more likely to get an Adult response. Allow him to take responsibility for his own actions and to learn from his mistakes. If he does not seem capable of learning from his mistakes, try to find the reason and possibly seek professional help. Allowing your child to make his own decisions without giving unasked-for advice can be very hard, but unless there is an obvious and serious reason for not allowing a decision, by all means let him go ahead.

Learn the difference between giving advice and discussing the various aspects of a decision and what the results might be. You are certainly within your rights to point out that drinking underage can result in arrest; that selling drugs to a friend can result in a jail sentence; that joyriding on a motorcycle can result in death or serious injury. You can certainly point out that if he takes the car without permission, he will not be allowed to have it again for a very long time; that if he is caught speeding, he will have to pay his own fines; that if he fails at school because he isn't trying, he will have to take the consequences; that if he drops out of school and takes a dead-end job, the chances are he will be stuck with that type of job for the rest of his working years. This type of information is just that — information from your experience given to a person with limited experience.

Give Him Support and Love

It is vital that your child know at all times that you are with him, not against him. Because he knows that he can't always depend on his own senses as a result of his disabilities, he needs to feel his parents are his rock — strong and dependable. Never stop telling your child that you love him and that you have confidence in his ability to come out on top. Then do everything in your power to support him without overwhelming him and trying to run his life.

The Impact of Immaturity

Learning-disabled children occasionally suffer from more than just neurological immaturity. Through an unknown and unfortunate set of circumstances, some children never appear to mature emotionally. While they are not mentally retarded, they do appear to be emotionally retarded. If a six-year-old has a violent temper, tends to fly into murderous rages, and lies and steals when he thinks he won't get caught, parents and psychologists tend to look upon it as a phase that parents must suffer through. They do not look as kindly on this type of behavior in an eighteen-year-old. This eighteen-year-old, especially if he has a learning disability as well, can be next to impossible to help. He may have had the best schooling and the maximum amount of support and help from loving parents, and yet he may not be able to bridge the emotional gap between childhood and maturity. He is the victim of immature, irresponsible thinking and behavior. The chief characteristic of these children appears to be their inability to learn from their own mistakes or profit from experience.

How can you recognize the warning signs while a child is still young enough to benefit from professional help? It is often hard to know. If a child's reaction to life situations remains on a very juvenile level, this might be an indication that there is trouble ahead. If he appears unable to cope with frustration, or to be more headstrong and wilful than might be expected even considering the fact that many learning-disabled children are emotionally immature, it might be wise to seek professional help These difficult children seem to be somewhat easier to deal with if their problems are tackled while they are still very young.

The Smiths have successfully raised three youngsters, one of whom had a learning disability, but feel that they have failed miserably with their fourth. He is a personable young teenager whose learning disabilities, while serious, haven't kept him back as much as his infantile behavior has. His mother has developed a heart condition as a result of worry. His father has all but given up. Recently this lad was arrested by the police for joyriding in a stolen car. His father asked him why he had done this when he knew he could have had his mother's car if he had asked for it. His answer was: "The keys were in it and it seemed like a good idea at the time."

Like many people of this type, this young man seems to be unable to resist his impulses and unable to learn from either

his own or other people's experiences. These childlike person-
alities can be very appealing and they are often manipulators
and con artists. They are also very hard to help unless the
potential trouble spot is discovered before their teens. Interpersonal maturity can be improved with psychological intervention, but good results take time. Unfortunately, it is often
very difficult to make the payoff for approved behavior as
attractive as the payoff for delinquent behavior.

Stopping Early Delinquent Behavior

Petty theft appears to be epidemic in certain urban areas, and
offers a special temptation to LD children. If they can excel at
petty theft, stealing things like chocolate bars and gum, they
become "heroes" to their peers. This eggs them on to steal
bigger and more expensive things. When we had a Gym Club
at one Toronto school, one of our youngsters who was at that
time in Grade 7 stole over $400 worth of merchandise from a
nearby mall. The authorities chose to make an example of him
because he had been picked up for petty theft so many times,
and he learned the hard way just how severe the consequences
can be.

The time to nip this type of misbehavior in the bud is when
it first starts. We are constantly appalled at the number of
parents who will pay for, or accept as gifts from a store
manager, something a small child has taken in a store. If
parents do this, they are not allowing their child to learn the
lesson about what is theirs and what is not theirs to take. This
is one area where parents *must* take a firm stand and allow
even a very small child to take the consequences of giving
back something he has taken, even if it means embarrassment.
This is one lesson which can pay handsome dividends as your
child gets older.

Another unacceptable behavior to which LD kids are prone
is cheating at school. Most children seem to try this at some
time or another, but it is very common with LD children because the difficulties they are having at school cause them constant embarrassment. Again, parents must take a firm stand
with their child and allow him to take the consequences if he
is caught.

Alan, a very bright child with dyslexia, was one of our early Gym Club members. Although spoiled and overprotected by his mother, Alan was still a nice child to have around because his disability didn't seem to affect his behavior to any great extent. Alan's teacher came to watch one of our Gym Club sessions, and took Joan aside afterwards. Alan, she confided, had developed a habit of cheating and she was having a difficult time making him face up to the problem. He constantly denied that the work he handed in was not his own. Finally he was confronted with an exact copy of someone else's work, but he was spared the consequences of his actions when his mother went to the principal and begged him not to punish Alan because of his trouble with reading. Unfortunately, Alan never did learn his lesson. He cheated his way through secondary school by copying other people's assignments and cheating on exams, but he was finally brought up short at university when he was expelled for plagiarizing a major assignment.

Problems with Self-Esteem

For the average parents of a learning-disabled child, the most difficult problem they will be faced with is their child's brittle self-esteem. It takes very little to break down what you have taken years to build. If by secondary school your child is still experiencing difficulties, he may be told that he needs a different type of school from his friends. While they go to a school oriented toward the student with no disabilities, your child may be channelled into a vocational school, or a combination school which can still provide needed help in problem areas. This is the child who is more likely to succumb to peer pressure to try alcohol or drugs, not because he really wants to try them, but because he wants to belong, to be an accepted member of some portion of his peer group. If at this crucial stage he falls in with a group whose pursuits are hedonistic and irresponsible, he may have serious problems. Positive feedback from children his own age when he steals from his family to buy drugs or booze, or when he shoplifts or commits acts of theft from houses, can be very a strong force. He wants to belong. He likes the benefits he reaps, not only in an accepting companionship, but also because he finds he enjoys the money, the drugs, the booze, the parties. They all combine to give him a false feeling of being an O.K. person.

If this happens to your child, you will have a difficult time convincing him that his new life-style is not the best life-style. In fact, as his parent, you may very well have no impact on him whatsoever. Sometimes experts in juvenile behavior can turn this warped thinking around by getting a young person to face the future and what that future might hold for him. It is important to realize, though, that for some of these children there *is* no tomorrow. If they see themselves as losers in the game of life, they will only live one day at a time. Making them face facts as they are, not as they wish they were, is a very difficult task that is best undertaken by experts. If you even suspect your child is heading in this direction, run, don't walk, to your school's guidance counsellor and ask for help in locating a professional, or an agency, who can provide effective intervention.

Detecting Potential Problems

The juvenile department of the police in this area tell us that by far the largest majority of children who come through their hands, or who end up in juvenile court, have learning disabilities. We get a similar report from agencies dealing with teenage drinking and drug problems. Everyone agrees that the best way to prevent these things from happening is to have parents alert to warning signs. Here are a few you would do well to be aware of:

- From junior high school on, watch for long absences from home with no explanation forthcoming about where he was, whom he was with, or what he was doing. You might get answers like: "Where were you?" "Out." "Who were you with?" "You wouldn't know them." "What were you doing?" "Nuthin'." At a local junior high school, it was the "in" thing in Grades 7 and 8 to steal booze or beer from parents, slowly over a period of time so that it wouldn't be missed, and then have a big bash in a nearby wooded park. Parents were unaware of this until the police broke up one of the parties and ushered the culprits home. There were about twenty of them, all quite drunk, none older than thirteen.

- If a child seems to have lost interest in his studies, has been refusing to do his homework, is lethargic or sleeping a great deal of the time while he is home, or has undergone a distinct personality change, be suspicious about drugs. Marijuana is the chief culprit, and it is as easily obtained as a soft drink for almost any child who wants it. It is not only available but comparatively inexpensive, at least in the beginning. There is always someone ready to sell it to children as long as they have the price. They will share among themselves, passing a joint around, knowing their friends will have the cash some other time.

- Be especially suspicious if you are missing small amounts of money, or if your child has "lost" possessions he might have sold (one child pawned his tape recorder). Make sure you know what marijuana smells like. If you aren't sure, go to your local police department and ask them if they can let you smell a sample so you'll be able to recognize it. It has a sweetish, quite characteristic odor once you are familiar with it, and looks much like the herb oregano. We are not suggesting you make a federal case out of a little experimenting. Almost every child will do some experimenting on his way to maturity. You probably did. It is the emotionally immature child, the child with a poor self-image, who is most likely to develop a psychological dependence on any chemical crutch. That is what you want to prevent.

Your Child's Friends

Keep an eye on your child's choice of friends. If he has stopped bringing friends home, or if the friends he is bringing home seem less than desirable to you, check up on them as quietly as you can. Older children can sometimes help; so can a chat with a sympathetic principal or guidance counsellor.

If you find that your child has indeed become part of an undesirable group, it is difficult to know how to handle the situation. It seldom, if ever, works to forbid your child to see those friends again. He obviously is gaining something from their friendship or he would terminate it himself. About the only thing you can do is to try to give him as many opportunities as possible to make new, desirable friends and develop new interests. Make sure that he is getting the maximum amount of emotional support from sympathetic and understanding family members at home. Do not under any circumstances allow yourself or any family member to "put down" your child. He cannot withstand sarcasm or aspersions cast on his ability or himself as a person. If he is seeking positive strokes from an undesirable group, don't criticize the group, just try to make sure he get lots of positive strokes at home and at school.

Occasionally a change in school is called for. A girl in our Teen program was attending a school which had developed a reputation for its fast-living teenaged students. It was known as a hotbed of drugs and sex, according to an exposé in a local paper. Her parents laughed off the whole thing until they had an opportunity to question their daughter and the parents of other children who attended the same school. They discovered it was even worse than the paper had reported. The parents spent a good deal of money they could ill afford to send their daughter to a private school after this happened, knowing that she was still emotionally immature, very impressionable, and easily led.

The Problem of Drinking

If you suspect that your child is drinking and you know that he is not getting it from your home, do a little detective work to find his source of supply. While the drug-pushers are usually criminals, the suppliers of alcohol to children almost never are. They are ordinary men and women who are amused to be asked by a young teenager to buy them a bottle. According to many children who have done this for years, they are hardly ever refused. These adults wouldn't dream of giving a youngster any kind of drugs, but they don't think of beer, wine, or liquor as a problem. Alcohol is a socially accepted part of life. Like smoking, it is a mark of growing up to almost every child. TV commercials for wine, beer, and alcohol, ads in newspapers and magazines, life-style advertising showing young and attractive adults having a wonderful time complete with some form of alcohol — all these things contribute to the idea that drinking is a grown-up thing to do. Unfortunately there is an incredible number of teenaged alcoholics. Contrary to what most parents believe, alcohol has always been a much greater problem than all other drugs combined. Almost every large city now has at least one group of Alcoholics Anonymous for teenagers alone. Some cities have several. For the child with a learning disability, alcohol is an easy path toward feeling better about the world.

With learning-disabled children, particularly, it is important for them to understand the dangers of alcohol. You can obtain excellent information on alcohol and drug abuse from many different sources, including most secondary schools. See that your child is supplied. If he ignores this and laughs it off, persist. Al-Anon, an offshoot of Alcoholics Anonymous, can provide you with back-up information and runs support groups for families of alcoholics.

Shoplifting

If your child suddenly appears in new clothes that you didn't buy him, or has spending money he is evasive about, be suspicious. It is an unfortunate fact that the incidence of shoplifting among teenagers is epidemic. In fact, in many places it is a status symbol. If you question your child about new clothing you might be put off by an answer that indicates it belongs to a friend and is "on loan," or has been "traded." This may be true, especially among young girls. Track it down and find out. If your child says he made extra money doing some job for someone, check up on it as diplomatically as possible. If there is just one incident, there is probably no cause for alarm, but if this becomes a common occurrence, check it out.

Sex and the Teenager

If either a boy or a girl establishes a "steady" relationship, make sure that they have already had all the sex information they need. If you are in any doubt, get it to them fast. Again, emotional immaturity can work against the learning-disabled child. Not only does this young person need the feedback of a steady girlfriend or boyfriend to bolster flagging self-esteem, but he or she must also cope with awakening sexuality with an immature emotional system. Many of the girls become pregnant at an early age, often because of some of the weirdest "lines" imaginable that were fed to them by their boyfriends. Their innocence and gullibility are astonishing, and there are lots of young men out there just waiting to take advantage of them. If you suspect that either a son or a daughter is having sexual relations, make sure they fully understand the consequences, and make sure that they get to a doctor or a birth-control clinic immediately.

We have talked to girls who have gone through the devastating experience of giving up a child for adoption, and to girls who have never fully recovered from the psychological effects of a therapeutic abortion. We have also seen some of the sad results of young teenage mothers dropping out of school to work at some menial job to try to support a baby they insisted on keeping. A teenage boy can be as badly affected by this trauma as a girl, so make sure it doesn't happen to your child.

A Good Relationship

If you can develop a close yet open relationship with your teenagers, you will help them through their times of crisis. There are many good agencies available to give you a helping hand if you need it. The ACLD is always ready with answers to your questions. We hope that at the end of your child's teen years you will send him out into the world as a happy and confident young adult.

No one said it would be easy, but it is certainly worth every bit of effort.

CHAPTER 10

Organizing Your Own
Recreational-Learning Program

"Let's face it," Freddie's mother said. "Freddie was born a klutz, just like me! It's too bad, because his father and his older brother are both good at sports." Freddie is one of many children with learning disabilities who has both gross and fine motor problems. While his brother, who was eight, learned to do all the things kids that age love to do, Freddie was left sitting on the sidelines. He couldn't ride a two-wheel bike because he couldn't keep his balance. He was never chosen for a team because he was so poor at all team sports. Lonely and miserable, he ended up pretending he didn't want to play with the other kids, but his mother knew he was eating his heart out.

It was the plight of youngsters like Freddie that led to the first Gym Club. Ill at ease because of their disabilities, these children also tend to have trouble developing communication and social skills. They need opportunities to improve their motor development in a non-threatening environment where they will not be compared with other children who are free of coordinational difficulties. If your child is lagging behind in both his social and his motor development, he might profit from a recreational-learning program.

Joan's original Gym Club was based on developing gross motor skills through special exercises and game play. This gradually grew to include four different sections. The Gym

Club itself emphasized gross and fine motor development. To this was added a Learn to Skate program, and later a Learn to Swim program, especially designed for children whose poor coordination made it difficult for them to learn these sports. The Teen program came next, as the children from the original Gym Club grew into their teen years still needing help and support. While all the programs emphasized helping the children's disabilities, they were so much fun that they became the social focus of the children's week. It was a fun evening out that also gave them a chance to socialize with other children who would not laugh at their disabilities. From these early programs has developed a concept of recreational-learning programs which is being carried out year after year by parents determined that their children get all the help possible to overcome their problems.

We would like to point out that not every child with a learning disability is deficient in motor development, but almost every child with a learning disability can benefit from the social interaction provided by the Gym Club. Often these borderline children are the most difficult to help. They are frequently the trickiest to diagnose, are passed over in school by teachers who do not realize their problems, and are often misunderstood by both family and friends. Many are well on their way to becoming social misfits at an early age. In a good recreational-learning program, these children learn to understand their problems, which increases their cooperation and their ability to deal with new situations. They also learn the valuable lesson of how to listen to and follow instructions. Wherever possible the programs try to teach a child how to use his strengths to overcome his weaknesses and how to be independent and self-reliant.

The Teen Program is somewhat different from the other three, which are geared to help children aged five to nine and ten to thirteen master basic skills. By the time these children become teenagers, their needs have changed. In the Teen group, the sport activities are more challenging, and the crafts more demanding and more related to individual interests. Experts are occasionally invited to discuss special topics such as career opportunities, alcohol and drug abuse, birth control, heterosexuality and homosexuality, good grooming, social behavior, and fashions. All of this takes place in an informal and comfortable atmosphere with the children having ample opportunity to discuss problems privately if they wish. They often set up a buddy relationship with their volunteers (who are usually just a few years older), giving them someone outside of their immediate family with whom they can discuss problems and concerns.

This support system might well have saved one young girl's life. One of our volunteers came to us after the end of a Teen program, concerned about the turn that conversations with her young teenager had taken. Sarah was not a very attractive child, mostly because her glasses were always sitting halfway down her nose, her hair always looked greasy and untidy, and her skin was bad. Her posture and her general manner conveyed an air of defeat and low self-esteem. Sarah had been with the Gym Club for two years but had made very slow progress. Unfortunately, her mother did not really see Sarah as an individual and would often refer to her as "my ugly duckling," without thinking how this could hurt a young girl just moving into adolescence. Recently Sarah had become preoccupied with death and the subject of suicide. She had asked Sandy, her volunteer, if she had ever known anyone who had committed suicide. She questioned her about the most painless and surest method. Sandy, in a panic, came to Joan. Joan immediately spoke to Sarah's mother, who insisted Sarah was just trying to get attention. She finally agreed to take Sarah back to a psychologist whom she had seen some years before. As it turned out, Sarah was indeed suicidal, to the point where she was hospitalized for a short period. When she was released, the psychologist suggested that Sarah's mother take Sarah to a dermatologist, a good beautician, and a hairdresser to get her hair styled. These simple steps did wonders for her self-esteem, because, while the "ugly duckling" didn't turn into a swan overnight, she was so much more attractive and received so much positive attention that it helped her overcome her desire to escape from a life she was finding intolerable.

Setting Up a Recreational-Learning Program

While it may sound obvious to say begin at the beginning, frequently well-intentioned groups expect their enthusiasm to supplant organization and planning. Unfortunately their efforts fail because they did not consider the problems first. We suggest that your first step be to find a group of parents who would like to help form a recreational-learning program. If there is an Association for Children with Learning Disabilities in your area, contact them as soon as possible. Their cooperation and help can make your task much easier. If there isn't one, you might be interested in forming such a group, in which case you should get in touch with your nearest group or your provincial or state branch. If you are having trouble rounding up parents who wish to participate, contact your local schools, school boards, special-education teachers, in fact anyone who might know of other parents. Put notices on local bulletin boards, in newspapers, on public-affairs broadcasts.

Once your group of parents has been formed and you have established contact with a nearby ACLD, you have the nucleus from which to work. Divide your Parents' Committee into a chairman, two vice-chairmen, a secretary-treasurer, and whatever subcommittees are necessary. Get everyone involved. This is important, because many parents will feel much more positive knowing that they are finally doing something to help their child.

Begin with just one program, preferably the Gym Club, and aim to enrol about twenty to thirty children. If there are more children needing the program, it is better to organize for two nights a week. It has been our experience that too many children and volunteers milling around leads to confusion for everyone concerned.

Having decided on your committee, the executive should start the search for a coordinator. This choice can make or break the program, because the full responsibility for success or failure will ultimately fall on the coordinator's shoulders. It takes a very special kind of person, who is able to get along with both adults and children and who possesses exceptional understanding and insight. This should be a salaried position, not the job of a volunteer no matter how experienced, so that the executive can maintain control and can replace the coordinator if the results aren't up to expectations. Look for a person with a background in special education or someone who has worked successfully with learning-disabled children in some capacity outside a school setting. This person must understand the philosophy of the program and have a comprehensive understanding of learning-disabled children, plus the necessary expertise in gym-oriented recreation. A person with a background in occupational therapy and/or physiotherapy would be excellent if the other necessary qualifications were also present. Probably the single most important thing is a positive personality, mature yet resilient, able to control staff, volunteers, and children, and still enjoy the challenge of the job.

Once you have chosen a coordinator, he/she should be given complete responsibility for the program, without interference from the committee, which should undertake a review at certain specified times. If at review time a majority of the Parents' Committee is dissatisfied, the coordinator can be replaced. Beyond that, the coordinator should be given complete control. We can say from experience that it is a hopeless task to try to run a program with parents constantly telling you how they think things should be run.

The next step is to find a suitable place. Permission to use a school is usually obtained through the school board, and might be expedited by working through your local special-education department or the principal of your school. If possible, try to find a school with a swimming-pool, because, although you may not plan a swim program for your first year, you will probably wish to some time in the future. A gymnasium is a must, of course, and with luck you will be able to obtain permission to use such equipment as mats, trampolines, balance beams, and so forth. You may also get some help from your local Parks and Recreation department if there is one in your area. You will also need a room for crafts, preferably an art room with running water and a sink. If this isn't possible, any schoolroom will do, but care must be taken not to disturb the classroom more than necessary. Make sure your group cleans up after itself or you may jeopardize your good relationship with the school board.

Once the place has been established, the Parents' Committee must choose a time. Tuesday and Wednesday are usually the least committed nights of the week, and 7 p.m. to 8.30 p.m. is a convenient time for most parents. An hour and a half is long enough to include a variety of activities and short enough to keep the children's attention. Two hours is a bit much for the younger children at the end of their busy school day. Too long or too late a program tends to add to disciplinary problems. Your group will probably function from September until the end of the school year, with breaks during scheduled school holidays.

Financing these projects is not easy. First, a decision must be made by the Parents' Committee about the fee schedule. It probably won't be possible to finance your whole program through fees in the beginning, but it is important to establish an amount you can count on when you are working on a budget. Each program must adjust its fee system to suit the people involved, charging so much per week, payable in advance for the complete program, or in two instalments in September and January. For further financing you might try service clubs, church groups, and other similar organizations. If possible, supply speakers to interested groups to inform them of your purpose. Once you have some idea of how much money is coming in, you can budget for salaries and supplies. In the beginning, pare all costs down to absolute essentials, borrowing and scrounging where possible, and wait until your program proves successful before allocating more money for those areas that really need it.

Hard feelings can be avoided by keeping all interested parties informed of the progress of your plans. Let parents, school board, school principal, teachers, and donors know how things are going. If a secondary school is being used, the teachers can be invaluable in helping you find suitable teenage volunteers. The special-education teachers are valuable sources of help and the art teacher can help you get supplies. Both can advise you if there are supplies at the school that you can use, such as pencils, scissors, paint brushes, jars for mixing paint, and so on. If the children's teachers are advised, they may be able to suggest specific ways you can help their pupils. With the school principal's permission, you might arrange to send home with any child a teacher feels could benefit full particulars about your Gym Club.

It is of the utmost importance to get as much publicity as possible. If people don't know about the program, it will fail. Use whatever media are available to let the parents in your community know what the program is, how much it is, when and where it will be held, when registration will begin, and how long the program will last. Designate members of the Parents' Committee, preferably those who have had experience in publicity or public relations, to send out news releases to radio stations, to TV and cable companies, to the education editors of local newspapers, and even to local clergymen who might be willing to announce a nearby program or place the information in a church bulletin. Have everyone phone anyone they think might be able to spread the word. Make sure everyone is prepared to answer questions, and give or send sheets with full information to anyone who wants it. Put ads in local papers, and post them on bulletin boards at schools, supermarkets, community centers, anywhere you think parents might see them. In short, leave no stone unturned to spread the word.

Training Volunteers

Once the basics are well in hand, you must discuss with your coordinator what you want the program to encompass. The coordinator will select personnel to handle each section, although the Parents' Committee should feel free to make suggestions.

Your program is going to be based on a one-to-one ratio — one child to one volunteer. It is important to assign each volunteer to a compatible child and to maintain that pairing for the entire program. Our preference is for senior secondary school students, or students majoring in one of the behavioral sciences at a community college or university. The most important qualifications for a volunteer are love of children, reliability, and patience. The volunteers must be made to understand that these kids need consistency and that if they are erratic in their attendance they will do their charges more harm than good. The use of a volunteer "contract" outlining expectations and conditions will help to instil responsibility in volunteers. Parents should not be used to work with their children in lieu of volunteers because they need a rest from their child, they can profit from the interaction with other parents, they can learn a great deal from guest speakers, and also it gives their child an opportunity to relate to a new person, which will help their social adjustment.

The best way to obtain volunteers is to pay a visit to your nearby secondary schools. Both the principal and the guidance counsellor can be of help. They will put notices on the bulletin boards explaining the program and its purpose, announce it in assembly, and possibly arrange for you to speak to any interested teenagers in an after-school meeting. You might be surprised to find that many of the students interested in becoming volunteers either have had, or still have, some learning disabilities of their own. They may hope to derive some benefit from the program themselves.

We allow three nights for instruction of volunteers, two hours per night. You may prefer to do the training in two nights immediately before the program begins and one about four weeks into the program. Most of your first night will be taken up giving further information about the Gym Club and the importance of not missing a class once a commitment has been made. You will also need names, addresses, and telephone numbers of all those who decide to participate. Now is the time to make sure each potential volunteer understands exactly what a learning disability is, how the program functions, and how you hope it will help the children. Point out the importance of relating to the child assigned to them. Explain that it is no disgrace if they simply cannot relate to their assigned child; ask them to report this fact as soon as possible so that another child can be assigned to them. It is important that they understand from the beginning what specific learning disabilities their assigned child has and how you hope to help him. One thing they must understand very clearly: it may be necessary for them to *earn* the trust and friendship of their child. Explain that many of these children have been defeated and let down in the past and that their egos are badly in need of bolstering. Some have been hurt and disappointed so many times that they have built a shell of hostility and indifference around themselves as a protection. These children need to be able to depend on their volunteer to help restore their trust in people. It may take some time to win their confidence but it is well worth the effort.

On the other nights of training, stress that these children are not mentally retarded, and that they will likely have behavioral problems, but that they will eventually learn to manage these. Impress on them the importance of talking to their child's parents, and to his teacher if possible, and of reading the results of any tests as well as comments from instructors. The more the volunteer knows, the easier it is to plan a program and choose the method best suited to his child's specific problems.

Explain fully how the gym part of the program will be implemented and how the crafts will be run. Emphasize that a volunteer must not do things *for* a child. It is all right to assist, but no child can learn if he manages to get other people to do things for him. Explain, also, that these children tend to be very good at manipulating people and warn them to be on the lookout for this.

Here are some suggestions to help volunteers elicit the response they want from their child when working with him in either gym or arts and crafts:

- *Increasing Motivation* The child needs to *want* to play the game, and to do the exercise or the craft. Sometimes children will not try for fear of failure, but will tell their volunteer they "really don't want to do that." Try to increase motivation by pointing out the benefits, or by simplifying the task, or altering it in such a way that the child can succeed. Consult the instructor if necessary.

- *Lowering Restraints or Standards* If a game, activity,

or craft seems to be beyond the child's capabilities, simplify even further so the child can succeed. If this is impossible, slowly steer him into another game or project, or consult the instructor.

- *Structuring the Environment*   You will need to keep an easily distracted or hyperactive child away from other children and keep work areas as uncluttered as possible. Guide the child from one step to the next and gently discourage jumping from one thing to another without finishing the first.

- *Patterning*   If it seems impossible for a child to begin any phase of a game, activity, or craft because he has a problem understanding the instructions, try putting his hands, or legs, or body through the necessary motions. Don't do a craft project yourself, but put his hands through the motions. With games and activities, you might show him, then explain as you do it yourself and put his body through the motions. This will help a child get the "feel" of how something should be done. Sometimes you might need to repeat these motions more than once before the child is able to do it for himself.

- *Imitation of a Model*   Because many children with learning disabilities are unable to conceptualize ("picture" in their mind what something looks like) or have auditory problems which make verbal instructions difficult to follow, we always made a very simple model for arts and crafts to give them a basic idea. We would often embellish this with another model to show some of the variations that a child could use to personalize his craft. We always aimed to have something a child could take home with him each night. Volunteers can show the model to a child, and explain it in detail, but they should be cautioned not to make the model themselves.

- *Verbal Instructions* These must be given clearly, slowly, and distinctly so that a child can follow them easily. Be sure to try to make eye contact. If a child is intent on watching you, he is more likely to really hear what you say. You may even have to hold his head to get his attention if he is very easily distracted.

- *Trial and Error* This is often the best teacher. Suggest that volunteers use discretion in stopping a child from committing an error in a craft or activity. Sometimes it is better to allow him to go ahead and then discuss where he went wrong and help him to learn from his mistake.

- *Shaping* This is the basic technique that makes these programs work. We take the child to the lowest point where he can succeed and make sure he is congratulated and feels happy with his success. Next time he must do a little better before he earns the praise and encouragement, so that he will want to continue to improve. If done subtly, shaping can elicit the desired response without the child's being aware that he is being conditioned. Explain this to your volunteers and also explain that it will take a great deal of patience on their part but that it is probably the most successful method of helping these children.

The Parents' Program

The information and exchange of ideas available to parents while their children are involved in the program are of equal importance to the improvements the child makes during the sessions. These parents often need help and support, which they have hitherto been unable to find. There will be some parents who have never had an opportunity to talk to another parent with a learning-disabled child. From the very beginning it is important to emphasize that this is *their* program as well as their children's. However, you must also firmly discourage the use of the program as a baby-sitting device. It should be understood that at least one parent per child is expected to remain throughout the evening. We ran into several instances of parents dropping off their child and being late picking him up, which made their child feel deserted and panic-stricken. In one particular case an unfeeling parent asked a baby-sitter whom the child had never seen before to pick her up without telling the little girl in advance. The child was terrified and refused to leave with a complete stranger. By the time the parents were phoned and finally arrived, their child was hysterical.

A Parent Program Coordinator should be selected from among the parents at the beginning of the sessions to work with the coordinator to organize speakers, discussions, and special films and events. During discussion periods you will find that feelings of resentment, guilt, frustration, and shame will surface from many parents who for the first time have the opportunity to relate to and discuss problems with other parents, or with experts in the field of learning disabilities. There is a thirst for knowledge and a need for help, and it is important that parents be made aware of what support the community has to offer. Many schools are negligent in keeping parents abreast of their rights, what is being done for their child, and what can be done for their child outside of the school. Parents should be made aware of diagnostic clinics, good tutors, what books are available, and anything else that will help them cope with their "different" child.

There is one type of parent who is unlikely to involve himself with your program. This parent, for pride or some other reason, refuses to acknowledge that there is anything the matter with his child. He (and it usually is the father) is the type of parent who says, "He could do better if he tried harder," or "He'll grow out of it," or "She's just a girl. What does she need an education for, anyway?" These negative remarks hide a determination not to admit anything is wrong. Not only does this attitude make it more difficult for the child, but it also often destroys a marriage. Everyone is the loser.

It is hard to draw this type of parent into the program, but if he can be persuaded to come on an evening when you have an interesting and informative speaker or a particularly good film, sometimes the general discussion which follows will draw him into voicing his reactions, often with good results. Sometimes a visit at home from a psychologist or an understanding and knowledgeable parent of the same sex can help. It is preferable to have someone of the same sex call on this type of parent, because he is otherwise likely to respond with: "What would you know about it, you're just a woman (or man)!" Do what you can to help this type of parent, but understand that some will never come around.

Extending Your Program

When you have proved that your program is needed and successful, you may want to branch out into other areas. Both the Learn to Skate and Learn to Swim programs were very popular with children in our club because they helped them be less different and more like their peers. These programs offered great fun in a completely unthreatening situation. Because we were willing to make progress slowly, at a child's own pace, most of the children were finally successful in both of these programs, which did a lot for their confidence and self-esteem. The Teen program will be a natural outgrowth as the children in your program approach adolescence. We had some children with us right through primary school and into secondary school. These were the ones who needed both physical help and psychological support. Others were so much improved after one or two years that they were ready to join other after-school programs such as Scouts and Guides.

It is well worth the effort to work hard to make your recreational-learning programs a success. It is hard to determine just how important they are to the children involved, but it has been our experience that even the help they receive in their social adjustment is well worth the effort. Many of these children have gone on to become volunteers themselves.

PART TWO

Games and Activities for Helping Your Child at Home

CHAPTER 11

Your Plan of Attack

Every parent is a teacher, whether or not he recognizes the fact. Mother is usually the first adult to whom a child responds and she is his first teacher. The purpose of this chapter is to help you develop techniques to aid your learning-disabled child, which you can use in the form of games and activities in the following chapters.

In today's busy world, not all parents have as much time to spend with their families as they would like. Many feel guilty about this, but we think that the quality of the time you spend with your learning-disabled child is more important than the quantity. Inventive, creative use of the time you do have available will make learning opportunities out of everyday experiences. You may make up your own games as well as using some of the ideas in this book.

From your child's assessment you have a picture of his strengths and his weaknesses, and how he learns best. Your plan of attack should be to use his strengths to help his weaknesses. If he learns more easily through his eyes than through his ears, you will want to place emphasis on games and strategies which will help remediate his auditory problems. If he learns more easily through his ears, you will want to use aids that will help him improve his visual ability. Just remember, all these games and strategies are supposed to be fun. Keep them that way. Only use these aids when your child wants to play a game or cooperate in a strategy. Be ready to stop when he appears bored or tired. If he doesn't seem to be succeeding, restructure the game, but do follow through with it. A child needs to learn to finish what he has started. In the beginning, establish the rules of the game, make sure your child understands them, and then be sure to stick to them. It is often tempting to make it easier if you see he isn't succeeding. Much better to start with a simple game where you know your child can succeed and build toward the more complicated games.

If You Are Helping with Schoolwork

Not all parents are equipped to do remedial work with their own children. Not all parents have the patience. Sometimes a parent suffers from the same learning disability as the child. Not everyone can learn to be objective, which is necessary when you switch from being a parent to being a teacher. Don't feel guilty if you can't cope with remedial work. Save your efforts for those everyday learning situations which are of inestimable help to your child. If you do decide that you would like to try to help your child with schoolwork, be sure to coordinate your efforts with your child's teacher. Here are some guidelines:

1. Choose the time of day that is best suited to your child. You will probably know whether he is at his best in the early part of the day, or later in the afternoon. If you aren't sure, a few days of careful observation will probably confirm it for you. Make sure that you aren't choosing a time that is important to him for some other reason (a favorite TV program, for instance). The time should be right for you, too. It just isn't possible to help a child while you are busy trying to prepare dinner or get another child ready for school.

2. In time, you will be aware of whether your child works best with you or independently of you. If he needs independence, take advantage of program texts such as Sullivan Reading and Mathematics Programmed Texts. Your child's teacher will be aware of these and help you obtain them. They help

your child by using constant repetition for over-learning and self-correcting. If he works better with you or with specific guidance, there are many materials available which can be put on tape so that you don't have to be by his side every instant.

3.   Be careful not to impose your learning style on him. Your learning-disabled child may *need* to get up every so often and stretch his legs or pat the cat. He may actually work better with soft music in the background to help him relax and concentrate.

4.   Lessons should be daily and short and for only as long as you feel you are holding your child's attention. With very young or hyperactive children, lessons may be initially as short as a few minutes and gradually increased so that you are working from thirty minutes to an hour each day, depending upon his age and grade. The use of a timer is very effective to mark the passage of time for specific activities: "See if you can finish this page before the bell rings." If you agree with your child that you will work for a specific number of minutes, *stop* when that time is up; don't continue for just a few minutes more.

5.   If possible, establish a quiet place free of any interruptions and use the same place each day. Your child might enjoy having a special pencil, a special book, or something else that makes this a special time. A few minutes alone with him at the end of the lesson can be cherished by both of you.

6.   It is essential that any task be finished. This establishes a pattern that will always be important to your child. If you find that the task set is too difficult for your child, restructure, don't abort. You want to establish the precept "Always finish what you start." Be cheerful, but firm. This is a favorite time for children to try to manipulate parents. If you ignore a temper tantrum and your child realizes that all his temper is doing is prolonging his task, he will soon learn that it isn't worth while and will resign himself to regular lessons which must be finished. You are trying to help your child establish a learning attitude that will carry over into school.

7.   Reinforcements may include a logical one such as a chart on the wall showing his progress, plus strokes like a pat on the back, a hug when he does something well, or a small treat.

8.   Use simple, one-sentence instructions with a specific task. Use simple words like "Add the numbers" or "Color the dog green."

9.   If both parents are involved in teaching the child, they should be careful to divide their duties. It is much more effective to work individually than to confuse the child by making him feel that he must please more than one person at a time.

10.   Know what you want to teach, break it down into short steps, and determine how much time you feel it will take your child to complete the task.

11.   Begin at a level where you know your child can succeed and work toward more complex activities. If your child finds a task difficult, consider the number of things with which he must cope. He may not be able to think of an answer and write it down at the same time. He should be allowed, then, to answer first, then write it down. Be sure to allow him enough time to think out his answer.

12.   Don't be discouraged if progress seems slow.

13.   If possible, try to incorporate the academic skills you are teaching into some type of social or game activity around the house.

14.   Whenever possible, allow your child to help structure his time himself, but again, watch out for manipulative behavior. If he makes promises, see that he keeps them. If you make promises, see that you keep them.

15.   Please remember, above all, never to say, "I knew you could do it if you would only try."

Planning Everyday Games and Activities

The points made concerning schoolwork done at home can be applied to games and strategies in many cases. Start simply, with easy-to-understand directions. If other children are going to participate in any of the games, make sure your child is going to be able to perform well enough to compete on a more or less equal footing. Try not to let him get involved in games where you know he can't possibly succeed. He is liable to be laughed at, which is a terrible blow to self-esteem and self-assurance. Under no circumstances should you begin a game your child enjoys if he has been misbehaving, hoping it will improve his behavior. You will just reinforce bad behavior.

Helping Teenagers with Studies

Sometimes all the years of effort can backfire on parents when their LD child reaches his teen years. As these children grow away from parental support, they are determined not to be spoonfed by the parents in daily academic sessions. "I feel like a baby!", "I always thought I was a retard and now I know it!", "Everything's the same, year after year. It never gets any better!" are just a few of the comments that have been reported to us by the parents of teenagers. When continued reading support is needed through the teen years, the use of tapes can be a significant strategy. Once a child establishes the importance of using tapes as a learning strategy, he will use them all his life. Some taped textbooks and novels used in English classes are already available through school libraries, public libraries, or Institutes for the Blind. Many secondary school Specific Learning Disability teachers will make these tapes available. Many are also working with parents to augment the tapes in school libraries. In your local library you will also find current books and magazines on tape under the heading of Talking Books.

Both of Norma's daughters have small tape recorders that they take into university lectures and then use when studying. They clarify their notes on tape and use them over and over. These tapes are much in demand by other students, who find them an ideal way to study for exams.

Another strategy that works with teenagers who have poor reading comprehension is to read aloud so that there is the reinforcement of hearing as well as seeing. If, at the same time, he makes notes, another reinforcement is added. This is a particularly effective way to study for exams, especially if your child studies in his own room without any outside interference.

The use of calculators for children with severe memory problems in mathematics has proved a boon in the last few years. Many schools now allow calculators to be use extensively, but it is best to discuss this with your child's teachers and/or the principal. There are many learning-disabled children who are skilled at problem-solving but are poor at the basics of math because of a difficulty with long-term memory. For them, a calculator can be a lifesaver if they learn to use it properly. A calculator is only as good as the information punched into it, so careful instruction is a necessity. If the school approves, teach your child how to use a calculator.

It's Your Right

Don't be put off by educators who tell you that parents are only supposed to be parents. You will hear such things as "You will only confuse him," "He will feel pressured," "Let him just enjoy being a child at home." Like it or not, all children learn at home from parents and siblings, so why not make use of this fact. In addition, these same educators will not come up with alternative strategies for the child who needs help during all his waking hours. Many of our best experts in the field of learning disabilities were once the parents of learning-disabled children themselves. They saw how much they could help and gave it their best shot. When their children no longer needed their help, they moved on to the broader field of educating other children with learning problems. Parents teach good manners, values, practical living skills, behavior, and many other things that children, when grown, feel they have just learned by osmosis. Why should they not help their child cope with their academic problems if they are able?

CHAPTER 12

Visual Games and Activities

Before a child begins to read, he must learn to discriminate and see likenesses and differences between sizes, shapes, forms, colors, configurations, and finally letters and words. He must be taught to *perceive*. This is called "reading readiness" and is the basis for many kindergarten activities that prepare a child for reading. Looking at pictures in books, magazines, or catalogues and classifying similarities and differences will help your child develop reading readiness. This prepares him to look carefully at the shapes of letters and small words when he first begins to read. When appropriate, show your child that pictures and words are sequenced on a page moving from the left side to the right side and from the top of the page to the bottom.

Many of the following games will help develop more than one aspect of visual ability as we have indicated.

Candid Camera

Focus: *visual acuity, visual memory*
Method: Without any advance warning, have your child shut his eyes and describe what a person is wearing. This may be a person seen from a car, someone in the room with him, someone seen on television, or even what you are wearing yourself. *Variation:* Have him describe what he himself is

wearing, something he has just seen, or a picture he has just looked at. This is a good visual game to play in a car with more than one child.

I Spy

Focus: *visual acuity, color discrimination, visual closure*
Method: A game for two or more people, each one taking a turn. The person whose turn it is calls out the color (size, shape, beginning consonant) of something in plain sight. The players try to guess the object from the clue given. The first person with a correct guess takes the next turn. No cheating allowed! *Variation:* As indicated, any property of an object can be used. An excellent game to help a child differentiate shapes if played as "I Spy Something Round."

Scavenger Hunt

Focus: *visual and auditory discrimination, visual and auditory recall, ability to follow directions, tactile discrimination, motor coordination*
Method: This popular old game can be played by the whole family or a group of your child's friends. The objects to be found must be of a specific color, size, shape, texture, or taste. *Variation:* You may require abstract reasoning to determine what they are supposed to find. Some examples might be: "Find something in the kitchen that is sharp," "Find something in the bathroom that is shiny," "Find something in the bedroom that is soft," "Find something in the yard that is round and red."

Travel Fun

Focus: *visual acuity, auditory recall, arithmetic skills*
Method: Before you start, help your child to prepare a list of the things he may see on a trip. These might include such things as cows, horses, and dogs for very young children or, for older children, unusual items such as Corvette cars or cemeteries. Parents and children will decide ahead who con-

stitutes a winner: the one who gets the largest number, or sees the most unusual item or the greatest variety, or sees the most things first.

Concentration

Focus: *visual memory, visual acuity, visual discrimination*
Method: A commercial game of Concentration may be bought or a regular deck of cards or two decks of cards may be used. You can also make a duplicate set of words or pictures on three-inch-by-four-inch cards with one word or picture on each card. Spread the cards out, with the picture down, in random order on the table. Allow a player to turn up two cards to try to get a matching set. If the try is unsuccessful, the cards are returned to their original face-down position and the next player tries. Each player tries to remember the location of cards after they have been returned to the face-down position in order to make as many pairs as possible when it comes his turn to play. If a player is successful in matching a pair, he is allowed another turn. The person with the greatest number of pairs wins.

Snap!

Focus: *visual discrimination, matching, fine motor training*
Method: Deal out all the cards in a deck face down to up to six players. Each player at the same time turns over one of his cards from the pile which he has placed in front of him. When a pair is made with any other player, the first player to call Snap! takes the matching card from the other player and sets the pair aside. When the cards are all played, the player with the most pairs wins. A commercial game of Snap! is also available.

Kim's Game

Focus: *visual discrimination, visual memory*
Method: Place a number of small objects on a tray, starting with just a few and working up in later games to a larger

number. Allow the players to look at the tray for a few minutes and then remove or cover the tray. Now allow the players to recall as many items as possible. The player who remembers the largest number wins.

What's Missing?

Focus: *visual memory, visual discrimination*
Method: Remove an article from a room or an article of clothing from a person and then ask the players to try to guess what is missing. The first player to guess wins and has the chance to plan how the game will be played next round.

Scrapbooks

Focus: *visual discrimination, fine motor training, laterality*
Method: An inexpensive scrapbook may be purchased or made. At the top of each page list one letter of the alphabet. Allow your child to find pictures from magazines and catalogues that start with the given letter, and paste them on the appropriate page. He can also draw his own pictures if he can't find the picture of an object.

Picture Sorting

Focus: *visual discrimination, fine motor abilities*
Method: Give your child a pile of magazines, newspapers, and catalogues (old travel brochures are colorful to use) and allow him to cut out pictures which he can then sort into categories, by color, by size, by type of object, or by what room an object belongs in. With young children you may wish to use concrete items that could be sorted by some category such as color or size, like buttons, marbles, silver, socks, ribbons, etc.

Flashlight Fun

Focus: *visual tracking, concentration*
Method: In a darkened room or at night you can trace a

pattern with a flashlight against a wall and allow your child to follow it with his eyes. Later, as his visual tracking improves, you can draw simple patterns such as squares, triangles, or circles which your child can follow with his eyes and identify. *Variation*: As your child improves, allow him to take his own flashlight and follow your pattern as you make it, or duplicate it after you are finished. He can then make his own patterns for you to identify.

Boat Race

Focus: *visual tracking, concentration*
Method: This is a good game to play on vacation where there is a small bridge over a stream. Each player chooses a stick or a leaf of approximately the same size. They are all dropped into the stream at the same time to see which will reach a previously established "finish line" first. A convenient, easy-to-see rock or log is the usual choice. With practice a child will learn to observe the river current so that he can drop his "boat" in the most advantageous place.

Shell Game

Focus: *visual tracking, visual memory*
Method: Using three eggcups and a button, devise your own version of the old "shell game." Allow your child to watch under which eggcup you put the button, then move the eggcups around. He is the winner if he can guess under which eggcup the button is located when you have moved the three eggcups around several times.

Card Sorting

Focus: *visual memory, visual sequencing*
Method: Spread out on the floor or a table a complete deck of well-shuffled cards. Ask your child to put the deck in order by suit and then by number from ace through all the numbers to queen and king.

Eye-Openers

Focus: *visual acuity, visual memory, visual discrimination*
Method: How well does your child visualize? Ask him which is larger, a quarter or a nickel. How many wheels on a freight car? What color is your school janitor's uniform? What letters are on a telephone dial? What arm does Daddy wear his watch on? What color are your sister's eyes? You can devise any number of similar questions which help develop a child's powers of observation as well.

Comics

Focus: *visual discrimination, visual memory, visual sequencing*
Method: Read comic strips to your child, then cut them out and mix them up. Have your child rearrange them (a) in proper order according to the captions, (b) to make a different story.

Nifty Newspapers

Focus: *visual discrimination, visual memory, visual sequencing*
Methods:
For the very young child:
— Have him find pictures in the newspapers and tell you what they might describe.
— Have him find pictures of animals, people, houses, etc.
— Get him to cut out specific letters from headlines.
— Have him describe where these letters were located, such as top, bottom, middle, left side, right side.
— Have him circle with a marker all of certain letters in a headline, or words that are the same.

For older children:
— Help them develop research skills by asking them to find specific things you know to be in the paper.
— Have your child find an ad for the sale of a bicycle, then ask him to write an ad he thinks is better and tell why.

— Use weather reports of your area for a week or more to make a weather chart.
— Use colored pictures to make jigsaw puzzles. For younger children you might cut a picture into just three or four parts or use a whole newspaper page cut into five or six parts.

Map-Making

Focus: *visual discrimination, visual memory, visual sequencing*
Methods:
1.   For very young children, get them to make a map of their own room (a floor plan with the position of furniture marked), their house, their yard, their neighborhood, their school.
2.   Help your child make a map of how to get to school, how to get downtown, or to a friend's house, or to the local movie theater, etc.

With older children, plan an imaginary trip to a distant place and help them to trace it on an atlas or a globe with a marker. Plan different ways of arriving at a given destination. This can be great fun as a family project, planning either an imaginary trip or one that someone in the family is going to make.

When Norma's older daughter was in Grade 6, she was fortunate enough to have an excellent and highly imaginative teacher. For Social Science he came up with an unusual project that got the whole family involved. He told his pupils to pretend they were *voyageurs* leaving Quebec City in the summer of any year before 1810. They had four canoes and must cross Canada by water and portages right to the West Coast. They had from September until the end of the Christmas Break to plan their trip. They had to tell what they would take with them, how they planned to live off the land, where they would winter, what hostile Indians they might meet, what help they might expect from friendly native people. You can rest assured that when this interesting project was finished, the whole family knew a lot more about Canada, including how to draw a map of the country and how to plan a cross-country canoe trip.

Picture Story

Focus: *visual discrimination, visual memory, visual sequencing, expressive language*

Method: For the young children: Help them make up a simple story and then cut out pictures that could be used to illustrate their story. These pictures could be pasted into a scrapbook, or made into a panel to go on his bedroom wall. For the older child: A more elaborate story might be told in picture form, with printed subtitles under the picture. Some children like to cut out their characters from magazines and use comic-strip-type balloons to print in conversation. This can be a very absorbing pastime for a rainy afternoon. For older children, especially if there is more than one participant, the stories can be told to the rest of the children at the end of the play period

Marbles

Focus: *visual tracking, fine motor control*

Method: This fine old game is a good way for children to learn to use their fingers adroitly and to track the marbles with their eyes. The usual method of playing the game is to draw a circle on the ground and have each player place two or three marbles inside the circle. Each player takes a turn trying to knock out one or more marbles by flicking a marble into the center with thumb and forefinger. If he succeeds in knocking out a marble, he gets another turn. The beautiful alleys the children use these days will also help children who are having trouble remembering their colors.

Ball Games

Focus: *visual tracking, eye-hand coordination*

Method: There are many games that can be played with a ball, from games played on a beach with a large ball, to games played in a small space with a small ball. Many are played with two or more people; a few can be played by yourself. Try some of the following and invent others of your own:

- For very young children, sit on the floor spread-legged and roll the ball back and forth between you. As your child improves, give the ball a small bounce and allow him to catch it first with both hands, later with just one hand.
- Place an object on the floor and allow your child to "bowl" it over with a ball.
- Using plastic bowls, let your child try to throw a ball into a bowl. As he becomes more adept, move the bowl farther away. This is excellent "target" practice.
- Practise catching a ball by bouncing it back and forth at increasing distances as your child becomes more adept.
- Show your child how to bounce a ball off an outside wall and catch it. Allow him to stand close to the wall at the beginning, gradually moving farther back when his skill improves.

Paper and Pencil Games

Focus: *visual discrimination, fine motor skills*
Method: There are many pencil and paper games that will interest children from the preschooler to the teenager. Here are just a few:

Hangman: An old game most youngsters learn in their early school days. Draw a gallows. Under the gallows draw a dash for each letter of a word your opponent must try and guess. For each letter he has wrong, you draw a part of the "hanged" person's body. If a complete person is drawn before the word is guessed, the person challenging is the winner.

X's and O's: This simple game is still a good one.

Join the Dots: You can make these yourself by drawing a simple picture in a faint outline, placing numbered dots on the picture quite close together, then rubbing out the original outline. Allow your child to join the dots to see what the picture is. You might start a young child with something as simple as a square, a triangle, or a circle. There are many books with these Join the Dots pictures.

Flannel Board

Focus: *visual discrimination, visual memory, visual sequencing, fine motor skills, tactile sensitivity*

Method: There are so many uses for a flannel board that only a few of them can be mentioned here. We suggest a board about twenty inches by thirty inches, although smaller or larger ones may be used. If you do not have facilities for making the frame, a picture frame or a frame used for stretching canvas will do just as well. Cover the frame with flannel or use a firm piece of board covered with flannel. The advantage of using a frame is that you can pin things on it as well as using the clinging nap of the flannel. The best fabric to use is felt, but an old flannelette sheet is quite adequate. Cut various shapes and objects from different felt or fabric. You may also use certain paper products such as paper table napkins and paper towels. Use these as the basis for lessons or storytelling. Play games by mixing up shapes and allowing your child to put them back into the original order. Let him tell you a story using the flannel board. There seems to be no limit to the number of games you can devise with a flannel board and a little ingenuity.

Silhouettes

Focus: *visual discrimination, visual closure*

Method: This is a variation of the old game where a person, using two hands, makes the silhouette of an animal against a blank wall, using a strong light to throw a shadow. For very young children, you can use familiar objects which are easy to recognize in silhouette: cups, mugs, a ball, a teapot, a coffee pot, a pitcher, etc. It is also a good way to help children identify different shapes. Cut out shapes of circles, triangles, squares, and oblongs, and silhouette them against the wall. Be sure your child is sitting in front of you where he can see only the silhouette, not the object itself.

CHAPTER 13

Auditory Games and Activities

There is a vast difference between hearing and listening. These games and activities are intended to help train the ear to listen. We are born with the ability to hear, but only with training do we learn how to listen effectively. Listening enables a child to respond effectively to music, stories, instructions given by parents or teachers, and the conversation of friends. By giving a child the opportunity to develop listening skills we lay the groundwork for the child to get the most from future educational experiences.

I Hear with My Little Ear

Focus: *auditory discrimination*
Method: Don't take for granted that all the buzzing, boilings, ringings, and so forth around your home are easily recognized by your child. You can say, "I hear with my little ear something that is making a buzzing sound. What is it?" and ask your child to identify the sound. This can be used for sounds inside and outside your home, farm sounds, city sounds, animal noises, etc.

Mother, May I?

Focus: *auditory discrimination*
Method: This is a game to be played with friends or brothers and sisters. All the players stand behind a starting line. The game is started with the idea being to get to the leader first and touch him. The leader is standing at a distance facing the players. The leader says, "Johnny, take four baby steps." Johnny must ask, "Mother, may I?" before taking the steps. The leader replies either "Yes, you may" or "No, you may not." Players must be sure to obey instructions or else they are penalized according to the leader's wishes. Then the leader will say, "Janie, take two hopping steps." Janie then must ask, "Mother, may I?" If any player forgets to ask, he must return to the starting line.

Little Sir Echo

Focus: *auditory memory, fine motor, rhythm*
Method: Tap out a series in a set rhythm and have your child duplicate the rhythm. Begin with short patterns or number sequences, then develop into longer patterns, using familiar nursery-rhyme rhythms or tunes your child knows.

Story Records

Focus: *auditory memory, auditory sequencing*
Method: Allow your child to listen to stories on records or tapes and then ask him to repeat the story he has heard back to you in his own words and in proper sequence. This will take a little training, as a rule, because children tend to remember best the part of the story they liked the best and either place it in the wrong sequence or give it the whole emphasis. As part of training to listen, encourage your child to listen carefully and remember all the things that happened and in what order.

Word Train

Focus: *auditory discrimination*
Method: You give your child a word such as "lap" and he must then give you a word which starts with the final consonant, for example "pill." This continues as long as you want to play or until one player can't think of a word. It can be played with several players, a player having to drop out if he can't think of a word. *Variation:* This can also be played with a standard Scrabble board with older children who know how to spell.

Categories

Focus: *auditory association, auditory memory*
Method: Give your child a "category," which can also be a place, and he responds with examples which belong in that category or place. For example, if you say, "Category: kitchen," he might respond with stove, refrigerator, pots, pans, dishes, etc. If you say, "Category: animals," he might respond with dogs, cats, cows, horses, etc. This can be played with several players. For older children, you might play Categories in a more specific way. The leader will say, "Category: animal found on a farm, five letters," and the players have to guess the specific animal — in this case, "horse."

Radio Romps

Focus: *auditory discrimination, auditory memory, imagination*
Method: Children brought up on TV have little chance to absorb information without visual clues. Radio encourages attentive listening and imagination. Especially good for this type of ear training are such specific things as news broadcasts, weather reports, sports news, broadcast sporting events. Ask your child for a brief review afterwards, or suggest he tell a joke he heard to the whole family at dinner. Suggest he keep a record of weather reports over a period of time to see how accurate they are. Have your child listen to stories on children's

radio programs and describe how he pictures the setting, characters, costumes, and so on.

Ear-Openers

Focus: *auditory discrimination, auditory memory*
Method: This is a good activity in any situation, but especially out of doors. Ask your child to be very quiet and listen to the sounds around him. Ask him what he hears: does he think the sound is close or far away? can he locate the sound? You might hear country sounds such as a cow mooing, birds singing, a stream babbling, wind in the trees. In the city you would hear cars, trucks, a street-car, a bus, people talking, a locomotive whistle, etc.

Answering Service

Focus: *auditory discrimination, auditory memory*
Method: Allow your child to answer the phone and later try to guess whose voice it was. Ask indulgent relatives or friends to call and test discrimination skills by asking "Do you know who this is?" As a child becomes used to a telephone he can be allowed to take short messages. *Variation:* Most larger cities have special numbers with recorded messages. Ask your child to dial one of these numbers and report what he hears.

Reading Aloud

Focus: *listening skills, auditory comprehension*
Method: You should read aloud to your child from the time he is able to understand even simple sentences. Start with nursery rhymes and gradually increase the length and complexity of the stories you read. Be prepared to stop if your child begins to fidget. When a story is finished, ask questions so that you can assess his comprehension.

Following Directions

Focus: *auditory memory, following directions*

Method: Begin by sending your child with a simple message to a person in another room. Give him the message, ask him to repeat it, then ask him to take the message to the person you designate. After he has delivered the message, check to make sure the message was delivered correctly. Messages may become progressively more complicated or silly as your child's ability to remember the spoken word improves.

I Packed My Bag

Focus: *auditory discrimination, auditory memory, auditory sequencing*
Method: This can be played with one or several players. The leader picks a place and says, "I packed my bag to go to the cottage, and in it I put . . ." He then names one thing. The next player repeats this whole sentence, adding one item of his own. The next player again repeats and adds an item. A player must drop out if he forgets to repeat an item or can't think of a new item. The "trip" could be any place where a child might have some idea of what to take, such as the North Pole, the jungle, summer camp, etc.

Simon Says

Focus: *auditory discrimination, following verbal directions, body image, motor coordination*
Method: Any number can play this game. It was a favorite with the Gym Club, where a large number of children and volunteers were frequently involved. The players stand in a row facing the leader. The leader will give directions about what the players must do, prefacing it with "Simon says." If the leader does *not* say "Simon says," the players are not to follow the directions given. If a player follows the directions anyway, he or she is eliminated. The leader might say, "Simon says: put your right hand on your left elbow"; then "Simon says: take one giant step forward"; then "Take a small step backward." Those who follow this last direction will be eliminated. The last one to remain in the game is "Simon." *Variation:* To reinforce auditory skills, you might ask your child to

do what you say, not what you do. Then you might say, "Simon says: touch your toes," while you actually touch your nose. The opposite can be used to reinforce vision — have your child do what you do, not what you say.

Odd Word Out

Focus: *auditory discrimination*
Method: Give your child four different words, three beginning with the same initial sound, one beginning with a different sound. Ask your child which word is the Odd Word Out with a different beginning sound. *Variations:* You can play this game with similar final consonants, rhyming words, or different categories of words such as all toys but one, all animals but one, all items of clothing but one, etc.

Changeover

Focus: *auditory discrimination*
Method: Make up a number of cards with families of rhyming words, one word per card. Make several cards with "changeover" printed on them. Shuffle the deck and give five cards to each player. Put the rest in the middle. One person begins play by putting a card in the middle and saying the word on the card. Each following player tries to put a rhyming card on top, saying the word as he does so. If he cannot play, he draws a card from the table and then plays if possible. If a player cannot play on the rhyming family, he can play a "changeover" card, if he has one, and start a new family of rhyming words from a card in his hand. The first player to get rid of all his cards wins.

MacNamara's Band

Focus: *rhythmic response, auditory perception*
Method: This can be used with just one player or with several. Put on a good rhythmic record, possibly a march. Allow each child to have one "instrument" that he can bang or blow. Two pot lids, a spoon and an old pot, kazoos, tin

whistles, horns, drums, anything that makes a noise can be used. The children then march up and down and keep time to the music.

Name That Tune

Focus: *auditory discrimination*
Method: Hum or play on the piano the beginning few bars of a song familiar to your child, but don't use the words. Ask him to identify the tune. If he can't, play a little more, or sing a few bars. Let him do the same thing, allowing you to guess what he is humming.

Who Said It? #1

Focus: *auditory discrimination, auditory memory*
Method: You can ask your child, or a group of children, who is most likely to have said one of the following (or any that you can think of yourself):
1. Going up? (elevator operator)
2. Open wide, please. (dentist)
3. Time for bed. (Mom or Dad)
4. Strike three. (baseball umpire)
5. Line up. (teacher)
6. All aboard. (train conductor)
7. Stop. (policeman)
8. He shoots, he scores. (hockey broadcaster)
9. Wash behind your ears. (Mom)

Who Said It? #2

Focus: *auditory discrimination*
Method: This is a good birthday party game, or at any time when there are quite a few children present. Everyone covers his eyes with his hands (no peeking!). The leader taps one player to say a line such as "The cat chased the dog down the street." The other players are then asked to identify the speaker. The person who guesses the largest number of speakers first wins the game. The leader should keep score so there will be no mix-ups.

Silly Rhymes

Focus: *auditory discrimination*
Method: Take a familiar rhyme such as a nursery rhyme and change the rhyming word; for instance, change "Hickory Dickory Dock" to "Hickory Dickory Doe" and ask your child to make a new sentence, such as "There was a boy named Joe," or "The mouse ran up my toe." For younger children, you may wish to give them the second line and ask them to supply the last word only, rather than the whole line.

Cutout Capers

Focus: *listening skills, visualizing from memory*
Method: Make a card and on it tape a picture of some category such as an animal, a piece of clothing, a piece of furniture, etc. Put a string through the card and hang it around your child's neck so that the picture is suspended at the back. He is then told what category his "cutout" is and is allowed to ask questions of other members of the household to determine what he is. Limit the number of questions or the length of time (use your timer).

Your Order, Please

Focus: *auditory memory, listening skills*
Method: Allow your child to take orders in a restaurant or take-out food place and give them to the waiter. Start with just the two of you, but allow him to try to do this for more people as he becomes more adept.

Buzz Saw

Focus: *auditory discrimination, thinking*
Method: This is a version of the old game of Hot and Cold. One player is removed from the group and must go out of the room. An object is chosen as the target of the game, or a small object might be hidden in the room. If the object is in plain sight, it might be something like a picture on the wall. A

spoon might be hidden behind one player's back, and so forth. The child then comes in and tries to discover what the target object is. The other players indicate whether he is hot or cold by the buzz sound they make: louder if he is "hot" and softer if he is "cold."

Go Find

Focus: *auditory discrimination*
Method: Give your child one of the sounds of the alphabet or a word with an initial consonant, and ask him to bring you one or more items from the house that start with the same sound. For example, you might use the word "pen" and your child might bring you a "pencil."

Musical Glasses

Focus: *auditory discrimination*
Method: Use eight glasses partially filled with water to give a close approximation of the eight notes of the scale. Show your child how he can play a simple tune by tapping the glasses with a spoon. Play one for him and ask him to play it back. Now allow him to play tunes he knows or make up tunes for you to play back to him.

How Many Words?

Focus: *auditory discrimination, auditory memory*
Method: You say to your child, "How many words can you carry in a bucket?" and he names one word for each letter in the word "bucket." Then you might say, "How many words can you put on the back of a horse?" and your child replies with five words, each starting with one of the letters in "horse." He can also be allowed to give you a word.

CHAPTER 14

Games and Activities To Improve Language Skills

Using language involves the process of listening to and understanding other people, and producing language oneself that is easily understood by others. To help children with learning disabilities you must understand how language works. These children usually learn vocabulary more slowly than their peers and may have trouble recalling words from memory. They understand a particular word when someone else says it, but may be unable to retrieve that word from memory for their own use in conversation or in answering questions.

Learning-disabled children may have deficits in processing and producing language. These may be difficult to detect because the children work hard at compensating.

Teachers observe that children who are slow at acquiring the linguistic rules for word and sentence formation usually have learning disabilities, but often it isn't until they have reached Grades 3 or 4 and haven't acquired spelling and reading skills that their problems can be definitely diagnosed as learning disabilities.

Developing Language Skills

1.   Begin by talking to a child when he is just an infant. You can't begin too soon to accustom him to the sound of the

human voice and the sound of words. If a child is seldom spoken to, he is much slower developing effective speech.

2. As soon as your child begins to speak, allow him every opportunity to use language and learn new words.

3. When he begins making simple sentences, you can start to discuss things with him, such as what he wants to eat, what clothes he would like to wear, etc.

4. To ensure correct grammatical usage, try to speak correctly yourself. If he makes a grammatical error, rather than correcting it directly, repeat his sentence in a conversational tone using the correct grammar.

5. Children with language problems are more easily identified at kindergarten level than those with other disabilities through their verbal interaction with parents and teachers. Often we will limit our speech to the child with language problems — talk down to him or show him — so that he will understand more easily. This in fact is harmful to the child, as it restricts his experiences with oral language and denies him the reward of processing and understanding what we say. We interact verbally more often and at more length with the child who we know understands and appreciates what we say. We take a delight in a child who appreciates the subtleties of a joke and short-change a child who doesn't.

6. Although it can become tedious at times, do try to answer all the questions your child asks and encourage the use of who, what, when, why, and how.

7. To encourage your child to talk to you, listen to him carefully and allow him to know that you are interested in his ideas and opinions.

8. If a preschooler begins to stutter, don't be disturbed unless it lasts for a long time. Many children, especially little boys, will stutter for a while but will soon stop as long as you don't make a fuss about it. In any event, don't let him think it is abnormal or he will just get worse. Don't allow anyone to tease him about it. *Give him ample time to finish a word or a*

sentence and don't be tempted to finish the sentence for him. If the stuttering persists, consult your doctor.

9.   When your child starts to school, make sure he has access to books and then discuss them with him. Encourage him to talk about things in which he is interested so that you can get further information for him in the form of books or magazines.

10.   Improve vocabulary by teaching your child how to use a dictionary. You might like to help him make a simple dictionary of his own. If he uses a "sound alike" word in the place of a correct word, be sure he knows the difference.

11.   If you have read a book or a magazine article that might interest him, tell him about it so that he will realize that you, too, enjoy reading.

12.   Read to your child. Use rhymes and verse to develop his appreciation of language, rhythms, and word play.

13.   As soon as he is able, allow your child to read to you. Encourage him to look up any words he doesn't know. Be sure to have a good junior dictionary on hand.

Games and Activities

Puppet Theater

Focus: *expressive language, vocabulary, fine motor*
Method: One or more children may be involved. They may be encouraged to make their own finger or hand puppets from old gloves or socks, or they can use purchased puppets. As they get more dexterous, they might like to use string-controlled puppets which they can make from papier-mâché. The children should be encouraged to write their own stories or use a theme from TV or a storybook and adapt it to use with their puppets. It is a good idea to keep a bag of scraps of wool, fabric, felt, old socks and gloves, old nylon pantyhose, and so forth to be used to make puppets.

Guess Who

Focus: *receptive and expressive language skills, visual memory, powers of observation*
Method: Have your child guess whom you are describing when you speak of someone you both know or have watched frequently on television. Encourage your child to describe someone for you to guess.

Guess What, Guess Where

Focus: *expressive language, syntax, visual discrimination, visual memory*
Method: As above, describe an object or a place and ask other players to identify it. It could be something in plain sight, it could be something with which everyone is familiar, and it could be a place all the players have heard about but not necessarily seen. The person who guesses first chooses the next place or object.

Identikit Game

Focus: *expressive language, receptive language, visual memory, visual discrimination*
Method: Cut out two of each of the following shapes, each shape being in a different color: large circles, small circles, large squares, small squares, large triangles, small triangles. Ask your child to use one set to make a design, describing to you how he is doing it. Without looking at what he has made, follow his directions and try to duplicate his design. When you are both finished, compare the designs to see how similar they are. You then make a design and describe what you are doing so that your child can make his design according to your directions. Be sure to emphasize the use of words such as under, over, beside, top, bottom, right, left, to reinforce the child's understanding of direction.

What Sound Do You Hear?

Focus: *expressive language, receptive language, auditory memory*
Method: Describe what you are doing and ask what sound it would make; for example, rowing a boat, walking through tall grass, walking on gravel, using a typewriter. *Variation:* The other senses can be included as well, so you might play What Do You Taste (or See or Feel or Smell)?

I Went to the Store

Focus: *vocabulary, expressive language, auditory memory and sequencing*
Method: The first player says, "I went to the store to buy something to put on bread. It is sweet and thick and red and is made with a small red fruit. What is it?" Answer: strawberry jam. The next player thinks of something else that might be bought at a grocery store and describes it for his opponent to guess.

If We Were Going To . . .

Focus: *vocabulary, expressive language, auditory memory*
Method: You start the game by saying, "If we were going to bake a cake, we would have to have: eggs, butter . . ." and each player adds an ingredient or adds a method of preparation. *Variation:* "If we beat eggs and flour and butter together, and then added sugar, etc. . . . what would we have?"

Let's Pretend

Focus: *vocabulary, mimicry, imagination, receptive and expressive language*
Method: There are many methods of playing this ancient game. If your child likes to dress up, allow him to put on a collection of old clothes (keep a bag of old clothes for this game) and pretend to be someone. He must make you guess who he is by what he has on and the way he talks.

What Did I Say?

Focus: *vocabulary, auditory memory, articulation*
Method: Repeat a simple tongue-twister and ask, "What did I say?"; for example, "Peter Piper picked a peck of pickled peppers" or "Rubber baby buggy bumpers." Have your child repeat it to you. *Variation:* If you are helping a child to improve his vocabulary, you might use a sentence or a phrase with an unfamiliar word. Ask him to repeat it, then ask him what he thinks the unfamiliar word means.

A Special Day

Focus: *vocabulary, auditory memory*
Method: Cut out a picture of a special day, or have your child draw a picture to represent a special day such as a birthday, Christmas, Passover, Easter, St. Patrick's Day, etc. Ask him to write on the paper all the words he can think of that might be associated with that day.

What Happened?

Focus: *vocabulary, sentence formation, syntax, imagination*
Method: Begin a sentence such as "Johnny and I went to the store and on the way . . . ," then ask your child to finish the sentence by telling what happened. *Variation:* This can be a marvellous beginning to a continuing story to which several children can contribute. You might begin with something unusual enough to stimulate the children's imaginations, such as "Bingo and Beezo were two monkeys who drove a dump truck. One day Bingo and Beezo were driving down the road and do you know what happened? . . ." Each of the children takes a turn telling part of the story, and you may want to play for days.

Word Bingo

Focus: *vocabulary, auditory discrimination*
Method: Make up a Bingo card using all the consonants

except c and k. Call out a word and ask your child to cover the first consonant of the word with a button. When he has made a row in any direction, he wins Bingo. Several children can play this game.

In Command

Focus: *expressive language*
Method: The players choose one person to go first. He reaches into a bag and takes out a hat or some other piece of wearing apparel, or a badge that makes him an army general, a navy admiral, an Indian chief, the boss of a group of construction workers, etc. He then gives orders that the others must obey as long as his turn lasts. Set the timer so there won't be any disputes about when someone's time is up. This is similar to Let's Pretend, except that the child doesn't know ahead of time who he will be and must improvise.

Showtime

Focus: *vocabulary, enunciation, imagination*
Method: This is an extended form of Let's Pretend. Along with your bag of old clothes for dress-up, have a box full of the names of TV and story characters, experiences, and the names of specialized occupations. The child (or children) picks a person or situation and produces a "play" about it. This can be simplified for your child when he is young and made more complicated as his self-assurance increases. These little skits can be performed just for you or for the whole family, or they can be shared with playmates. At first you may find it necessary to help develop a story line, but children seem to be natural actors and will soon catch on to how it is done. This is also a good way to help children act out their frustrations in a non-threatening situation. If he has been having trouble relating to a certain person or occupation (if he doesn't like his teacher or is afraid of firemen, for instance), the reason behind the feeling may come out if he is allowed to role-play the person that bothers him. Under these circumstances, you may sometimes wish to ask questions as one of

the characters in the skit. Do participate if your child wants you to. It's great fun!

Radio Station H.O.M.E.

Focus: *expressive language, imagination, organization*
Method: Radio station H.O.M.E. is basically a news station — first with all the news about your neighborhood. Have your child gather any bits of news he knows or funny things he can make up for a newscast that can be weekly, two or three times a week, or daily. He can tell about the weather or coming events, play a favorite record, tell what is happening at school, and so on. As his skills increase, he may wish to write a script ahead of time. Set up a simulated radio station for the broadcast. You might use a child's desk or table with a chair behind it and a small sieve as a microphone. If you can, you might take your child to a real radio station before he starts his "broadcasts" so that he can see just how it is done in real life.

Let's Play School

Focus: *expressive language*
Method: Even children who are not enthralled with school often like to play "school." Take advantage of this to have your child "teach" you or someone else something he is learning, or has just found out about. It might be the rules of a new game, a new card trick, something concerning his latest hobby or interest, a joke or story that he wants you to "learn" and then tell someone else. Use your imagination to make this a learning experience for both of you.

Singulars and Plurals

Focus: *vocabulary*
Method: While many plurals in English just add an "s," there are many which are totally different words or which don't change in the plural. Make a list of these words as you think of them and use them as the basis for a word game

where you give the singular and your child gives the plural. This can be played with a group of children, the one getting the most correct answers getting a small prize. To get you started: sheep (same in singular and plural), house and houses (change in pronunciation), calf and calves (change of spelling and pronunciation), mouse and mice (different word). *Variation:* You might like to try male and female words for animals, such as cow and bull, doe and buck, etc. Another variation could be how groups of animals are named, such as a covey of quail, a herd of cows, a flock of sheep, and so on. Your imagination will produce others.

CHAPTER 15

Games and Activities To Improve Body Image and Spatial Concepts

When a child is born, he has no idea of who he is or what he is. Gradually his awareness of himself as a separate entity increases as his perception of his environment increases. As his eyes focus, he is aware of large, strange figures hovering over him. He very soon comes to know the familiar ones and to respond to them. Soon he discovers fingers, then toes. He finds he can do interesting things with his body, like roll over or kick his legs. As his neck and back strengthen, he tries to sit up, because the world looks so much better from this position. The infant is growing into a child, and as he does so, he is learning about his own body. Finally he crawls, and then walks. By the time he is mobile, he is becoming more aware of himself as a separate entity.

It is very important for a child to understand his own body and its place in space. Not all children learn this easily and these games and activities are to help your child be aware of himself and the space he occupies. You will find that a full-length mirror is very helpful in allowing a small child to identify his body parts. It can be the basis of many games and activities. Spatial understanding allows a child to relate sizes of objects and positions of objects to each other. Is the tub bigger than the basin? Will it hold more water? Is my bed farther from the door than my chair? Is it bigger? Is the airplane higher than my kite? And so on.

This Is Me

Focus: *body awareness, body image, spatial perception*
Method: Have your child lie down on a large piece of paper. If you can't find one large enough, cut open brown paper bags and join them with tape. With a crayon or magic marker, draw an outline of his body. You might like to make more than one of these outlines. One could be used as a nap mat; one might be hung on your child's wall where he can color in the eyes, nose, mouth, and hair (with some guidance from you). If you put this beside a full-length mirror, he will have a much better idea of where various things belong. He might like to draw in fingernails on the four fingers and the thumb of each hand, and then do the same for his toes. He might like to "dress" the figure with clothes done in crayon. If you wish to make a figure from flesh-colored felt, you can make rough approximations of some of his favourite clothes that can be put on the figure. You might like to make a fabric outline and stitch it onto a quilt for his bed. You could outline his hands, or allow him to outline them, and stitch them onto pillows, blankets, even a shirt that he wears. All these things help your child establish a sense of body image. Keep these outlines to show how much your child has grown from one year to the next. They love it! *Variation:* Outline your child in sand the next time you are at the beach, then allow him to draw an outline of you. Compare the sizes.

Play Clay

Focus: *body awareness, body image, spatial awareness, fine motor skills*
Method: Small children love to press their hands or feet into clay, and this imprint can give a child a real sense of the space his hand or foot occupies. He can also use his handprint or footprint to make a priceless gift for a grandparent. Place soft, self-hardening clay in a form, such as a foil pie plate, and allow your child to press his hand or his foot into the center of the clay to make an indentation deep enough that it could be a small dish to hold pins or paperclips. Allow the clay to harden thoroughly and help your child paint it a skintone.

Then have your child decorate it around the edge. When the paint has dried thoroughly, apply one or two coats of glaze according to the directions. Kits of self-hardening clay with the paints and glaze included are relatively inexpensive and can be found in most stores that sell craft supplies.

Winter Wonderland

Focus: *perceptual constancy, body image, body awareness, cross-modality perception*
Method: There are many fun games to play in the snow. We will mention only a few, but we are sure you will think of more.

1. *Angels in the Snow*   Have your child lie on his back and move his arms and legs back and forth. Help him to his feet so that he can see his "angel." You might make a "Snow Angel" beside his so that you can compare sizes together.
2. *Giant Footsteps*   Have your child make footsteps in the snow; then you make footsteps beside him and compare the sizes. He would enjoy putting on Daddy's overshoes and making even bigger "Giant Footsteps" all by himself.
3. Look for and identify other footprints such as those of dogs and cats, or wild animals and birds of the neighborhood.
4. Get your child to press his hands into fresh snow. Beside these prints, press his favorite ball, so that he can see the size of his hands in relation to the size of the ball.

Simon-Without-Seeing

Focus: *establishing midline, kinesthetic/tactile body aware-ness and image, auditory perception, sequencing*
Method: This is a version of Simon Says in which all except the leader wear blindfolds. Blindfold your child and then say, "Simon says: place your left hand on your right elbow." Do this with other body parts so that your child will have a tactile awareness of his own body without actually seeing it. Be sure that you follow the rules: if you don't say "Simon says," your child loses. If he can go right through the game without missing once, he is the winner.

Measure Me!

Focus: *body image, body awareness, laterality, number concepts, developing vocabulary, establishing directionality*
Method: Using a tape measure, measure your child's height, the length of his arms and legs, how big he is around the waist, etc. Compare this to similar measurements of other family members. If there are other children in the family, they might enjoy measuring each other and comparing their size. Children love to keep these measurements to show how much they've grown or how much bigger their muscles are.

Pin-Ups

Focus: *body image, body awareness, vocabulary, visual memory, expressive language*
Method: First, find a picture of your child, or of someone else, that is large enough to print on all the parts of the body — eyes, ears, hair, arms, legs, etc. Do the same with pictures of familiar animals such as a cat, dog, elephant, and so on. Leave these pictures up for a period of time until you are sure that your child is quite familiar with the different parts as labelled. You are then ready to proceed to a game based on these body parts. This is a form of Pin the Tail on the Donkey, only you can use a human figure, or animal figures. Make a drawing on a piece of paper of a figure minus one part. Draw the part separately, such as the trunk of an elephant or the arm of a man. Have a blindfolded child "pin" the part on the figure which is hung on the wall. You might also want to "pin" a rose on a person, a "star" on a sheriff, etc.

Sing a Song of . . .

Focus: *body image, body awareness, directionality, auditory perception and memory, cerebral dominance, motor coordination*
Method: Put actions to this little song, sung to the tune of "Sing a Song of Sixpence":

Sing a song of people
Standing in a line.
They each have two hands
And I have mine.
I also have arms 'n' legs
Eyes, ears, and a mouth.
And I've got two feet down there
If I reach away down south!

Other "body" songs you might like to try with your child are "Do the Hokey Pokey" (Put your right hand in, put your right hand out, put your right hand in and turn it all about. Then Do the Hokey Pokey, Do the Hokey Pokey. That's what it's all about!) The parts of the body can be changed as the song progresses. Another one you will probably remember from your own childhood is "Head and shoulders, knees and toes . . ." One that is very popular with youngsters is "Dem Bones, Dem Bones, Dem Dry Bones . . ." (Now the foot bone's connected to the ankle bone, etc. . . .) There are many more of these songs that reinforce body image for young children.

Footsteps

Focus: *establishing laterality, body awareness, motor co-ordination*

Method: Have your child take a pair of his shoes (he can do this with his shoes on if he is able and trace an outline on a piece of paper. Cut out this shoe pattern, both left and right, a number of times from heavy cardboard or paper. Make several sets. Make all the left feet with a large L and all the right feet with a large R. Your child will need help cutting these out if you use cardboard, but he can probably manage heavy paper himself if he is adept with scissors. These footsteps are then used to make patterns on the floor in dance steps, hopping two Left and two Right, or any other combination that is fun. He might enjoy this if it is done to appropriate music. Your child can place his foot either on or beside the footprints, whichever is easier for him.

Hopscotch

Focus: *establishing laterality, gross and fine motor coordination*
Method: This traditional game is usually played outside where numbered squares are drawn with chalk on a driveway or with a stick in dirt. The child throws something (a flat stone, a string with several buttons attached), and hops between squares, landing on one or both feet, and picks up the stone without losing his balance or stepping on a line.

Soldiers on Parade

Focus: *establishing laterality, auditory perception, auditory sequencing, gross motor development, balance and rhythm*
Method: This is a fun way to help your child develop many skills. Let him pretend to be a soldier on parade and you are the sergeant-major. Order him to come to attention and then march off while you count left, right, left, right. When he has this down pat, try reversing his parade with "About turn!" or "Left turn" or whatever different direction you would like to give him. This will familiarize your child with the meaning of such terms as forward, backward, etc., as well as helping his sense of direction. As he becomes more adept, you might like to set your parade to marching music.

Treasure Hunt

Focus: *establishing laterality, listening skills, auditory sequencing*
Method: Hide some small prize in the house, or outside in the yard, and prepare a map for your child to follow to find it. The map should give written directions which you will read out to him first. For the younger child, you might wish to give him just oral directions. For example, if you hide an apple on the back porch, you might start your child from the living-room and tell him: "Take six large steps to the living-room door. Now turn left. Walk straight ahead until you come to the kitchen door. Now turn right. . . ." etc.

How Many?

Focus: *closure, eye-hand coordination, number concepts*
Method: This game can be played in many different ways, but it is based on the old game often found at fall fairs: "Guess the number of beans (or coins, or?) and win a prize." Allow your child to guess how many oranges or apples it will take to fill the bowl, how many glasses of water it will take to fill the basin, how many small steps to cross the room, how many giant steps to cross the room, etc. You may then reverse this and fill a bowl with fruit or nuts and ask him how many he thinks are in the bowl. Then allow him to count them and see how close he comes. If you are playing this as a game with a number of children, you might give a small prize to the one who gets the closest to the right answer.

Jigsaw Puzzles

Focus: *conceptualization, eye-hand coordination, figure-ground perception, fine motor control*
Method: Don't throw away all those beautiful greeting cards. Use them to make jigsaw puzzles. Many are heavy enough to cut without anything backing them. Others are better pasted on light cardboard. Your child will enjoy making his own puzzles, putting them together again, and sharing them with his friends. Start with as few as three parts and gradually make the puzzles more difficult as your child becomes more adept.

Copycat

Focus: *visual closure, spatial perception, visual memory and discrimination, fine motor control*
Method: You may use a regular pegboard divided in half, or two separate boards. With colored pegs, make a design on the board, and then ask your child to duplicate the design on the other half or on her own board. You may also insert pegs in a design and use colored string or elastic to form a design around the pegs. This is more intricate and better suited to

older children. These pegboards may be purchased, or you can make them at home. You may make a design, have the child study it, put it out of sight, and have him attempt to reproduce it from memory.

Obstacle Course

Focus: *directionality, spatial perception, gross motor control*
Method: All youngsters seem to enjoy obstacle courses, which can be used to give them a better idea of higher, lower, bigger, smaller, and other spatial concepts. You might set up an obstacle course with a barrel to crawl through, a smaller one to crawl over, a swing to step over and possibly one to reach up and swing on with both hands, a cardboard carton to climb into and another to crawl through, and so on.

Shape Up

Focus: *perceptual constancy, classification, conceptualization, fine motor skills*
Method: Using different colors of lightweight cardboard, cut out two of several different-sized squares, some almost the same size, some noticeably larger or smaller. Do the same with triangles and circles. Spread these out in a random way on the top of a desk or table and allow your child to make pairs of the same size and shape. If you make enough of these shapes, the game can be played by several children, with a prize for the one matching the greatest number of pairs.

Tricky Toast

Focus: *spatial perception, visual discrimination*
Method: When you give your child a piece of toast, cut it into interesting shapes and ask him to put it back together. You might start with just squares and triangles, then use a cookie cutter to make more interesting shapes that fit together. You can do the same thing with sandwiches. Suggest that your child eat a circle, or a triangle, and so on. This is also a good way to get children to eat if they are picky.

CHAPTER 16

Games and Activities
To Improve Motor Skills
and Tactile Sense

At birth, our five senses are working independently of each other. As we mature, muscles, nerves, brain cells, and neural pathways gradually become coordinated. By the time an infant is one year old he is often walking, feeding himself, and trying to speak some words. Our senses are used to explore our environment and to convey information back to our brain so that we can act on the information. A hot pot touched by a finger sends an immediate warning to the brain to withdraw the finger quickly. If a big dog comes running toward us, our eyes relay this information to the brain, which immediately tells our feet to run.

All these complex acts are the result of the senses sending information to the brain, which transmits impulses to our gross motor (large) muscles and fine motor (small) muscles.

The development is first in the large muscles, later in the small muscles, but in learning-disabled children the smooth functioning of this complex system is often interrupted. The result is that many LD children lack the coordination to enable them to do many of the things that are easily done by other children their age. They might have trouble learning to ride a two-wheel bicycle, learning to skip rope, learning to swim. They may have trouble controlling the muscles in their fingers and hands so that they can print or write clearly. Their eyes and hands may lack the smooth coordination necessary for many activities.

As well as games and activities to help motor coordination, we are including some designed to improve the tactile sense. Many aspects of our environment are explored by the sense of touch, from the time we are small infants. Because they have perceptual problems in other areas, many children with learning disabilities depend on their tactile sense to understand the world around them.

Improving Gross Motor Skills

The average child who is moderately well coordinated moves through babyhood into childhood with a fairly predictable motor development. No one expects a four-year-old to be as good at such sports as hockey or baseball as an eight-year-old. For most sports, large muscles must have a chance to mature and learn to work together. There are some eight-year-olds, however, who function at the four-year-old level simply because their coordination hasn't caught up with their age. They need extra help to educate their large muscles to do what their brain tells them. If this child also has a visual-perception problem, he also needs help interpreting what he sees and translating it into action. Many may also need help with organizational skills.

We recommend starting with the simplest game or activity, where a child can easily succeed, and allowing him to advance at his own speed. The following games and activities will help any child, but you might find that some are just right to help your child with a specific motor problem. We are giving you a rough outline of what is expected of the average child by age so that you will have some idea where your child fits.

Level 1 — Ages 5 to 8. At this level, we work on organizational skills, helping the child to organize both the game he is playing and the actions of his own body. For example, a small child throwing a ball usually puts his whole body into the motion and sometimes the ball still falls from his fingers. Ball skills may have to begin with how a ball is held before a child even attempts to throw it. When he is older, he can throw a ball smoothly with little body movement, and a projectile use of the arm and shoulder muscles. A child also needs to practise the simple art of running without falling over his feet. If a child is awkward and clumsy, this can take a lot of practice. The next step would be rolling a ball back and forth between partners, working up to bouncing and throwing with both hands.

Level 2 — Ages 7 to 10. When a child reaches this level, he is better organized but still needs practice. He is running well enough to enjoy tag games. His ball skills are improving, as is his ability to move smoothly and rhythmically to music. He will still play the games and activities of Level 1 but in a form that demands more skills. He will develop his ball skills, for instance, to work toward such games as baseball and tennis.

Level 3 — Ages 9 to 12. Many children will move into this level in some areas while still needing help at Level 2. At Level 3, a child may join in team sports, such as soccer, football, volleyball, basketball, and so on. He may begin to play racquet sports if his eye-hand coordination is functioning smoothly. If the child has trouble adapting to the social aspects of team sports and finds himself being left out or teased, encourage him to try sports like swimming or skating, where he is competing against himself or the clock, until he gains confidence.

Imitation

Focus: *cross-modality perception, gross motor, body awareness, directionality, laterality*
Method: You are going to have your child copy your body movements. He may do them in a jerky manner at first, but the more often he repeats a movement, the smoother it will become. Stand with your child in front of a large mirror, so that he can see what you are doing. Now go through

various movements which will help your child identify body parts and will exercise and stretch large muscles. You might start by using simple semaphor-type signals with your arms. You can pretend to be letters of the alphabet. Use your imagination to make this into a game situation similar to Follow the Leader. If you know your child has balancing problems, have him balance on one foot, turn on the spot, and so on. You will discover as you play with your child what areas need most work. If he tends to be clumsy, try to emphasize smooth, precise movements with as little motor overflow as possible.

Animal Walk

Focus: *laterality, gross motor development, imagination*
Method: This is an all-time favorite with children, and we have found it to be an excellent way to help a child to relax. You can do these with him, or allow him to do them himself. He may think up walks and ask you to guess what he is. He will enjoy trying any of the following:

1. *Bunny* Raise the hands to the side of the head with the fingers pointing up, hop on both feet, wiggle the "ears."

2. *Baby Chicks* Stoop low to the floor. Hold hands facing down, join thumb and second fingers. Open and shut the hands to show how the chick pecks for food.

3. *Rocking Horse* Stand with hands on hips and legs astride. Rock forward lifting heels off the floor, then rock backward lifting toes off the floor.

4. *Rooster Walk* Holding the head and chest high, strut forward with knees straight and hands at the side of the chest. Wiggle the elbows like flapping wings.

5. *Bear Walk* Bend over from the waist and touch the floor with the hands. Keep the legs stiff. Move forward walking the hands and the feet. Keep the head up.

6. *Birds* Stand on tiptoe and wave arms slowly up and down. As the "wings" move faster, run around on tiptoe as if you

were flying. As the flapping slows down, the "bird" comes to a stop.

7. *Elephants* Bending forward at the waist, allow the arms to hang limp, the hands held together. Big, lumbering steps should sway you from side to side as you walk, giving a good imitation of an elephant and his trunk.

8. *Ostrich* Bending forward at the waist, grasp the ankles. Keep the knees stiff as possible. Walk forward stretching neck in and out.

9. *Kangaroo* Stand with feet together, bend elbows out from the body, leave hands dangling limply. Do a deep bend with the knees and jump forward.

10. *Duck* Do a deep knee bend, place hands behind back with the outsides together to form the duck's tail. Walk forward one foot at a time in the knee-bent position.

11. *Frog* Do a deep knee bend with your hands on your hips. Extend one leg to the side and return, then the other leg.

Walk the Plank

Focus: *laterality, balance*

Method: In Gym Club we used first a four-inch, then a two-inch, board for these games and activities. If you have a narrow, heavy plank, by all means use it. If not, you can mark the width and length on the floor with masking tape. First, allow your child to walk back and forth a few times, one foot in front of the other, until he gets the feel of it. When he can walk the length without losing his balance, you might try him with some of these activities:

1.   Walk forward, arms held out sideways, then return walking backwards. If he can't manage the backward walk at first, allow him to turn and walk back.

2.   Walk the length and back sideways with the weight on the balls of the feet.

3.   Walk forward with arms out forward, and return backwards.

4.   Walk forward with arms folded on chest, and return backwards.

5.   Walk in one direction with the right foot always in front of the left and return with the left foot always in front of the right. You will be able to think of other ways of "Walking the Plank" to help improve balance, such as carrying an item in one hand, then the other, then overhead, and so forth.

Skipping-Rope Activities

Focus: *gross motor coordination, eye-hand coordination, laterality, body awareness, large-muscle development, balance*

Method: Many children have trouble learning to use a skipping rope. It is best to break down this activity into small parts and have the child master the skill gradually.

1.   Put a line across a floor with chalk or masking tape. Allow your child to step over it, then jump over it, back and forth.

2.   Place a skipping rope in the same position and have your child repeat the above directions.

3.   Have two people raise the rope very slightly and allow your child to jump back and forth over it.

4.   Now have the two people swing the rope slightly back and forth while your child jumps over it. Work on this until your child feels comfortable.

5.   Now show your child how to hold the rope and how to turn it. Allow your child to practise this until she feels quite confident.

6.   Get your child to jump over the rope at the bottom of its full swing, stopping between jumps. She can repeat this many times until she feels she is ready to actually begin skipping. Give her lots of time to practise.

There are many other games and activities that can be played with a skipping rope. Here are just a few. Use your own ingenuity to think up more.

1.   Swing the rope in a large circle on the ground and have your child jump over it each time it comes around. Using a steady rhythm will be easier for him, and will help him

develop his sense of rhythm, which is important in many sports.

2.   Have your child hold one end of the rope and turn it while you hold the other end. See if he can establish and maintain a constant rhythm. Now try to have him turn it in the opposite direction so that he will have an awareness of the difference in direction.

3.   Have your child turn the rope using just shoulder movements, just elbow movements, and just wrist movements. Make sure he is aware of the different movements.

The Suspendable Ball

Focus: *gross motor development, visual perception, eye tracking, eye-hand coordination*

Method: The suspendable ball is a basic tool for many activities. It can be suspended from the branch of a tree, from a hoop over a garage door, or from a rafter in a barn for older and taller children. For the smaller fry, all you need to do is hold it over your head and well away from your body so that it can swing freely. The longer the string, the more slowly it will swing, but the swing will always be rhythmic. The distance the ball swings is also directly related to how hard your child hits it. Many other activities are based on your child's holding the ball.

We are breaking the Suspendable Ball activities into two separate sections:

To Develop Body Image

1.   Hit the ball with the forehead, then the chin, then the left side of the head, then the right side of the head.

2.   Hit the ball with the right shoulder, then the left shoulder, then the right elbow, then the left elbow; with both the front and the back of first the left and then the right wrist.

3.   Hit the ball with the palm and then the back of first the right and then the left hand; then try to hit the ball with a karate chop using the side of each hand.

4.   Hit the ball with the fingertips, then one finger at a time.

5. Hit the ball with each fist, then with the hands clasped together.
6. Hit the ball with the chest, then the right hip, then the left hip, then the back.
7. Hit the ball with each knee, shin, and foot.

To Improve Visual Tracking

For these activities, the ball is not suspended but held in the hands. The child can hold the ball himself or you can hold it for him. It should always be a minimum of eight inches from his eyes, preferably farther.
1. Track the ball from left to right with the eyes, then from top to bottom, then in a clockwise and counterclockwise direction.
2. Track the ball with the eyes in a diagonal direction, first from upper right to lower left, then upper left to lower right.
3. With you holding the ball, he can track it, following it with the right hand from left to right, then with the left hand, then with the two hands clasped together.
4. Do the same, tracking the ball from top to bottom. There are many variations of this that you can dream up for yourself.

Ball Activities

Focus: *body image and awareness, gross and fine motor coordination and eye-hand coordination, eye tracking*
Method: There appear to be an unlimited number of games played with a ball, and we will only mention a few. What we would like to emphasize, first, is a method of helping your child handle a ball with comparative ease. As we mentioned before, many children of eight or ten are still trying to throw a ball the way a four-year-old might throw it. In order for your child to feel comfortable with a ball, he might need to be taught, step by step, how to use it.
1. Sit on the floor and roll a large ball back and forth between you. Try to establish a roll-and-catch rhythm.
2. When your child is adept at this, have him lie on his

stomach and roll the ball to you, then turn on his back and roll the ball.

3. Now, try a bounce. Have your child catch the ball after once bounce, then after two bounces. This will also help eye tracking. You might need to practise this if your child has visual-perception problems. Now, have him bounce the ball back to you, well enough for you to catch it.

4. It's time to try a toss. It can be started with a larger ball, then, as the child progresses, switched to a smaller ball. Stand quite close together at the beginning until your child is catching the ball with ease. Then move farther apart. Start by throwing underhand, then begin to throw overhand, again close together in the beginning and gradually moving farther apart. *Note:* When you move to a smaller ball, be sure your child is holding it right. Don't try to influence which hand he throws with — let him decide that for himself. At first he may not be sure and try both right and left hands. Later he will show a preference.

Here are some games to play with balls:

1. *Wall Dodge Ball*   One person stands in a marked-off area in front of a wall. A person with a soft ball (nerf ball) stands a specified distance away from the wall. The object is for the person with the ball to throw it and try to hit the other person below the shoulders.

2. *Squareball*   This is similar to a free shot in basketball. Outline a square on a wall with chalk or masking tape. Stand your child at a designated spot and have him throw the ball and try to land it inside the square. You may need to start him quite close in the beginning, but you can move him farther back as he becomes more proficient.

3. *One-Pin Bowling*   Place an Indian club or a plastic bottle (or anything else that will serve the purpose) on the floor. Stand your child a distance back from it and have him roll a ball and attempt to knock over the "bowling pin." You can increase the distance between target and child as he improves. Both Squareball and One-Pin Bowling can be played with several players; the one scoring the most points is the winner.

Dipsy Doodle

Focus: *laterality, spatial perception, motor coordination, body image, body awareness*

Method: This is an eight-part exercise that is most fun if it is done to music. If you can play the piano, start a piece slowly and speed up when your child becomes more proficient. You might like to walk through the instructions with your child before you start. The starting position is feet together, hands at the sides.

1.   Jump to a straddle position, at the same time bending the right elbow and bringing the right fist to the chest.

2.   Bring legs together and bring left hand to chest.

3.   Jump to the straddle position and extend right arm upward.

4.   Bring legs together and extend left arm upward.

5.   Jump to the straddle position and bring right arm to chest.

6.   Bring legs together and bring left arm to chest.

7.   Jump to the straddle position and bring right arm down to the side.

8.   Bring legs together and bring left arm down to the side.

Tube Tumbling

Focus: *laterality, body image, spatial awareness, gross motor coordination and balance*

Method: If you can obtain a large inner tube, the type used for airplanes and large trucks, you can provide a great deal of fun for your child, as well as help his motor development. The larger the tube, the more easily a child will be able to bounce. Here are a number of good activities especially designed for use with a large tube:

1.   *Knee Bounce*   From a standing position near the tube, bounce onto knees and return to a controlled standing position. Repeat three or four times. If your child does not hit both knees on the tube at the same time, he might be thrown off-balance. Practice will help.

2. *Feet Bounce* From a standing position on the tube bounce on both feet, bending the knees slightly. To obtain height, raise arms forward and upward. At the beginning you should hold your child's wrists until he is sure of his balance. He will find it easier if he does this in bare feet.

3. *Bouncing Forward Roll* This is more complicated and means coordinating several actions together. From the inside of the tube, have him try a knee bounce to a standing position, and then another knee bounce from the inside to the outside of the tube ending in a forward roll.

4. *Jack-in the-Box* Have your child stand with his back to the tube. By kicking his feet out he can hit the tube with his seat and bounce back to an upright position.

5. *Stomach Drop* From a standing position, drop onto the tube, extending the body as it drops. Drop the stomach into the center and push with both hands to recover on the knees.

6. *Rabbit Bounce* Start with a knee bounce, followed by hands extended forward to the other side of the tube to another knee bounce ending in a roll. Start your child slowly on this one.

There are many variations of the above activities. Invent some yourself and allow your child to improvise as his skill improves.

Game Skills

Focus: *laterality, muscular control, eye-hand coordination for team sports*
Method: We are now moving into Level 2 activities and games. This group is designed to help your child fit into his peer group in team sports. We will assume that he is now capable of throwing the ball with one hand. If he is still uncertain in this area, try the following:
1. Beginning with a large ball such as a beach ball, work on the two-hand underhand throw, proceeding to a throw from the side and a two-handed overhead throw. Passing from the

chest, as you would in basketball, comes only after the other throws have been mastered.

2. Use progressively smaller balls, down to a small ball of the size usually used in a playground. By the time your child gets to the smaller balls he will find it easier to use one hand.

3. For basketball, target practice is necessary. Rather than starting with a ball that is bouncy, try a crumpled newspaper shaped in a ball. Find a suitable-sized box or wastebasket and allow your child to just drop the newspaper ball in to start with, so that he will know it will actually fit into the receptacle. Then stand him away from the "basket" and allow him to shoot at it with the newspaper ball, moving him farther away as he improves. When his accuracy improves, switch to a basketball, or one closely resembling it in size. Have him practise throwing from the chest. You may need a large target in the beginning, such as a large carton or a laundry basket.

4. For football, a child needs to learn to use his body easily and change direction on demand. Football skills need to be broken down into small components so that your child can work on one skill at a time. First, he must become competent at running. If he tends to be clumsy with his feet, let him practise until he feels comfortable running. After this, try to combine running and dodging as he tries to get past you. Then runs, stops, pivots, etc. You will need a football for him to practise throwing and catching.

5. For baseball, practise both underhand and overhand one-hand throws. This is a skill that must be worked up to gradually. Be sure the ball is small enough to fit his hand. To practise batting skills, you might like to start your child with a paddle-shaped board. Throw a crumpled newspaper ball for him to hit to start with. You will need to stand quite close in the beginning so that he will have no trouble seeing and hitting the "ball." If your child has eye-hand coordination problems, this will take a good deal of practice. As he improves, you can switch to a ball, and then to a bat.

6. Racquet sports are started in much the same way as baseball, except that throwing the ball is not as important. Start your child with a board or a light-weight tennis racquet, allowing him to hold it with two hands in the beginning. Use

crumpled newspaper to start with, as with baseball practice. Allow him to bounce a tennis ball up and down to get the feel of it. Then begin tossing it to him, standing quite close to him, until he becomes adept at hitting it. Once these skills are mastered, you can work on tennis as a sport. Squash and racquetball can be worked on in the same manner. For badminton, your newspaper ball more nearly approximates a bird than an actual ball can. Switch from the newspaper ball to a bird when you feel your child can see and hit something that size.

Fine Motor Activities

We will include in this section activities to improve eye-hand coordination. Most crafts are excellent for fine motor training. We will give a few simple projects, but you will be able to think of many more. Like gross motor coordination, fine motor skills develop at different rates in different children. Learning-disabled children tend to have problems with crafts because of clumsy and awkward movements, poor visual motor memory, a poor spatial perception of space and size, and sometimes a very short attention span. For hyperactive children, you will need to keep the crafts very simple, or break them into small segments which can be done at different times. You will find, however, that your hyperactive child is usually much quieter while working on a craft he enjoys. When planning crafts and activities, stress the following:

- Grasping, which will help in learning to use a pencil.
- Finger-thumb coordination, as in pulling and fringing.
- Winding, as in winding yarn or string.
- Sequencing, an important reading skill. Be sure that your child always works from left to right and from top to bottom.
- Mirror images are often a problem with children who have trouble reading. To help them understand the difference, you can get your child to cut out letters from folded paper so that he can unfold them and see the "mirror image."

- Names of colors, shapes, and textures.
- Imagination; make the skill more than mere imitation.
- Make sure everything is washable!

For craft supplies we suggest a wide range of colors, textures, and shapes. For example: *soft* felt, fur, velvet; *hard and bright* beads, sequins, nuts and bolts; *gritty* sand, sandpaper; *pliable* leather, pipe cleaners; and so on.

Decorated Cans

Focus: *fine motor skills*
Method: This is an easy craft for children, and the end result is both attractive and usable. Remove the contents from a can of soup or vegetables, and wash and dry it thoroughly. Sit your child at a table or a counter and spread newspapers out in front of him. Although this isn't a particularly messy craft, there are bound to be a few drips. Have your child cover the outside of the can with water-soluble white craft glue. Holding the can by the closed end, wind concentric circles of yarn or coarse string around it, starting at the left and working toward the right. Your child may not be able to get an even row-after-row effect, but that doesn't matter, since unevenness is just as attractive. Finish by adding a little extra glue to the end of the yarn or string and smoothing it against the last row. Allow this to dry thoroughly. The next day your child might like to paint the string or yarn with poster paint. After it is all finished, you can seal the finished product with a coat of polyurethane as a preservative. These make great gifts to hold pens and pencils. Using larger juice cans, your child can make cookie tins. By using different-size tins with plastic covers, he can make a canister set. *Variations*: The tins can be covered with paper, felt, or fabric and decorated with cutout designs. If you wish, you can spray-paint a few cans ahead of time and have your child decorate them in any way he wishes with cutout designs. Be sure he uses scissors with blunt ends. If he is left-handed, left-handed scissors might be easier for him to use.

Parchment Pictures

Focus: *fine motor, imagination*
Method: This is a spring, summer, and autumn craft when done with fresh flowers, grasses, and leaves. Cut two pieces of wax paper of exactly the same size. Laying one piece on the table, waxed side up, instruct your child to arrange a design of flowers, grasses, or leaves in the center, leaving a border around the edge. They should be in one layer with little or no overlapping. After he is satisfied with his design, place the second piece of paper, waxed side down, on top as a cover. If there is less than a one-inch border, remove a bit of the design. Now press over the whole surface of both sides with a warm iron. This will cause the two pieces of paper with the design in the middle to meld together to form a parchment picture. Tape this on your child's window where the sun can shine through it. *Variation:* For Christmas or other holidays you might like to help your child cut out decorations from paper serviettes, old cards, or wrapping paper. Proceed as above.

Mobiles

Focus: *manual dexterity*
Method: Use drinking straws and pipe cleaners of various colors. Allow your child to choose what colors he likes, and twist straws and pipe cleaners into interesting shapes joined together. When he has finished, attach a string to his mobile and hang it in his room.

Young Architect

Focus: *manual dexterity, imagination*
Method: You can save craft sticks from popsicles or you can purchase them inexpensively at a craft store. These craft sticks are a wonderful building material for youngsters who have problems handling the commercial toy building materials such as Meccano and Leggo. Start them off with these sticks, and when they become proficient, move them on to the Leggo and Meccano type.

Pile interlapping sticks on top of each other in the shape of a square to make a log cabin; cut a roof from craft paper. You can make a great fort with a wall and buildings. You can use the sticks with small boxes and cartons to create a toy city. You can overlap and glue them to make picture frames. You can lean them together to form the structure of a tepee and then cover with tissue paper. They can be glued with white glue, or just left to be used another day. Allow your child's imagination free rein to design all kinds of interesting buildings, roads, bridges, etc.

Brown Baggies

Focus: *fine motor, color sense, imagination*
Method: There are so many craft projects that can utilize brown paper bags that we can only mention a few:
1.   Use the large-size grocery bags to make Hallowe'en masks, or masks to use for skits. Have your child paint on eyes, nose, mouth, and hair, or use frayed yarn for hair.
2.   Use large bags to make "gingerbread men," decorating them as you would the cookie variety. With different sizes of bags you can make a whole family.
3.   Smaller brown paper bags can make excellent puppets. Your child can make the kind that fit over the hand, or use a larger bag to draw body parts and attach them together at the joints with flexible tape or the push-through type of metal paper fasteners. Made this way, they can be operated with string.

Peepshows

Focus: *fine motor, imagination*
Method: Constructing peepshows is an excellent craft to help your child acquire a variety of skills with scissors and glue. Acquire a shoebox, or something similar which has a removable lid. Explain to your child that this is to be a three-dimensional picture. He may not understand what you mean, so it might be wise to show him how it works. You don't need another box; just use a piece of cardboard the same size as the

end of the box and make a picture with standing figures in the foreground, cars, etc., in the middle distance, and buildings or other scenery in the background. Place the picture at one end of the box. Help him to get started on his peepshow, and when it is finished to his satisfaction, cut a hole in one end so that you can peep into the box. We used to light the whole scene with a pencil flashlight, or you can cut a large piece out of the top and cover it with tissue paper so that light can shine through. Your child may charge family members a marble or a penny to be allowed a peep. *Note:* Save all your old magazines, catalogues, and travel brochures for this.

Budding Rembrandt

Focus: *fine motor, imagination*
Method: Encourage your child to paint pictures of whatever he fancies. All you need to do is provide some old clothes, a smock, or an old shirt for him to wear and a space for him to work. He can use finger paints, watercolors, poster paints, brushes and cotton-tipped swabs, crayons, magic markers, pencils, and so on. Provide your child with lots of paper — it needn't be expensive — and let him go to it. Help him learn his colors by having him repeat the names of the ones he is using. His more creative efforts might be put on display, and you might like to take a picture of any that are his particular pride and joy. Think how much he'll enjoy seeing the snaps of his art in years to come!

Collage

Focus: *tactile sense, fine motor*
Method: Almost any type of material that can be glued onto heavy paper or bristol board can be used for a collage. You can, of course, combine all these various bits and pieces with paint as well. This is an excellent method of training the tactile sense by using bits of yarn, sand, sandpaper, fur, absorbent cotton, felt, foil paper, and so on. As well, the finger-thumb grasp is helped by using dried beans, peas, macaroni, corn, seeds, etc. Beautiful sky effects can be created by using

light-blue tissue paper and white glue. Fluffy white clouds can be white tissue paper, or pulled-out bits of absorbent cotton. Buildings can be cut from paper or can have a three-dimensional look if built up with broken spaghetti, dried pea "stones," or red kidney-bean "bricks." Sheep and lambs can be puffy cotton balls, trees can be bits of cedar or other evergreen, or they can be cut from green paper. There is no limit to the many things your child can do with a box of interesting bits and pieces, some white glue, tissue paper, barley, rice, dry cereals, and so on. Provide lots of washable white glue and let him make his own masterpiece.

"Stained Glass" Bottles

Focus: *fine motor, color discrimination*
Method: Any attractively shaped bottle will do for this craft, but some wine bottles and liqueur bottles make spectacular vases when done by even a rank amateur. Cover the bottle with white glue and layer on different colors of tissue paper torn into different-sized random shapes. Smooth these with the fingers as you put them on, but it is not necessary to get all the wrinkles out. When the bottle is completely covered, allow it to dry thoroughly. You can help your child make a wash for the outside of the bottle by thinning white glue with a little water. Cover the whole outside of the bottle with this wash and allow it to dry thoroughly. It will dry clear and give a hard, shiny surface.

Crayon Batik

Focus: *fine motor, color sense*
Method: This was always a popular craft with our children in Gym Club. The basic method of doing crayon batik is to draw a pattern on fabric, color it in in crayon, then place the cloth face down on paper towels. Now press it with a hot iron. The wax will melt into the paper towels, while the color remains on the fabric. We suggest men's old shirts, old sheets, and so on, for these projects. The favorite among our many classes was place mats. The children used to love making

personalized place mats for themselves and their families with names or initials and funny decorations. You can also make bags for carrying books or shoes, put a pattern on a shirt or blouse, or use the technique for many other projects. Have your child fringe the ends of the fabric; this is excellent for finger-thumb coordination.

Lively Fingers

Focus: *manual dexterity*
Method: There are many games played with the fingers which your child might enjoy:

1. "Here's the church, here's the steeple, open the doors and here are the people." Clasp hands together with fingers intertwined. Raise the two index fingers until the tips are touching to make the steeple. The two thumbs make the doors. Open the "doors" and unfold hands to show finger "people."

2. Here is a Beehive (one fist with thumb enclosed)
   Where are the bees? (point with other hand)
   Hiding inside where no one sees (shake head, point to eyes)
   They're coming out now (point with free hand)
   They're all alive (make circular motion with hand)
   One, two, three, four, five! (unfold one finger at a time)
   Buzz-zz-zz.

3. Patty-cake, patty-cake, this is me
   Here is my hair, here is my knee
   I feel my nose, and I see my toes
   Here are my fingers, I've ten of those

4. One little, two little, three little Indians
   Four little, five little, six little Indians
   Seven little, eight little, nine little Indians
   Ten little Indian boys (girls)

   Sing this with gestures, raising a finger for each number. When your child becomes adept, try it backward, counting back from ten to one.

5. Itsy-bitsy spider went up the garden wall
   Down came the rain and spider had a fall
   Out came the sun and dried up all the rain
   Itsy-bitsy spider went up the wall again.

Put gestures to this song, allowing the children to make their fingers "spiders," and acting out rain and sun.

Helpful Finger Skills

Focus: *manual dexterity*

Method: There are quite a few skills needed in everyday living that are dependent on manual dexterity and eye-hand coordination. Many of these concern a child's ability to dress himself. If your child is having trouble with buttons, bows, and zippers, here are a few tips:

1.   Available at most toy stores is a teddybear that has all these fasteners made just for little fingers to practise.

2.   If you don't want to go to this expense, you can make up many of them at home. You might find a zipper in an old pair of pants or jeans that is large and heavy enough for little fingers to manage. Try putting a few drops of cooking oil on the zipper, or running a bar of soap up and down it, if it is sticking. If you buy a zipper, try to get the extra-heavy-duty plastic type intended for bulky-knit sweaters. Sew it firmly to heavy fabric such as denim so that it will be easier to handle.

3.   You can try using a pair of Daddy's shoes for lacing, but, as a rule, large "eyes" and a shoelace that is easily grasped are better. There is a large plastic shoe just for this purpose available in many toy stores. If you wish to make something at home, try punching out holes in lightweight cardboard and using heavyweight twine with the ends waxed as the laces. For tying a bow, start with bulky yarns, pliable rope, or something easy to handle. Tying a bow takes quite a bit of practice, so you might anchor the two ends of yarn/rope on a board to make handling easier.

4.   To help your child manage buttons, you might find an old coat with a large button and buttonhole that can be cut off and attached to a firm, easy-to-handle surface. If you can't

find an old coat, buy the largest button of that type that you can find, make a buttonhole to fit it in a piece of firm cloth, attach the button to another piece of the fabric, then anchor them both on a firm surface.

Recipes for Fun

Focus: *fine motor, tactile sense, organization*
Method: It is not always necessary to buy craft materials. Many interesting crafts can be made with scraps, throwaways, and everyday things around the house. The following are some recipes for craft materials that you could help your child to make.

1. *Play Dough #1*
   1 cup salt
   2 cups flour
   2 tablespoons vegetable oil
   food coloring, and a little more oil if necessary
   Knead and keep in plastic bag to retain moisture.

2. *Play Dough #2*
   Mix equal parts flour and salt, moisten with just enough water to make a stiff mixture. Color with food coloring.

3. *Play Dough #3*
   Crumb several pieces of day-old bread (remove crusts first). Add enough white glue to make a stiff dough. Knead well. Keep in plastic bag. This gets very hard and is easily painted.

4. *Play Clay*
   ¹/₂ cup salt
   ¹/₂ cup hot water
   ¹/₄ cup cold water
   ¹/₂ cup cornstarch

   Mix salt and hot water in a pan and bring to boiling point. Stir cold water into cornstarch until cornstarch dissolves. Add cornstarch mixture to boiling water. Stir vigorously to prevent lumps. Cook over low heat, stirring constantly, until mixture is like stiff pie dough. Remove from heat and turn onto a breadboard to cool. As soon as it is cool enough to handle, knead until smooth and pliable. Play Clay has a grainy texture and is excellent for flattening with a rolling pin and cutting into shapes for mobiles, Christmas tree decorations, etc. It dries and hardens in from one to three days, depending on thickness.

5. *Paper Paste*
   1 cup flour
   1 cup sugar
   1 cup cold water
   4 cups boiling water
   1 tablespoon powdered alum
   $1/2$ teaspoon oil of wintergreen (optional)

Mix flour and sugar and slowly stir in cold water to form a paste. Slowly add boiling water, stirring vigorously to prevent lumps. Bring mixture to boil, stirring constantly until thick and clear. Remove from heat and stir in alum.

6. *Finger Paint*
   $1/2$ cup cornstarch
   $3/4$ cup cold water
   2 cups hot water
   2 teaspoons boric acid solution for preservative
   1 tablespoon glycerine (obtainable from a drugstore)
   baby-food jars
   food coloring

Mix cornstarch with $1/4$ cup cold water to make a smooth paste. Add hot water, stirring to prevent lumps. Cook over low heat, stirring constantly, until mixture begins to boil. Remove from heat and add $1/2$ cup cold water and boric acid solution. Stir until well mixed. Add glycerine to mixture to slow up drying process. Divide into separate jars. Add food coloring to jars. Stir until color is completely blended.

Young Sculptors

Focus: *fine motor, visual discrimination, body image*
Method: There are many materials that can be used by a young sculptor. Most of the above, plus sand, pipe cleaners, papier-mâché (made with torn-up bits of newspaper and paper paste), and many others. If you are using sand, try adding some warm melted wax to the sand. It remains quite pliable for some time and can be softened in a warm oven. All these materials can be used to sculpt the human figure or body parts.

Found Fun

Focus: *fine motor*
Method: There are many very simple crafts which use cast-off bits from around the house that usually find their way into the garbage. Here are a few:

1.   *Styrofoam platters*, which are often under meat purchased in the supermarket, can be carefully washed and dried and used for découpage. Have your child cut pictures from magazines and glue them with white glue to the styrofoam. When he is happy with his picture, dilute white glue with water, half and half, and brush the mixture over the entire surface. When it is dry, give it a second coat. The pictures can be used as trays for keys, pins, etc.

2.   *Styrofoam egg cartons*, which come in three or four soft pastel colors, can be used to make beautiful Christmas tree ornaments. Cut two adjoining "cups" out of the box but leave enough of the styrofoam to act as a hinge. Bring the two together and close with cellulose tape. Decorate with sequins and glitter, and attach string to the top.

3.   *Old candles* can be melted down to make new candles. You must do this for your child, over hot water, not over a direct-heat burner. When the wax is melted, allow it to cool until it is soft and pliable. For several minutes it can be worked with the hands into interesting shapes. Incorporate a

bit of the wick in the center so that it can be lit. You might like to have your child pour the cooled wax into waxed cat-food tins for personal candles, inserting a bit of wick as it hardens. You can also use old milk and cream cartons. Fill with wax. In this case, braid ordinary string, dip it in the wax while it is still liquid, and show your child how to suspend it in the center of the wax, holding the wick in place by curling the top over a pencil.

4. *Dried weeds and seed pods* can be collected from fields and ditches and painted for decorations. They can be spray-painted (for the older child) or painted with a brush and poster paint.

5. *Old burlap bags* can be washed and used to make wall hangings. Cut out a suitable-size piece, have your child fringe three sides and make a design or picture with glued-on bits of leftover felt or fabric. Bits of yarn, a few sequins, old buttons (sew these on), and so forth can be used as well. Fold over the unfringed end and tack onto a piece of wood to facilitate hanging.

6. *Old nylon pantyhose* can be washed and used for stuffing "animals." Have your child make a whimsical animal pattern on paper, cut it out, then cut the design out of scrap fabric. Use the nylon pantyhose to stuff the stitched animal, then put eyes, etc., on with glue or magic marker.

7. *Nuts, bolts, wire, washers,* and other bits and pieces from Daddy's workshop can be used to make attractive "jewelry" for the young miss. Clean and polish them if necessary and allow your child to string the nuts and washers on wire, pipe cleaners, twine, or yarn. She can make necklaces and bracelets for herself and all her friends.

Roll-Around

Focus: *kinesthetic/tactile experience for the whole body*
Method: Give your child every opportunity possible to experience different tactile sensations over his whole body.

Put cornstarch or bubble bath into his bath so he can experience the silky feeling of the water (cornstarch is soothing to irritated skin, as well). Wrap him in a fur coat with the fur side in. Allow him to curl up on a mohair blanket or some other blanket with a long pile. Persuade him that there is no more fun in the world than rolling around in a pile of freshly raked leaves, or on a carpet of pine needles in the woods. Bury him in sand up to his neck. We are sure you will find many other ways to stimulate the tactile senses of your child's whole body.

Feelie Bag

Focus: *visual memory, tactile discrimination, vocabulary, expressive language*
Method: Put several different items into a brown paper bag, such as a toy soldier, a ball, a small stuffed animal, a plastic cup, etc. Ask your child to put his hand inside and feel the objects. He then tries to identify them by feel alone.
Variations: As a child develops his tactile sense, you might try putting in pieces of fur, velvet, sandpaper, foil, thin silk, and other things that have a distinctive feel. Allow your child to touch these before you put them in the bag, making sure he knows the names of all the fabrics and the other objects. Now, put them in the bag and allow him to identify them by touch alone.

The Matching Game

Focus: *categorization, tactile discrimination, conceptualization*
Method: You can use the same method as in Feelie Bag, using either one or two bags. If one bag is used, put in quite a number of small items in pairs such as pairs of buttons, two small spoons, two plastic eggcups, etc. Allow your child to pair them by feeling them without looking. You might also try this by putting one of each pair in two different bags, allowing your child to feel one bag with his left hand, and one with his right to make the pairs of items.

Touch and Tell #1

Focus: *tactile perception*
Method: This is to help children tell the differences between common items by touch alone. In a series of small
dishes or on a long piece of paper, place small amounts of a
number of items with different textures that are quite characteristic. You might start with items with different shapes and
textures from the kitchen, such as salt, sugar, dried peas, rice,
oat cereal, macaroni, etc. Then you might try familiar things
from the yard such as sand, pine needles, a leaf, pieces of
grass, a flower, etc. This can be as simple or as complicated as
you wish, depending on your child's level of competence.
Blindfold your child, of course!

Touch and Tell #2

Focus: *visual memory, tactile perception*
Method: This is a game even adults can enjoy playing.
When the family or a group of friends are gathered together,
choose one member who is then blindfolded. Another member
of the group is asked to step forward so that the blindfolded
person can feel his face and hair to identify him. *Variation*: At
a children's party, form the guests into two teams and blindfold one member of each team. These two then try to guess
each other's identity by feel. The team with the most correct
guesses wins.

CHAPTER 17

Everyday Activities To Improve Other Skills

Helping a Poor Memory

Many parents complain to us that their learning-disabled child "never listens to what I say." Sometimes this is true, especially if parents are critical and demanding, but often it is just that the child has a poor memory and forgets what he hears. All the strategies for training listening ability will help this child, but there are a few other things you might try as well. These children often have poor auditory recall — that is, a poor memory for what they have heard. Along with this they might have a short attention span, which means they can only attend to one short directive statement at a time, or they may have an inability to associate what they have heard with past related experiences. Any or all of these problems can be present with a memory disability, and they impose a severe handicap on educational, social, and emotional growth and development. Here are a few strategies you might try at home:

1. Encourage your child to speak in whole sentences rather than one word or one phrase at a time.

2. Work toward getting him to verbalize full replies to questions. For example, if you ask him "Where have you been?"

don't accept "Outside" as an answer; insist on something like "I was outside playing on the swing."

3. It will often help if you ask your child to repeat instructions. If someone asks him to do something, ask him to repeat the instructions before he goes off to do it.

4. Assess exactly how much he can take in at one time. You may need to start building on short, simple sentences with one idea only. If he fumbles for words in reply or when repeating instructions, supply the words, then ask him to repeat again. Supplement all these instructions whenever possible, using visual aids, touching, and gesture as reinforcement.

5. Encourage him to memorize anything he can enjoy — jingles, slogans, telephone numbers, rules for games, limericks, etc.

6. Encourage him to exercise his memory by retelling the story of a TV program (in proper sequence), a visit to a friend's house, a favorite comic strip, etc.

7. While driving in the car you might like to play memory games such as "On the way we saw . . . (a mother cat and kittens, two lakes with boats on them, a black cow by the fence, etc.)." Each item is to be repeated by the next player, who must drop out if he can't remember an item. I Packed My Bag is another game of this type.

8. Many card games are good for memory exercise.

9. When your child is learning the name of something unfamiliar, name the whole thing, including its properties: for example, a convertible car; a collie dog; a Chinese man.

10. Encourage your child to repeat names, properties of things he knows about, relationships, and anything else of this sort that should be committed to long-term memory. Constant rehearsal will help a great deal. Sometimes repeating something aloud will give added reinforcement.

11. Drawing or cutting out pictures and pasting them in a scrapbook helps to rehearse familiar objects so that he won't forget their names or functions.

12.   Expose him to as many interesting learning situations as possible. Children remember much better if their memory is reinforced with interest and curiosity.

Helping With Arithmetic Problems

Many children find ordinary arithmetic an almost insurmountable problem. In many ways it is related to the previous memory problems, as is poor spelling. While he may have no trouble applying reasoning ability to problem-solving, he may have a great deal of trouble remembering the basic addition, subtraction, and multiplication tables. In fact, many children can't even learn to count easily because of sequencing and visual-memory problems. There are many strategies to help your child in this area.

1.   *Black Jack or "21"* is a great game to help addition skills. You might also change this to 11, 31, 51, 65, or whatever. The dealer can remove face cards, or give them an even value of ten. The ace is eleven or one. The dealer places one card down in front of each player and himself. Now place a card face up in front of each player. Players "peek" at their down card to see if they want another (for "21") or the play continues in the same way until someone gets exactly "21." If everyone goes over, the dealer wins. If any player gets the designated number, he wins; otherwise it is the person who comes closest (including the dealer).

2.   *Greater or Less* is a card game which uses only the numbered cards. Put a pile in the center and have each of two players draw a card. Have your child tell you whether his card is greater than, less than, or equal to your card. He wins if he is right more times than he is wrong. When he gets better at this method of playing, you might like to switch to more than two players. Each player is given a card face up; the one with the highest card (or lowest if that is the way the game is being played) takes all the other cards. The one with the most cards at the end of the game is the winner.

3. *Pairs* Make two sets of flash cards, one set with addition, subtraction, multiplication, or division problems, the other set with the corresponding answers. More than one player can play. Cards are shuffled and each player is dealt five cards, with the remainder being placed in the center. The player on the left of the dealer plays first. If he finds upon picking up his cards that he already has a pair (for example, one card reading 6 x 3 and another reading 18), he lays them down in front of him, reading them aloud as he does so. He then may draw one from the pile and discard one face up next to the "kitty" pile. The next player may pick up the discarded card or take one from the top of the "kitty." The first player to go "out" wins.

4. *The Circle Game* is used to drill number facts. The circles can be cut out of cardboard or drawn on a chalkboard or on paper. Inside the circle, place six or seven numbers. In the center put any arithmetic operation you want to reinforce, for example ÷3, ×4, +6, −2, and so on. The operation is then performed on each number in the circle. This can be a game you might play with your child alone, or with two children as a test of speed, the one getting the most right answers in a given time being the winner.

5. *Cribbage* is a fairly simple game to teach children if you play yourself. They love learning an adult game and many of them become very good at it. It is an excellent reinforcement for basic addition skills.

6. *Counting Games* of any sort are good for children who are having difficulty establishing number sequence. Have your child count the sidewalk squares from his driveway to a neighbor's, the number of steps going upstairs, or down to the basement. He might count the number of houses on the street and find out if any numbers have been skipped.

7. *The Tile Game* is another counting game which can be varied as a child progresses. Many stores have packages of floor tiles at a very reasonable price. Get twenty of these tiles

and mark them with magic marker from 1 to 20. Put them in sequence on the floor and have your child stand on a specific number as you call it out. When he is experienced at that, you might call out "Stand on the number that comes after 9" (or before 4, etc.). Later you can use simple addition, such as "Stand on the number that is the answer for 2 plus 3." Heavy cardboard cut from cartons can also be used, or carpet samples if they are available.

8. *Dice* are an excellent way to help children with simple addition. They can also help them understand number concepts if you show them that the three dots on dice are the same as the number 3 and so forth. Most children find the small dice rather hard to handle at first, but you can make large dice quite easily. Obtain square boxes (gift shops will often give you two), blocks of wood, or large squares of commercial soft foam and use them to make a pair of dice. You can use magic marker or paint for the dots. As well as simple number sequences and addition, the children who play the game together might enjoy using the dice to make a problem from the numbers which come up. They might take turns calling what the next problem would be, such as addition, multiplication, division, or subtraction.

9. *Coins* are a good way to improve math skills and are a necessary part of a child's education as well. Every child should be taught about money as soon as he is able to understand. The concepts of more, less, and equal can be strengthened with coins. You should teach that the size of the coin has nothing to do with its value. If a child is having math problems, making change can be difficult. It is worth while teaching your child to always add up to an amount rather than try to subtract when making change; for example, if you are given a two-dollar bill for a purchase of $1.59, you would give one penny to make $1.60, and four dimes to total $2.00. This is much easier for most people than trying to subtract $1.59 from $2.00 in their heads. Your child might like to figure out what other combinations of coins he could use.

Everyday Games and Activities

It is not always possible for a busy mother, or a mother who works outside of her home, to have the time to participate in games and strategies with a learning-disabled child. There are, however, many chances to teach and reinforce in the circumstances of everyday living. With a little ingenuity you can make many everyday occurrences a learning experience for your child, such as doing laundry, setting a table, going shopping, and so on. Use the television set, which is probably your learning-disabled child's favorite amusement because it is completely non-threatening. Here are just a few to get you started:

Going Shopping

Focus: *visual memory and discrimination, auditory memory, categorization, arithmetic, fine motor, organizational and planning skills*
Method: Whenever your child accompanies you on a shopping expedition, allow her to help with making a list by checking what articles you are out of. Ask what sound (or what letter) a certain item begins with. Ask her to count the number of items on your list. If you are using coupons, ask her to match coupons with items as you place them in your cart. Ask her to compare prices and tell you which is the best buy. Explain unit pricing to her. If you are only buying a few items, ask her to make a note of the items and add the bill. Allow her to handle the money when you are paying and check the change to see if it is accurate. Have her help unpack and put away groceries in the proper spot. All of these activities are excellent help for a learning-disabled child.

Table-Setting

Focus: *sequencing, left-right discrimination, manual dexterity, visual memory*
Method: Allow your child to assist with setting the table, showing him how the cutlery is placed at left and right, where

other items are placed on the table, where each member of the family sits, and so on. Soon he will be able to do it without assistance.

Doing the Laundry

Focus: *visual discrimination, sequencing, color discrimination, shape differentiation*
Method: Have your child sort socks and mittens into pairs, put matching pillowcases and sheets together, sort items by color, size, or shape.

Making the Bed

Focus: *sequencing, visual and auditory memory, gross motor*
Method: While you are making a bed, have your child watch you and then repeat to you the sequence you used. What did you do first? Second? And after that?

In the Workshop

Focus: *visual perception, categorization, sequencing, visual memory, gross and fine motor*
Method: All children enjoy being with Daddy when he is in the workshop. Your child can sort nuts, bolts, nails, screws, and so on into their proper piles. He can sort them out by size as well. A large piece of board, a paintbrush, and some washable paint are satisfying tools for art expression. Later let him try using a hammer and saw.

Cleaning the House

Focus: *rhythm, manual dexterity, eye-hand coordination*
Method: While you are doing routine tidying and dusting, sweeping and vacuuming, have your child do the same to music. Roll up newspapers in a ball and fire them at a wastebasket. Count number of things picked up off the floor, help put them in piles according to whose they are, help put them away.

Cooking

Focus: *arithmetic skills, auditory and visual sequencing, following directions, reading*

Method: Whenever you are following a recipe, have your child watch and learn. Show him how to use measuring cups and spoons. Allow him to read out the instructions for you if he can. Later, allow him to cook on his own with your supervision. Make sure he cleans up afterward, showing him the sequence of rinsing, washing, and drying. You might also use cooking as a method of helping memory by reading out one item or direction from a recipe and asking your child to repeat it. Teach all children how the stove works and what all the dials mean. Older children can also help with preparing vegetables, which aids manual dexterity. They can also get out ingredients for recipes, foods from the refrigerator, and so forth, and then put them back in the proper place, which helps visual memory.

Television

Focus: *visual and auditory perception, discrimination, and memory sequencing*

Method: We will assume that you are discriminating in what your child can watch. Certain programs containing a good deal of violence seem to be especially upsetting to children with learning disabilities, possibly because of their lack of maturity. Use the television as a learning medium by allowing your child to watch good educational programs as well as programs especially written for children. Ask questions about what he saw and heard: What happened first? How was the hero dressed? What color was the heroine's dress? You might ask him to retell the story in his own words, making sure it is in proper sequence. If it is a story about some distant place, ask him what he learned about that place. Ask him what sport he has been watching, who the teams were, who won, how the game is played, the names of any players he remembers. He might like to repeat rhyming commercials. You will think of many more.

Tape Recorder

Focus: *auditory discrimination and memory, expressive language*

Method: We have mentioned before how useful a tape recorder can be. Here are a few more suggestions. Tape familiar household sounds such as a boiling kettle, the vacuum, a bath running, different people's voices, and so on. Play them back and ask your child to identify them. Allow your child to put stories on tape and play them back. Take a tape recorder with you on shopping expeditions, visits to the zoo, etc., and play back sounds later for identification.

Telephone Skills

Focus: *sequencing, auditory memory, visual memory, manual dexterity*

Method: Explain a telephone dial to your child, showing him how the combinations of letters and numbers work to get a dialled number at the other end. Allow him to try himself. Ask him why he thinks certain letters are omitted. Show him how a push-button telephone works. Buy or make a personal telephone book for him. Help him look up the numbers of his friends and relatives and write them in his own book.

Piano

Focus: *auditory discrimination*

Method: Play high notes, then low notes, without your child seeing your hands. He can cover his eyes or turn his back. Ask him to stretch his hand high for high notes, and to crouch low for low notes. Some children quickly learn to name the notes as you play them; others find this impossible to learn because they can't distinguish the differences in pitch. Try teaching your child a simple sequence of notes such as the first phrase in "Mary Had a Little Lamb." There are many games you can invent if you play the piano yourself.

General-Knowledge Questions

Focus: *visual and auditory perception, memory, logic, expressive language*

Method: Make everything you do a learning situation to stimulate your child's powers of observation, to help him with logical thought processes, to aid problem-solving. Using the Socratic method when children ask questions can often help them answer their own question with just guidance from the person they have asked. Here are a few examples:

1. Suppose your child asks why there are clouds in the sky. Rather than a straightforward answer, try asking "What do you think clouds look like?" You might get an answer something like a ball of cotton, a white blanket, foam on the seashore, etc. Try to lead him to something that is liquid. Ask him if clouds remind him of anything in the kitchen or the bathroom. Try to elicit an answer of steam from a kettle or a bath. Then go on to help him answer his own question by telling him that clouds are water vapor that is heavy enough to see because it is cooler up there than down here. Ask him why he thinks clouds move, why they are sometimes dark, and so on.

2. If your child asks what makes grass grow, or something similar, you might ask him what it would look like if you didn't cut the grass. Ask what he thinks helps make the grass grow. Show him the grass roots, explain the function of rain, the earth, fertilizer, etc. Explain that all our cereal crops come from grains which are grasses. Most questions of this type can only be explained fully to an older child, but even very young children, when they are at the who, what, when, where, why stage, can be helped to think for themselves by using a simplified version of this method.

What Is It?

Focus: *conceptualization, categorization, auditory and visual discrimination, memory*

Method: This is an amalgam of several other games played in various ways. This can be changed to suit circumstances, but it is an excellent game to play to amuse a child while driving in the car, or waiting in a doctor's office, or while you are doing some type of work in which he can't participate. Ask him to discriminate between two similar-sounding words such as cat and bat or father and bother. Ask him to discriminate between two familiar sounds such as a kettle boiling or the tap running. Ask whether birds lay eggs in nests or vests; whether chickens have feathers or sweaters; did Mother cook or book the dinner, and so on. With sounds, you might ask him to discriminate between the sound of the tap in a basin and the tap in a bathtub; you might hide a ticking clock and let him find it; you might ask him what the washing machine is doing when it switches in sound from washing to emptying, and so on.

Comparing

Focus: *spatial awareness, tactile discrimination*
Method: When you are in the kitchen or any other area where this might apply, help him compare big and little, smooth and rough, same as and different from, hard and soft, short and long, above and below. With both wet and dry measure, help him understand which holds more, which holds less, which holds the same amount. Ask him how he can tell.

Water Fun

Focus: *sensory awareness, reasoning power*
Method: When you are in the kitchen, there are a great many activities which will help your child understand the world around him, and improve his tactile senses and his fine motor coordination. Here are a few:
1.   Scraping and washing unbreakable dishes can help fine motor coordination.
2.   Put into water things that will sink and some that will float. Discuss what the difference is. Ask him to guess whether an article will sink or float and have him put it in the water. Discuss his answer.

3. Discuss such words as sink, float, plastic, soap, detergent, bubbles, etc.

4. Put some baking soda in a glass of water and allow your child to stir it to make it fizz. Discuss this with him.

5. Place a paper towel on the surface of the water so that it floats. Discuss why it eventually sinks. Make a boat out of a piece of foil and discuss why this continues to float.

6. In the bath, try different objects to see whether or not they will float. Discuss why turning a jet of water on bubble bath fills the tub with bubbles. Discuss how mixing taps work.

Things To Do Outside

Focus: *sensory awareness, observation, gross and fine motor, expressive language*

Method: There are many ways to use out-of-doors activities as learning experiences. Some of the following have already been mentioned but are worth repeating; others are new. You will also think of many yourself.

1. When you are going for a walk, notice colors and shapes, read signs, listen to noises and identify them, watch for the change of seasons, try to name birds that you see, etc.

2. Introduce your child to the local library and inquire if they have any programs especially for children. Help your child pick out a book for himself, and explain how the library works.

3. Play different types of ball games to improve ball-handling and eye-hand coordination.

4. Use a skipping rope, as soon as your child can skip, to help coordination and counting, and help him remember some of the verses the children use in skipping.

5. Notice the weather, discuss what causes it, show your child a weather map and explain how it works. Discuss what kinds of clothes you wear for different types of weather, and why.

6. To help number sequencing, count cars, houses, people, anything you pass on your way to the store, the library, or anywhere.

7. Play such games as hopscotch, hide and seek, tag, Simon Says, May I? and so forth.

8. Draw pictures of things you saw after you go back in the house. Discuss what you saw to improve memory.

Keep a Junk Box

Focus: *creative imagination, fine motor control, tactile discrimination*

Method Nothing can be as satisfying to a child as being presented with a box full of interesting bits and pieces which he can use to create and play with to his heart's content. Here are a few of the things you might like to put in such a box:

1. Miscellaneous items: rope, string, sandpaper, sponges, shoelaces, old pantyhose, clothespins, wool, wood scraps, and so on.

2. Boxes: paper-tissue boxes, small and large boxes which held matches, milk and cream cartons, boxes both with and without lids and of various sizes.

3. Meat and vegetable trays in plastic, foil, cardboard, and styrofoam. Include pie plates and tart tins.

4. Odds and ends of fabrics, lace, feathers, beads, shells, buttons, empty spools, yarn, carpet pieces, tiles, pine cones, and so on.

5. Tubes from toilet tissue, paper towels, wax paper, aluminum foil, Christmas wrapping.

6. Bits and pieces of other items such as washed tin cans both with and without labels, wallpaper, wrapping paper, greeting cards, magazines, catalogues, travel brochures, pipe cleaners, paper plates and cups, odd socks and mitts.

How can you use all these delightful bits and pieces? Here are a few suggestions, but your child is sure to come up with many more.

1. Use boxes and odds and ends to make planes, cars, trucks, cameras, garages, houses, barns, a whole town, etc.

2. Make puppets from socks and mitts.

3. Use meat trays for collages, sewing practice, cutting out figures, making the roof of a building, etc.

4. Use cards, magazine pictures, and travel brochure pictures to make your own jigsaw puzzles. The smaller ones can be pasted onto meat or vegetable trays. The larger ones can be mounted on cardboard.

5. Use catalogues to identify items, tell what room in the house they should be in, cut them out for a play-house.

Little Skills

Focus: *general knowledge, visual acuity*
Method: There are many little skills that most people take for granted that your child might have to be shown several times and allowed to practise. We have mentioned skills connected with getting dressed, such as buttons, bows, and zippers. Here are some others:

1. Telling time on a regular or digital clock and watch.
2. Reading a calendar.
3. Reading a speedometer.
4. Reading a thermometer.
5. Reading his weight on a scale.
6. Learning how to use a dictionary, telephone book, catalogue, cookbook, or book of instructions.
7. Using a calculator.
8. Reading maps.
9. Answering a telephone correctly.

Glossary

The definitions in this glossary are meant to supply parents with a basis for understanding the language used in other books and reports, and in discussions they may have with the various professionals who deal with their child. As we review the literature about learning disabilities, we find considerable confusion in terms, which we have tried to reduce by mentioning other similar terms under certain glossary entries. Overall, we have attempted to explain the most commonly used terms in easily understood language, within the specific context of learning disabilities. We advise all parents to become familiar with the terminology, because they will hear and read it constantly as their learning-disabled child proceeds through the school system.

Agnosia: The lack of ability to gain information through one of the senses, even though the receiving organ is not impaired.

Alexia: The inability to read due to a central-nervous-system dysfunction. (A partial loss is known as *Ayslexia.*)

Aphasia: An inability to comprehend oral language and/or an inability to express oneself properly through speech. It is an impairment in the use of meaningful symbols.

Apraxia: Difficulty in doing a purposeful motor movement.

Auditory blending: The ability to bring together the various sound units in a word in the correct sequence so that the word can be recognized as a whole.

Auditory discrimination: The ability to hear differences between sounds, syllables, and words.

Auditory memory: The ability to recall sounds, syllables, and words.

Auditory perception: The ability to interpret and organize information received through the ears.

Auditory reception: The ability to hear.

Basal Reader Approach: A method of teaching reading using a set of basal readers. The authors provide a sequence of skills, content, vocabulary, and activities through the teacher's manuals and the student workbooks which accompany the series.

Behavior modification: A means of attempting to change human behavior by structuring the environment to reinforce the desired response.

Body awareness: The ability to identify the parts of one's own body.

Body image: The ability to relate body parts to each other and to the outside environment.

Brain-injured child: A child who before, during, or after birth has, by either illness or injury, suffered damage to the brain. This damage may prevent or impede the normal learning process. Central-nervous-system dysfunction is often referred to as brain damage or neurological dysfunction.

Cerebral dominance: The control of activities by the brain with one hemisphere usually being consistently dominant over the other. In most individuals the left hemisphere is considered dominant and is believed to control language.

Classification: The ability to recognize class identities and use them in establishing logical relationships (much like categorization).

Closure: A technique used in testing reading comprehension. Words are deleted from a paragraph and exact word replacement is required.

Cognition: The act or process of knowing. Thinking skills and processes are called cognitive skills.

Comprehension: The ability to use judgement and reasoning in common-sense situations.

Conceptual disorder: An inability to formulate concepts because of the disturbance in the thinking process.

Conceptualization: The process of forming a concept or a general idea from a number of examples; for example, apples, pears, and oranges are understood as the concept of fruit.

Cross-modality perception: Also referred to as intersensory transfer, transducing. The neurological process of changing information received through one input modality to another system in the brain.

Decoding: The ability to associate a sound with a letter or syllable.

Delivery systems: The various ways of offering educational services to children: for example, regular class, special-education contained class, withdrawal class.

Developmental lag: Delayed maturity in one or several areas of development: for example, emotional, educational, social, physical.

Developmental task: Tasks or skills normally accomplished by a child in a predictable sequence. A learning-disabled child may not acquire these skills automatically because of his deficits and may have to be taught each task explicitly.

Diagnosis: The identification of a disorder or condition by its distinctive symptoms, and the conclusion reached.

Directionality: The ability to perceive and label directions such as up-down, in-out, north-south, in front of-behind.

Dyscalculalia: The inability to perform mathematical functions.

Dysgraphia: The inability to perform the motor movements necessary for handwriting.

Dyslexia: A disorder of children who, despite conventional classroom experience, fail to attain the skill of reading.

Echolalia: The parrot-like repetition of words or phrases spoken by another person, without any understanding of the language.

Encoding: The comprehension and relating of incoming stimuli: for example, as someone speaks to you, you understand what is said.

Etiology: The cause or origin of a condition.

Expressive language: The production of language for communication with others. Speaking and writing are forms of expressive language. A marked discrepancy between writing and speaking skills may indicate a learning disability.

Eye-hand coordination: An example of cross-modality perception. This skill is necessary for both gross and fine motor tasks such as eating and penmanship.

Eye tracking: The ability of the eyes to maintain focus and to move smoothly in following a moving object or in reading a line of print.

Figure-ground perception: The ability to focus on one thing in the visual field, allowing everything else to drop into the background.

Fine motor skills: The use and coordination of small muscles to perform precision tasks such as manipulating a pencil, zipping a zipper, doing up buttons, tying shoes.

Gross motor skills: The use and coordination of large muscles to perform tasks in which balance is often important: for example, walking or swimming.

Hyperactivity (hyperkinesis): Constant and excessive movement and motor activity. The result is that a child finds it difficult to attend to a non-motor task for an extended period of time.

Hypokinetic: The absence of the normal amount of motor activity; listlessness.

Impulsivity: The characteristic of acting upon impulse without consideration of the consequences of the action.

Individualized reading: A method of teaching reading. Learning is structured using the child's own interests to select the reading books and the teacher acts as a counsellor.

Inner language: The process of internalizing and organizing experiences without the use of linguistic symbols.

Kinesthetic method: An approach to learning using the muscular sense. It is usually combined with the tactile sense, as in learning letters and words by tracing them in sand.

Language arts: Part of the school curriculum, namely those activities that use language: listening, speaking, reading, writing, spelling.

Language experience: An approach to reading based on the child's own experience. Stories are written down by the teacher as told to her by the children after an experience such as a trip to an apple orchard. The child may also write his own stories.

Laterality: The awareness that there are two sides to one's body and the ability to recognize these two sides as left and right.

Learning disabilities: See page 7.

Learning style: The way a child is best able to understand and retain learning. We all learn best through one or more channels: visual, auditory, motor, or a combination of these.

Mainstreaming: Placing of children with handicaps and learning problems into the regular classroom.

Memory: The ability to store and retrieve, on demand, previously experienced sensations and perceptions. May also be referred to as "imagery" and "recall."

Midline difficulty: A child may be said to have difficulty crossing the midline (an imaginary line drawn from the middle of his forehead down through his body, separating it into left and right halves). He may have problems with eye tracking from left to right, eye-hand coordination, or putting his right hand across the midline to touch some body part on the left side.

Modality: A pathway by which a child receives information, such as vision, hearing, touch, taste, and smell. Each child will have a preferred modality.

Number concepts: The ability to count and use simple numbers to represent quantity.

Ocular pursuit: Same as eye tracking.

Perception: The process by which the brain organizes, integrates, and makes sense of the information gathered by the senses.

Perceptual constancy: The ability to perceive that an object remains the same regardless of changes in distance and position. For example, a beach ball is a beach ball whether it is in the house or on the beach.

Perceptually handicapped: A person who has problems in learning because of a disturbance in the perception of sensory stimuli.

Perseveration: The senseless continuation or repetition of an activity that has been started. The child is unable to change or stop the activity even though it has become inappropriate.

Phoneme: The smallest unit of sound in any particular language. The sound made by the letter "t" is a phoneme. It becomes a grapheme when it is written down.

Phonetics: The study of the sounds of speech and how they are produced.

Phonics: The use of phonetics in the teaching of reading. It is the linking of the phoneme of the language with the equivalent written symbol (grapheme).

Psychoeducational diagnostician: A specialist who diagnoses a child who has learning difficulties.

Psycholinguistics: A field of study that blends psychology and linguistics and examines the total language process.

Reading comprehension: The ability to understand what one has read.

Receptive language: Language spoken or written by others and received by the child: for example, listening and reading.

Retrieve: To recover from memory for use in producing language.

Sensory motor: A term meaning input of sensation and output of motor activity; for example, you feel heat and you move your hand away from the fire immediately.

Sequencing: The ordering of skills in the developmental pattern for growth (mathematics, development of language skills, etc.) that most children follow. They proceed from rote counting to knowing the days of the week in order — from the least difficult to the most difficult.

Social maturity: The ability to assume personal and social responsibility.

Social perception: The ability to interpret "signals" in social situations. Socially inappropriate behavior and lack of social perception are often associated with learning disabilities.

Vestibular system: The balancing system of the inner ear that regulates the adjustment of body movements to gravity.

Visual closure: The ability to recognize a whole picture even when one or more parts of the whole are missing.

Visual coordination: Same as eye tracking.

Visual discrimination: The ability to discriminate between forms and symbols in the environment.

Visual memory: The ability to accurately recall prior visual experiences.

Visual-motor memory: The ability to reproduce previous visual experiences using the motor modality: for example, remembering the picture of a boat and reproducing it on paper.

Visual perception: the identification, organization, and interpretation of sensory data received through the eyes.

Vocabulary: The ability to understand words. *Receptive vocabulary* refers to all the words a child can understand when they are spoken by other people.

Word-attack skills: The ability to analyze words visually and phonetically.

Association for Children with Learning Disabilities (ACLD)

THE ACLD is a national non-profit organization that emphasizes self-help for parents of children with learning disabilities. The ACLD works with parents and school systems, provides up-to-date information—about local resources and recent discoveries that pertain to defining or solving learning problems, and initiates opportunities for parents to get together and compare notes.

The national office contains a resource library of over 600 publications for sale and offers a film rental service. In addition, the ACLD publishes a bimonthly (6 issues a year) newsletter, "Newsbriefs," that covers current developments within the field.

Addresses for the fifty state affiliates and more than 785 local chapters, including offices in each Canadian province, change from year to year, but most states have at least one active chapter. Programs within locality vary, some offering activities such as regularly scheduled parent meetings, social gatherings for adolescents, and summer camp for younger children.

The addresses of active chapters are available from the national office, which will be happy to answer all requests and forward any inquiries to the appropriate state or province.

National Headquarters
(United States)

Jean Petersen
Executive Director
ACLD
4156 Library Road
Pittsburgh, PA 15234
(412) 341-1515 or
(412) 341-8077

National Headquarters
(Canada)

June Bourgeau
Executive Secretary
ACLD
323 Chapel Street
Ottawa, Ontario K1N 7Z2
(613) 238-5721

Useful Commercial Games

Most games bought for children help in some area or another, and games played by two or more people are useful in developing good social skills. Space limits our list, but we are including some that have proved to be particularly useful for children with learning disabilities.

Texas Instruments Educational Products

This company has a series of games and educational products which are at the top of our list for helping an LD child in a fun way.

Speak and Read for preschool through Grade 3 (later for children with reading problems) is a new learning aid that duplicates the human voice to build beginning reading skills. Comes with a colorful 64-page activity book and earphones. Modules are also available. Expensive.

Speak and Spell for Grades 1 through 8 uses the combination approach of hearing, spelling, and seeing a word. Modules available. Expensive.

Speak and Math, a sight-and-sound approach to teaching basic math skills. Students use sight, hearing, and touch to help learn more than 100,000 basic mathematical problems. Expensive.

The Little Professor for preschool through Grade 4 is a simpler form of math game combining the space-age game and the time-proven flash-card approach to basic math. Moderately priced.

DataMan for Grades 1 through 6 adds fun to math practice through the four basic math functions. Moderately priced.

Math Marvel for Grades 1 through 6 is an advanced and more versatile version of The Little Professor. Moderately expensive.

Spelling B for preschool through Grade 3 is a word-picture approach to good spelling. Moderately expensive.

Mr. Challenger for Grades 3 and up includes word games you can play by yourself or with a friend. Memory stretchers, riddles of pure logic, and simple guessing games are included. Looks like a small computer. Moderately expensive.

Touch and Tell for preschool to Grade 3. A new game for teaching preschool concepts. Modules also available. Expensive.

Games To Aid Visual Perception

All the following games are relatively inexpensive and are readily available at most toy, variety, and department stores. Design Blocks and Patterns, Dominoes, Doodles, Etch-a-Sketch, Hi-Spot, Jacks, Jigsaw Puzzles, Kaleidoscope Puzzles, Lite Brite, Magneto Drawing Stencils, Pick-up Sticks, Picture Peg, Ring Toss.

Games To Develop Language Skills

These are also readily available and inexpensive. ABACA, ABC, Anagrams, Animal Rummy, Animal World Cards, Clue, Coast to Coast, Consonant and Vowel Lotto, Grand Prix, Group Sounding Games and Group Word Games of different types, Kan-U-Go, Lexicon, Lotto Games, Park and Shop,

Password, Phonic Rummy, Play and Say, Probe, Quick Wit, Rhyme-O, Scrabble, Sentence Cards, Sentence Cube Game, Spell Power, and three similar games — Shake-a-Word, Spill and Spell, and Perquackey.

Games To Develop Mathematics Skills

These games help improve basic math skills and many also aid problem-solving ability. All are comparatively inexpensive. Bingo, Checkers, Chess, Confusious Counter, Finance, Heads Up!, Magic Brain Computer, Monopoly, Parcheesi, Rack-O, Rook, Snakes and Ladders, Steeplechase, Stockticker, Sum Fun, The Underdog Game, Watch Your Numbers.

Games To Develop Auditory Perception

Most of these are repeats of previously mentioned games but are also very good for auditory perception. The best games for improving this skill are Password, Simon, and Super Simon. The last two use electronics and sound patterns as an excellent auditory teaching tool. Any game which requires a child to listen attentively will help auditory skills. Here are a few: ABACA, ABC, Anagrams, Animal Rummy, Bingo, Heads Up!, all Group Word Games, Kan-U-Go, Lexicon, Lotto, Phonic Rummy, Play and Say, Quick Wit, Rhyme-O, Scrabble, Sentence Cards and Cubes, Spell Power, Spill and Spell, Sum Fun.

There are many new games introduced every year which will often be of help in specific areas. If you are in doubt, discuss a game with a knowledgeable person in a good toy store, or with your ACLD.

Reading List

The following is based on a very comprehensive list compiled by the Ontario Association for Children with Learning Disabilities. We have added a few books in special areas which we feel you might like to read or use for games and activities. Please read through our Bibliography as well. Most of the books there are intended primarily for professionals in the field, but many of them might be of interest to you. You may also find many interesting and informative books and pamphlets available through your local ACLD.

ALLEY, G. R., and DESHLER, D. D., *Teaching the Learning Disabled Adolescent: Strategies and Methods.* Denver, Co.: Love, 1979.

ANDERSON, L. E., ed. *Helping the Adolescent with the Hidden Handicap.* San Rafael, Calif.: Academic Therapy Publications, 1970.

BENTON, A. L., and BELL, P., *Dyslexia: An Appraisal of Current Knowledge.* Toronto: Oxford University Press of Canada, 1979.

BERNE, ERIC, M.D., *Games People Play.* New York: Random House, 1964; New York: Ballantine Books (pocketbook), 1973.

BLOOM, L., and LAHEY, M., *Language Development and Language Disorders.* Toronto: John Wiley and Sons, 1978.

BRUTTEN, M.; RICHARDSON, S.; MARGEL, C., *Something's Wrong with My Child: A Parent's Book about Children with Learning Disabilities.* New York: Harcourt Brace Jovanovich, 1973.

CROOKE, W. C., *Can Your Child Read? Is He Hyperactive?* Jackson, Tenn.: Pedicenter Press, 1975.

CRUICKSHANK, W. R., *Learning Disabilities in Home, School and Community.* Syracuse, N.Y.: Syracuse University Press, 1977.

DOWNING, J., *Reading and Reasoning.* New York: Springer-Verlag, 1979.

DREIKURS, R., and Soltz, V., *Children: The Challenge.* New York: Hawthorn Books, 1964.

ENGELMANN, S. *Your Child Can Succeed: How To Get the Most Out of School for Your Child.* New York: Simon and Schuster, 1975.

FEINGOLD, B. F., *Why Your Child Is Hyperactive: Behavior Disturbances and Learning Disabilities Caused by Artificial Food Flavors and Colors.* New York: Random House, 1974.

FISHER, JOHANNA, *A Parent's Guide to Learning Disabilities.* New York: John Wiley and Sons, 1978.

FREED, ALVYN M., *T. A. for Tots (and Other Prinzes); T. A. for Teens (and Other Important People); T. A. for Kids (and Grownups Too).* Sacramento, Calif.: Jalmar Press, 1973, 1976, 1977.

FURTH, H. G., and WACHS, H., *Thinking Goes to School: Piaget's Theory in Practice.* New York: Oxford University Press, 1974.

GADDES, W. H., *Learning Disabilities.* New York: Springer-Verlag, 1980.

GARDNER, R. A., *MBD: The Family Book about Minimal Brain Dysfunction; Part I for Parents, Part II for Boys and Girls.* New York: Jason Aronson, 1973.

GOLICK, MARGARET, *Deal Me In: The Use of Playing Cards in Teaching and Learning.* New York: Jeffrey Norton, 1973.

GOTTLIEB, ZINKUS, and BRADFORD, *The Learning Disabled Child: Current Issues in Developmental Pediatrics.* New York: Grune & Stratton, 1979.

GRUBER, H. E., and VONECHE, J. J., *The Essential Piaget*. Toronto: Fitzhenry and Whiteside, 1977.

HARRIS, THOMAS A., M. D., *I'm O.K. — You're O.K.* New York: Harper & Row, 1967; New York: Avon Books (pocketbook), 1973.

HEIDMANN, M. A., *Slow Learner in the Primary Grades*. Columbus, Ohio: Charles E. Merrill, 1973.

HENDERSON, HILDEBRAND; TOFTEY, J.; TOFTEY, T., *Back Up Books — Grades K-3; Back Up Books — Grades 3-6*. Skokie, Ill.: National Textbook Co.

ILG, FRANCES L., M.D., and AMES, LOUISE BATES, Ph.D., *The Gesell Institute's Child Behavior*. New York: Harper & Brothers, 1951; New York: Dell (pocketbook), 1960.

INGLISH, R. L., *A Time To Learn*. New York: Deal Press, 1973.

JAMES, MURIEL, and JONGEWARD, DOROTHY, *Born To Win*. Reading, Mass.: Addison-Wesley Publishing Company, 1971.

JOHN TRACY CLINIC, *Play It by Ear!* (for deaf children but excellent for LD children with auditory problems)

JOHNSON, D., and MYKLEBUST, H. R., *Learning Disabilities: Educational Principles and Practices*. New York: Grune & Stratton, 1967.

KALUGER, G., and KOLSON, C. J., *Reading and Learning Disabilities*, 2nd ed. Weston, Ont.: Charles E. Merrill Canada, 1978.

KARNES, MERLE B., *Helping Young Children Develop Language Skills*. Washington, D.C.: Council for Exceptional Children.

KEPHART, N. C., *The Slow Learner in the Classroom*, 2nd ed. Columbus, Ohio: Charles E. Merrill, 1971.

KIRK, S. A., and GALLAGHER, J. J., *Educating Exceptional Children*. Markham, Ont.: Houghton-Mifflin Canada, 1979.

KIRK, S.; KLIEBHAN, J.; and LERNER, J., *Teaching Reading to Slow and Disabled Learners*. Markham, Ont.: Houghton-Mifflin Canada, 1978.

KRAMES, J. E., *The Hidden Handicap*. New York: Simon & Schuster, 1980.

KRONICK, D., *Learning Disabilities: Implications for a Responsible*

Society; LD Children; A Word or Two about Learning Disabilities. San Rafael, Calif.: Academic Therapy Publications 1969, 1973, 1974.

KRONICK, D., and BLEIWEISS, S., *What About Me?* San Rafael, Calif.: Academic Therapy Publications, 1975.

LERNER, J. W., *Learning Disabilities,* 3rd ed. Boston, Mass.: Houghton-Mifflin, 1980.

LEVINSON, H. H., *Dyslexia: A Solution to the Riddle.* New York: Springer-Verlag, 1980.

MANN, L.; GOODMAN, L.; and WIEDERHOLT, J. L., *Teaching the Learning Disabled Adolescent.* Boston, Mass.: Houghton-Mifflin, 1978.

MUMA, J. R., *Language Handbook: Concepts, Assessments, Intervention.* Scarborough, Ont.: Prentice-Hall Canada, 1978.

MYKLEBUST, H. R., *Progress in Learning Disabilities.* Toronto: Longman (Canada), 1978.

O'CONNOR, K. H., *Removing Roadblocks in Reading.* St. Petersburg, Fla.: Johnny Reads, 1976.

OETTING, PHYLLIS N., *Everybody Wins.* San Rafael, Calif.: Academic Therapy Publications, 1974.

OSMAN, B. B., *Learning Disabilities — A Family Affair.* Mississauga, Ont.: Random House of Canada, 1979.

PEARSON, CRAIG, and MARFUGGI, JOSEPH, *Creating and Using Learning Games.* Palo Alto, Calif.: Learning Handbooks, 1975.

RAPP, D., *Allergies and Your Family.* New York: Sterling, 1981.

REGER, R.; SCHOEDER, W.; and USCHOLD, K., *Special Education: Children with Learning Problems.* Toronto: Oxford University Press, 1968.

REISTROFFER, M., and McVEY, H., *Parental Survival and the Hyperactive Child.* Madison: University of Wisconsin, 1972-73.

ROBERTS, A. C., *The Aphasic Child: A Neurological Basis for His Education and Rehabilitation.* Springfield, Ill.: Charles C. Thomas, 1970.

ROSNER, J., *Helping Children Overcome Learning Disabilities: A Step-by-Step Guide for Parents and Teachers.* 2nd ed. New York: Walker, 1979.

SHOENFELD, D., *Games Kids Like* and *More Games Kids Like*. Tucson, Ariz.: Communication Skills Builders, 1974, 1975.

SIEGEL, E., *Teaching One Child: Strategy for Developing Teaching Excellence*. Freeport, N.Y.: Educational Activities, 1972.

SIMON, SIDNEY B., *Negative Criticism*. Niles, Ill.: Argus Communications, 1978.

SIMPSON, E., *Reversals: A Personal Account of Victory Over Dyslexia*. Boston, Mass.: Houghton-Mifflin, 1979.

SMITH, B. K., *Your Non-Learning Child: His World of Upside-Down*. Boston: Beacon Press, 1968.

SMITH, S. L., *No Easy Answers: The L. D. Child* U. S. Department of Health and Welfare, 1978.

STEWART, M.,and OLDS, S., *Raising a Hyperactive Child*. New York: Harper and Row, 1973.

THOMAS, A., and CHESS, S., *Temperament and Development*. New York: Brunner-Mazel, 1977.

VALETT, R. E., *The Psychoeducational Treatment of Hyperactive Children*. Toronto: Copp Clark, 1974.

VAN WITSEN, BETTY, *Perceptual Training Activities Handbook*. New York: Teachers College Press, Columbia University, 1979.

WALLACE, G., and KAUFFMAN, J. M., *Teaching Children with Learning Problems*. Weston, Ont.: Charles E. Merrill of Canada, 1978.

WALSH, R. J., *Treating Your Hyperactive and Learning Disabled Child*. New York: New York Institute for Child Development, 1979.

WEBER, K. J., *Yes, They Can!* Toronto: Methuen, 1971.

WENDER P., *The Hyperactive Child*. Toronto: General Publishing, 1973.

Bibliography

BUSH, WILMA JO, and GILES, MARIAN T., *Aids to Psycholinguistic Teaching*. New York: Charles E. Merrill, 1977.

CHINN, PHILIP C.; WINN, JOYCE; WALTER, ROBERT H., *Two-Way Talking with Parents of Special Children: A Process of Positive Communication*. St. Louis: C. V. Mosby, 1978.

FOTHERINGHAM, J. B., *Counselling the Families of Children with Learning Disorders*. Toronto: Ontario Association for Children with Learning Disabilities.

HACKLER, JAMES C., *The Prevention of Youthful Crime: The Great Stumble Forward*. Toronto: Methuen, 1978.

HAWLEY, ROBERT C., and HAWLEY, ISABEL L., *Human Values in the Classroom*. New York: Hart, 1975.

HUDSON, FLOYD G., and GRAHAM, STEVE, "An Approach to Operationalizing the I. E. P." *Learning Disability Quarterly,* Volume 1, 1978.

JOHNSON, BILL, "What Parents Expect from Special Education." *School Progress,* January 1969.

KRUMBOLTZ, JOHN D., and KRUMBOLTZ, HELEN B., *Changing Children's Behavior*. Englewood Cliffs, N.J.: Prentice-Hall, 1972.

LERNER, JANET W., *Children with Learning Disabilities*. New York: Houghton-Mifflin, 1976.

LOSEN, STUART M., and DIAMENT, BERT, *Parent Conferences in the Schools: Procedures for Developing Effective Partnership.* New York: Allyn and Bacon, 1978.

McCARTHY, J. J., and McCARTHY, J. F., *Learning Disabilities.* New York: Allyn and Bacon, Inc., 1969.

MAYHEW, MARTIN and CHERILLE, *Fun with Art.* Cheadle, Cheshire, Eng.: James Galt and Co. Ltd., 1970.

MEREDITH, PATRICK, *Dyslexia and the Individual.* London, England: Elm Tree Books, 1972.

M. J. S., "Mainstreaming: 'I Don't Trust Them and I Haven't from the Beginning.'" A Case History. *The Exceptional Parent* magazine, August 1978.

————, "Mainstreaming: 'Jimmy's Teacher Doesn't Think She Can Work With Him Another Day.'" A Case History. *The Exceptional Parent* magazine, October 1977.

MULLIGAN, WILLIAM, "Dyslexia, Specific Learning Disabilities and Delinquency." *Juvenile Justice,* November 1972.

ROGERS, FLORENCE K., *Parenting the Difficult Child.* Radnor, Pa.: Chilton Book Company, 1979.

RUCH, FLOYD L., and ZIMBARDO, PHILIP G., *Psychology and Life.* Glenview, Ill.: Scott, Foresman and Company, 1977.

SCHLOSS, ELLEN, ed., *The Educator's Enigma: The Adolescent with Learning Disabilities.* San Rafael, Calif.: Academic Therapy Publications.

SCHLOSS, PATRICK J.; MILLIREN, ALAN P.; NEWBY, MARILYN P., *Learning Aids: Teacher-Made Instructional Devices.* Springfield, Ill.: Charles C. Thomas, 1975.

SHORT, JAMES F., JR., ed., *Delinquency Crime and Society.* Chicago: University of Chicago Press, 1976.

SIMON, SIDNEY B.; HOW, LELAND W.; KIRSHCHENBAUM, HOWARD, *Values Clarification.* New York: Hart, 1972.

SINCLAIR, C. B., *Movement and Movement Patterns of Early Childhood.* Richmond, Va.: Division of Educational Research and Statistics, State Department of Education, 1971.

T. V. PUBLICATIONS, *A Different Understanding.* T. V. Ontario.

TOUGH, JOAN, *Talking and Learning.* London, Eng.: Ward Lock Educational Publishing in Association with Drake Educational Associates, 1977.

UNDERWOOD, ROSEMARY, "How To Cope with Bureaucracy Without Going Completely Insane." Ontario Association for Children With Learning Disabilities, *Communique,* Volume 6, Winter, 1978.

WAGNER, RUDOLPH F., *Dyslexia and Your Child.* New York: Harper and Row, 1971.

WEISS, HELEN and MARTIN, *Home Is a Learning Place.* New York: Little, Brown, 1976.